Digital transformation leveraging SMAC technologies is one of the most happening areas in the banking and financial services industry. However, the buzzwords and noise surrounding digital often clutter the minds of those implementing digital transformation initiatives with misconceptions. Balaji Raghunathan and Rajashekar Maiya have ensured that they go beyond buzzwords in this book. They have not only demystified social, mobile, analytics, and cloud technologies for business owners, analysts, and product managers, but also provided a guide for implementing digital transformation initiatives.

As a leader of a digital practice providing solutions to financial industry customers for their digital needs, I can see that this book resonates well with the challenges faced by this industry and outlines a strategy for addressing these challenges. If you are one of the many who is in one way or the other involved in digital banking initiatives, this is the book you would have been waiting for.

Gaurav Mathur
Senior Director and Head–Financial Services Digital, India
Capgemini Technology Services India

We are at the cusp of a mega technology revolution that is changing every aspect of each industry. Banking is no exception. Social, mobility, analytics, and cloud as technology options provide every industry, including banking, a great deal of level playing field for all players. SMAC has democratized the technology and increased access, reduced the entry barriers, and made it affordable across the globe. As a leading banking group in the Middle East region, EmiratesNBD has always taken the industry-leading position when it comes to leveraging the technology, whether it is social, artificial intelligence, blockchain, robotics, mobile, or Internet banking, EmiratesNBD has been at the forefront. The book *SMACing the Bank* is timely and provides a comprehensive view of what's happening and how to leverage the technology to transform. It contains years of research, study, and first-hand experience coming together as a tool for bankers and technology specialists to start using immediately. The in-depth understanding of the subject by Maiya and Balaji is well articulated in the content and brought out in a very simplified manner. It clears many terminology misunderstandings, and this book will be a good reference point for many bankers.

Srinivasan Sampath
Sr. Vice President–Special Projects, Emirates NBD

The authors have done an excellent job demystifying the top trends that are transforming the digital banking and financial services industry today. I recommend this insightful book to anyone interested or involved in this space.

Amit Kabra
Experienced Digital Banking Professional

SMACing the Bank

How to Use Social Media, Mobility, Analytics, and Cloud Technologies to Transform the Business Processes of Banks and the Banking Experience

By
Balaji Raghunathan
and
Rajashekara V. Maiya

CRC Press
Taylor & Francis Group
Boca Raton London New York

CRC Press is an imprint of the
Taylor & Francis Group, an **informa** business

AN AUERBACH BOOK

CRC Press
Taylor & Francis Group
6000 Broken Sound Parkway NW, Suite 300
Boca Raton, FL 33487-2742

First issued in paperback 2020

© 2018 by Taylor & Francis Group, LLC
CRC Press is an imprint of Taylor & Francis Group, an Informa business

No claim to original U.S. Government works

ISBN-13: 978-1-4987-1193-7 (hbk)
ISBN-13: 978-0-367-65753-6 (pbk)

Library of Congress Cataloging-in-Publication Data

DataNames: Raghunathan, Balaji, author.
Title: SMACing the bank : how to use social media, mobility, analytics and cloud technologies to transform the business processes of banks and the banking experience / Balaji Raghunathan.
Description: Boca Raton, FL : CRC Press, 2017.
Identifiers: LCCN 2017022727 | ISBN 9781498711937 (hb : alk. paper)
Subjects: LCSH: Internet banking. | Banks and banking--Technological innovations. | Banks and banking--Information technology.
Classification: LCC HG1708.7 .R34 2017 | DDC 332.10285--dc23
LC record available at https://lccn.loc.gov/2017022727

Visit the Taylor & Francis Web site at
http://www.taylorandfrancis.com

and the CRC Press Web site at
http://www.crcpress.com

Contents

V

Foreword

Beginning in the 18th century, the world witnessed transformational changes due to mechanization and the invention of the steam engine. Large civilizations like India and China, who dominated world GDP, were overtaken by the Industrial Revolution, which made Europe and the West the dominant economic power for the next 200 years. The traditional industries dependent on human labor or animal power gave way to machines, increasing production, reducing costs, increasing standardization, and creating a massive explosion in the variety of goods. It led to the creation of new industries, like automobiles, shipping, aviation, and so on.

Today the IT revolution, led by artificial intelligence, robotics, IOT, 3-D printing, and the like, is transforming industry across the board, whether it is automobile, manufacturing, retail, logistics and distribution, textiles, transportation, and so on. We have never before seen such rapid changes in their business models, supply-chain life cycle, competitive landscape, and customer expectations.

However, banking is one industry where the business model hasn't much changed since the early 14th century. It has revolved around deposits, lending, and the transfer of funds for centuries. Traditionally, this business has been run by large joint-stock companies, government-sponsored organizations, then specialist banking corporations. But with the IT revolution, banking is getting disintermediated by non-banks. We are now in the midst of a historical change which will disrupt the industry. The change is driven by new players without legacy who are leveraging IT in new ways.

Digital disruption in the form of artificial intelligence and social, mobile, analytics, and cloud (SMAC) is not only making every service industry vulnerable, but also blurring the boundaries between manufacturing and consumption. Digital disruption has opened up markets to businesses that were not accessible earlier. It has provided the necessary reach to consumers like never before. SMAC is changing the role of consumers, enabling them to play multiple roles simultaneously—such as advisor, marketer, opinion generator, rater, reviewer, and indirect seller. SMAC has also helped businesses to reach and scale. With a stroke of a button, a business can reach millions of prospective customers with the least cost possible. SMAC has made financial services more affordable, accessible, faster, and transparent.

The changing industry landscape is also witnessing the entry of fintechs, retailers, and telcos testing the financial services area, as well as the entry of specialized entities such as payment-only banks, small-finance banks, and so on. Further, large tech corporations like Apple, Google, Amazon, and Alibaba are getting into financial services in a big way. Whether it is facilitating payment transactions or offering wallets, mobile banking, or mutual funds, corporations are leveraging social networking, delivering through apps on mobile devices, deploying cost-effective cloud infrastructure, and collecting lots of data about customer transactions, habits, opinions, and likes and dislikes by deploying analytics platforms. Traditional banks are struggling with a legacy IT landscape, whereas the new players are leapfrogging when it comes to using the latest open-source and open standards–based technologies.

Maiya and Balaji, who together have more than 50 years of experience in technology and banking, have captured the essence of what's happening today and how each of these technologies (artificial intelligence and social, mobile, analytics, and cloud) is breaking barriers when it comes conducting business digitally. This book provides their firsthand experience with more than 1,000 banks/corporates across all 6 continents, all these years. I am sure it will act as a comprehensive guide and framework for all banks in their transformational journeys.

T. V. Mohandas Pai

Chairman, Manipal Global Education Services and Aarin Capital
Member of the Board of Directors, National Stock Exchange
Former CFO and board member at Infosys Limited.
Co-founder of Akshaya Patra, the world's largest midday meal program

Acknowledgments

More than just our effort, this book is the result of contributions from many people.

We would like to make a special mention of Mr. N. R. Narayanamurthy, founder, Infosys; Mrs. Siew Choo from DBS Singapore; Mr. Sampath Srinivasan from ENBD; Mr. Ramadurai Ram from Fifth Third Bank, Cincinnati, Ohio; Mr. Amit Kabra from Dallas, Texas; and Mr. Gaurav Mathur from Capgemini (Financial Services) India, for their wonderful feedback on the book, helping us bring out the relevant context and banking expertise.

We would like to thank T. V. Mohandas Pai for his valuable comments and feedback on the book. We are grateful to have him write this insightful foreword despite his hectic schedule.

Our special thanks to Mr. Hans Moravec for granting us permission to summarize his research on "Evolution of Computer Intelligence," Vamsi Kiran Chemitiganti for granting us permission to summarize his research on "RoboAdvisors," and Michael McKinney for granting us permission to use a quote from the website LeadershipNow.com.

We would also like to thank Mr. Sarma.KVRS from Infosys for guiding us in referencing external content in the book, as well as Mr. Rajesh Sridharan from Infosys for reviewing four of the chapters from the perspective of technology and providing us his valuable feedback.

This book would not have been possible without the help received from Rich O'Hanley, Stephanie Place-Retzlaff, and Jay Margolis from CRC Press (Taylor & Francis), and Lara Silva McDonnell from Deanta. They patiently answered several of our queries and guided us through the entire journey of getting this book published.

Concerted efforts have been made to avoid any copyright violations. Wherever needed, permission has been sought from copyright owners. Adequate care has been taken in citing the right sources and references. However, should there be any errors or omissions, they are inadvertent, and the authors apologize for the same. The authors would be grateful should such errors be brought to their notice and assure that corrections would be incorporated in future reprints or editions of this work.

The authors acknowledge the proprietary rights of the trademarks and the product names of the companies mentioned in the book.

Balaji Raghunathan's Acknowledgments

Collaborating with Rajashekara Maiya (also called Maiya) in authoring this book has been an enriching experience for me. Despite his hectic travel across the globe, Maiya always had the energy to answer all my queries related to the banking and financial services industry on time. His clarity of thought, especially with respect to the state of digital adoption across the banking and financial service industry, has been key to this book's striking a balance between the industry view and technology view.

I would like to dedicate this effort of writing a book to my father, P. K. Raghunathan; mother, Kalyani Raghunathan; wife, Vedavalli T. V.; and my 13-year-old daughter Samhitha and eight-year-old son Sankarshan, who waited for me for several weekends over a period of more than three years to finish writing this book and spend time with them. Their understanding and patience helped me concentrate on the book and get it out in due time.

I'm also grateful to Mr. Sandeep Kumar from ITC Infotech for helping me get the necessary approvals from the legal team at ITC Infotech, as well as Mr. Ravindra Dekate from IGATE (now Capgemini) for helping me get the necessary approvals from the legal team at IGATE to publish this book.

I'll be missing Sandeep Karamongikar from Infosys, who is not alive anymore. Sandeep Karamongikar had been my mentor over the last six years and would always be the first to read my publications and provide his feedback.

Rajashekara Maiya's Acknowledgments

First, I would like to acknowledge my co-author Balaji's immense contribution in bringing out this book. His perseverance, patience, dedication, and never-say-no attitude have been the motivational factors in this collaboration. I remember vividly working over-time, during the week-ends and the holidays, and having countless discussions in Café Coffee Day and Starbucks.

My current and ex-colleagues have always encouraged and helped shape this book. This book is a culmination of all those experiences and interactions with bankers from more than 50 countries, spanning across six continents, in the last 20-plus years. I'm thankful to all those bankers with whom I have had the opportunity to exchange thoughts, discuss challenges, understand concerns, and share ideas.

I would like to dedicate this book to my parents, in-laws, wife Jyothi, and daughters Tanmayee and Samanvitha, who have provided constant support and have been a source of inspiration and motivation, patiently enduring me while I was writing this book. I'm grateful to my siblings and their families for their support and guidance.

I'm grateful to my friends of more than three decades, Sharavana, Tanuja, Ravichandra, Vinod, and Shankar Sadanand, who have played an invaluable role all along by supporting, guiding, and encouraging me to do what I have always liked the most. I will always be thankful to my life-long mentors, Mr. Sadanand, Mrs. Nagarathna, Mr. Praveen, and Mrs. Rashmi, who have constantly guided me in every aspect of my life.

About the Authors

Balaji Raghunathan has more than 20 years of experience in the software industry. As part of his current role as general manager of technology consulting and enterprise architecture at ITC Infotech, he is responsible for helping the clients of ITC Infotech simplify their technology landscape, assess their readiness for digital initiatives, modernize their technology architecture, and prepare them for their digital journey.

He has also led the delivery of digital projects for insurance, banking, and financial services customers, as well as helped them define their digital strategy. He has led strategy engagements for enterprise mobility initiatives, as well as developed, managed, and commercialized intellectual property (IP) during previous stints with Capgemini and Infosys. During the last decade, Raghunathan has been involved in crafting software solutions for the energy, utilities, publishing, transportation, retail, and banking industries.

Raghunathan's core areas of interest revolve around digital technology strategy, data privacy management, and enterprise mobility. He is an avid blogger on digital technology strategy and authored *The Complete Book of Data Anonymization—From Planning to Implementation* (CRC Press, 2013). He has also the co-authored the chapter "Mobility and Its Impact on Enterprise Security" for the book

Information Security Management Handbook, Sixth Edition, Volume 7 (CRC Press, 2013).

He holds a patent on system and method for runtime data anonymization and has a patent pending on system and method for categorization of social media conversation for response management. He is a TOGAF 8.0 and ICMG-WWISA-certified software architect.

Raghunathan has a postgraduate diploma in business administration (finance) from Symbiosis Institute (SCDL), Pune, India, and has an engineering degree (electrical and electronics) from Bangalore University, India. He has also completed a senior leadership certificate course from the Indian Institute of Management, Kozhikode.

Rajashekara V. Maiya has more than 25 years of experience serving the banking industry. As part of his current role as associate vice president and head of Finacle product strategy for Infosys, Maiya is responsible for charting the product strategy of Finacle, Infosys's flagship banking solution. This role includes responsibility for defining the detailed product roadmap, strategic acquisition and alliance partner identification, client engagement, and representation of the company before external stakeholders, such as analysts and media.

Maiya specialises in universal banking practices, risk management, regulations, compliance, blockchain, and artificial intelligence, and has been quoted on these and other topics in publications such as *Forbes, The Banker, Banking Technology,* and *The Economic Times.* He has worked as visiting faculty at many universities, and speaks regularly at SIBOS, Asian Banker, MEED, and other events. He is on the expert panel of the *McKinsey Quarterly,* a member of the XBRL Abstract Modelling Task Force (AMTF) Group, and an associate member of the Institute of Chartered Accountants of India (ICAI). He holds patents and patents pending in areas such as partner portals, delivery channels, offline banking, and customer experience.

Prior to joining Infosys in 1997, Maiya was an audit manager within an accountancy practice. He holds a master's degree in commerce, specializing in banking, costing, and taxation. He is an avid blogger on the aforementioned subjects and can be reached on Twitter at @rajamaiya.

Introduction

The coming together of social, mobile, analytical, and cloud technologies has disrupted the financial industry and unleashed the digital revolution on to this sector. It has provided more technological power to the consumer and is causing the current wave of computing investments by financial enterprises.

This book intends to de-mystify SMAC technologies, to look at their applications by financial enterprises, and to identify the typical challenges faced by these enterprises when they embark on their digital initiatives. It also lays out the approaches more and more banks are adopting to address these challenges.

This book starts off with the drivers behind the rapidly increasing investments in digital technologies, especially SMAC (Chapter 1). This is followed by an introduction to the *lingua franca* of the SMAC world (Chapter 2). We then move on to how SMAC technologies can benefit the banks in addressing the needs of their employees (Chapter 3), partners (Chapter 4), and customers (Chapter 5), followed by the culture, mindset, governance process, and operational shift banks need to imbibe to successfully transition to a SMAC-driven enterprise (Chapter 6). Finally, we take a look at the banking 2020 trends (Chapter 7).

This book should be helpful to the CEOs, CIOs, CMOs, IT directors, solution architects, program managers, and banking consultants, apart from the newly created roles of chief digital officer and digital directors.

However, this book is not intended to help developers of SMAC applications.

1

DIGITAL TRANSFORMATION OF BANKING

A 30,000-Foot View

I am excited, but very challenged. I keep wondering at night, "Will I have a bank the next morning, or will some technology company be doing banking without needing a bank?"

Uday Kotak
leading Indian banker, founder and executive vice chairman of Kotak Mahindra Bank[1]

Digital technologies revolving around social media, mobility, analytics (including big data analytics), and cloud (called SMAC going forward in this book) technologies have caused widespread disruption across industries. Banking and financial services enterprises are among the most severely disrupted ones.

More and more players from other industries like telecom, technology, and retail are providing services that have traditionally come within the ambit of banking and financial service enterprises. When it comes to mobile payments, we hear more about Apple Pay and Android Pay and devices like "Square." Even when it comes to lending, which is the primary focus area of banking and financial services enterprises, online lending companies like Kabbage and Lending Club get more share of the voice.

While the above names may be more familiar in developed Western economies, even in Cape Town, South Africa, startups like SnapScan, Peach Payments, Zapper, and FlickPay are gaining market share in the mobile wallet and payments spaces.

Telecom operators, given the enormous control they hold over wireless networks, have also become big players in the mobile financial services segment. Vodafone, with the M-Pesa mobile money offering, is a classic example of this.

Banks and financial enterprises have taken notice of the potential of SMAC technologies and are beginning to realize that more and more financial service innovations are happening outside their enterprise and are becoming more and more open to partnering with other industry players as well as startups.

American Express has launched new-age offerings like a Jawbone UP4 wearable-enabled contactless payment service in partnership with Jawbone, a leader in the consumer wearable devices segment. It has also enabled payments through Apple Pay. It has partnered with Walmart to set up an innovative banking service titled Bluebird, that is online and mobile-enabled. American Express is also working with social media platform companies like Facebook and Twitter for social media platform-enabled payments initiatives.[2,3]

Royal Bank of Scotland (RBS) has seen the value that the application programming interface (API) economy brings in. It has partnered with a set of financial technology startups and has set up an API platform to enable them to securely leverage their services to create new innovative services and applications for their customers. Its subsidiary, Ulster Bank, has begun to organize hackathons, which are typically organized by technology companies like Microsoft, Google, or Facebook, or Internet and mobile startups, to identify innovative apps (and developer talent).[4]

In early 2015, Ulster bank organized a two-day hackathon in collaboration with the Open Bank Project with the mandate to the participant developers to develop innovative apps revolving around inclusive banking. By 2017, this became a three-day hackathon with more than 250 participants developing their innovation ideas for solving future banking problems.[5]

Some of the leading institutions have also set up their own research and development labs to research not just leveraging social media, analytics, and big data, but also futuristic scenarios involving artificial intelligence, machine learning, robotics, wearables, automation, virtual currency, virtual reality, advanced data visualization and gamification.

Fidelity Investments has established the 80-person strong Fidelity Labs, a dedicated unit to research and experiment on early-stage technologies. This unit enables Fidelity to evaluate early-stage technology, "co-create" innovative applications with consumers leveraging early-stage technology, bring in the "Outside View," improvise these innovations based on customer feedback and work with Fidelity's business and technical teams to make successful innovations mainstream. Headquartered in Boston with offices in various other geographies, it partners with The Massachusetts Institute of Technology (MIT) and Stanford University to adopt breakthrough innovations and take it to the next level.[6]

Innovative applications leveraging technology have been frequently churned out of this lab. Key innovations include Stock City, a virtual reality investment analysis tool on Oculus Rift, a virtual reality device; secure cloud-based financial document storage service; smartwatch apps; and data visualization tools.[7]

American Express has set up a new tech lab in Palo Alto to focus on SMAC as well as futuristic technologies.[3]

BNY Mellon has invested in four technology labs across the United States and India to focus on building Google Glass Apps and smartwatch apps apart from analytical tools for their investor community.[7]

Information technology (IT) investments are also shifting toward SMAC technology capability building. There is a conspicuous shift in the investments toward "Systems of Engagement" from "Systems of Record." This essentially means that Chief Information Officers (CIOs) are not the only ones to have control over IT spend. Chief Marketing Officers (CMOs) are also getting more control over IT spend.

Shift of IT Investments in the Banking and Financial Services Sector

Banks have traditionally been directing their technology budgets toward initiatives focused on reducing cost of operations apart from regulatory compliance. During the last few years, they have begun to shift their investments toward innovative customer engagement initiatives involving SMAC technology apart from other digital innovations leveraging wearables and virtual reality applications. Even allocations from technology budgets toward "cost-reduction" projects tend to focus on migration of IT systems to "cloud" or integration with "cloud-based" systems and applications.

A leading global bank, headquartered in North America, has initiated a multi-million-dollar spend in building a next-generation mobile app for their consumers leveraging HTML5 as part of their strategic initiative to position mobile channel to support its customers.

Over the last three years, banking technology priorities have been shifting towards social, mobile, analytics, and cloud-based projects. In 2015, enterprise fraud-detection and risk management–leveraging analytics, innovative customer engagement, and digital transformation initiatives through social media and mobile apps with the aid of customer analytics were among the top ten priorities.[7] In 2016, actionable big data analytics and expansion of digital payments were among the top ten priorities.[8] In 2017, redesigning the digital experience and enhancing data analytics to identify customer needs are among the top ten priorities.[9]

SYSTEM OF ENGAGEMENT AND SYSTEM OF RECORD

Until the last decade, the focus of IT systems in banking and financial services sector was on maintaining a system of record (SoR) of their transactions with their end-user stakeholders, namely the customers, partners, and employees. Derivate applications of SoR were largely "uni-dimensional," and the fulcrum of these applications revolved around the "needs of the enterprise." These applications captured transactional information needed for "record" purposes from the stakeholders, and the stakeholders got to view whatever information the banking or financial service intended to convey, often due to regulatory needs. There was no intention to understand what the end users wanted. These systems had long implementation and rollout cycles largely because the objective was to "do it right the first time" and required large investments. The intent behind investment in these applications was to derive competitive benefits over their rivals in the banking and financial services segments.

SYSTEM OF ENGAGEMENT AND SYSTEM OF RECORD

During the current decade, IT investments in the banking and financial service enterprises have been shifting towards developing System of Engagement (SoE) applications. SoE applications are "bi-directional" and revolve around the needs of the targeted end-user stakeholders. The objective of these applications is to "engage" the end user by capturing the contextual parameters of the end user and provide "immersive and personalized experiences" to them. Given that "engagement" is a two-way process, user-generated content is as important as enterprise-generated content for SoE applications, and listening to end-user feedback is a necessary requirement for these applications. These applications are geared to benefit the business more from "collaboration with their stakeholders" than from "competition against their rivals." Rather than "getting it right the first time," the SoE applications are designed for "evolutionary" needs of the end user. Instead of one big bang release, these applications thus rolled out in multiple iterations and each iteration is rolled out within a short duration and is an improvement over the previous iteration.

Drivers behind the Increased Adoption of SMAC Technologies by Banks and Financial Institutions

Studies by leading industry analysts indicate that the banks and financial service enterprises investing big on the appropriate digital transformation initiatives are likely to see double-digit increases in revenues and high single-digit increases in productivity. Such gains are achievable given the intersection of the needs of the consumers aided by the technology (devices) they possess and the technological capability available for exploitation by the banking and financial services enterprises.

Singularity and the Rise of Smart Digital Assistants

Human beings can see "real" things through their human eyes. They can now see "real and virtual" things using virtual reality.

Human beings can smell and sense when something is wrong when nearby. Using sensors, they can even know about smoke if they are not present on the site and respond to the situation leveraging actuators. In fact, if the wrong situation is something that has occurred previously, the response can be automated through a system that has machine learning capability.

Human beings can take ages to go through mounds of banking transaction data and still may or may not be able to detect fraud. Leveraging big data analytics, terabytes of data can be analyzed within minutes and fraud can be predicted.

Welcome to a world where technology is increasingly taking on the role of smart digital assistants to human beings. These digital assistants can see, smell, respond, and even aid human beings in taking decisions. We live in a world where human beings get news from Twitter ahead of the newspapers, know about a person from LinkedIn, and share information with their friends on Facebook and WhatsApp. And no, the technology behind these smart digital assistants doesn't cost a fortune.

We seem to be heading toward the age of "singularity," a term coined by mathematician John von Neumann and popularized by futurist and science fiction writer, Vernor Vinge. Singularity refers to the age where technology will become more and more intimate, and artificial intelligence and machinelearning-powered, self-improving intelligent machines and computer networks would lead to the creation of recursive "super-human" intelligence. This would result in explosive progress in technological capabilities within a short period. This super-human intelligence will not be constrained by the biological limitations of the human brain and would enable the end users to find the solutions to hitherto impossible to solve complex problems and thereby lead the human race toward an unimaginable world of creativity and advancement.[10]

Ray Kurzweil, the accomplished futurist and acclaimed author of the book, "The Singularity is Near (published in 2005), predicts that by the end of the next decade, we will have computers which will be indistinguishable from Human intelligence in terms of the Turing test" (Turing test will be explained in Chapter 2).[11]

Consumerization of IT

The exposure of "employees" as "consumers" to advanced consumer technology experiences of mobile devices and cloud-based apps has resulted in employees expecting similar experiences from the employee-facing applications of their employers. Enterprises, as employers, are also realizing the benefits of consumer technology experiences for employees in terms of increasing their productivity and employee engagement and are increasingly adopting them. Most CIOs are now busy with programs and projects related to "bring your own device" (an initiative to help employees bring their own mobile devices to work and use them to access enterprise information), mobile app development for the employees, adoption of cloud-based solutions for file sharing, customer relationship management, and collaboration.

"Consumerization of IT" is a drastic change for the IT departments of an enterprise, from an era in which they used to first test out the technology and then provide access to their employees after understanding its security implications, to an era in which they have to adopt (and rollout) technology that the employees are already familiar with. Enterprises gaining access to technology before employees ensured that the enterprises had better control. This is not so with consumerization and thus brings with it additional security concerns. Enterprises are changing their security policies and processes to accommodate consumer/personal technology usage, but they are still struggling to figure out how to completely control use of "unapproved" technology by their employees for accessing enterprise information.[12-14]

Democratization of IT

Today's generation of stakeholders (who also form the consumers of the services and applications) of enterprises, namely the employees, partners, and customers, would prefer to have anywhere-anytime-any device access to self-service tools to enable resolution of their issues as against calling up a helpdesk phone number. Cloud-based infrastructure-as-a service tools enable individual users to provision their own IT environments without any dependency on their IT team.

Enterprises are also keener to provide access to self-service tools to their end users as it helps reduce their IT cost.

Within the enterprise, DevOps tools enable developers and IT teams to work seamlessly, and enable developers to create virtual machines needed for their development and testing environment needs without waiting for the IT team to provision the environment.

Virtual agents, aided by big data analytics, machine learning, and artificial intelligence, can provide personalized support to customers and address their queries. Dedicated social media communities are being deployed to enable end users help resolve the queries of other end users.

Thus, the world of IT is getting democratized, as the end users have access to support tools and processes as well as knowledge that was earlier available only to IT support teams, although the level of access may vary. This also helps improve the speed of fulfillment of end-user needs at reduced cost.[15,16]

Reduced Cost of Computing

Developing advanced analytics-based applications (working on any device) for generating recommendations and targeted offers for the customer do not need expensive hardware and software investments today. Consumer-based Internet companies like Yahoo, Google, and Twitter have made available to the public (open sourced) software frameworks like Hadoop, Kafka, and Storm, which enable enterprises and even startups to build intelligent applications to address complex needs of customers, partners, and employees. Bootstrap framework (open sourced by Twitter) enables enterprises to develop websites that can automatically adjust their user interface based on their screen resolution. These software do not need expensive hardware or mainframes to run. They can run on commodity hardware within the enterprise or the cloud. Amazon (as well as Google, Microsoft, and IBM) has enabled enterprises to rent their IT infrastructure per hour in the cloud. The cost of processing voluminous, high-velocity data in the cloud is hardly an entry barrier for today's enterprises. Given the serious competition among cloud platform vendors like Amazon, Google, Microsoft, and IBM, the cost of computing seems to be going only one way, which is downwards. As per the price cuts, announced in mid-2015 by Google (for usage of their cloud platform), a micro-instance would cost less than a cent for one hour of regular usage. The cost of renting computing infrastructure from other vendors also falls in a similar range.[17,18]

The drastically reducing cost of network bandwidth, storage, and computing power is proof enough that Moore's law still remains as relevant as it was 50 years ago, when Gordon Moore, the co-founder of Intel, made a prediction that remains the bedrock of the semiconductor industry.[19,20] This prediction talks about the doubling of the number of transistors in integrated circuits every two years. Thus, the size of integrated circuit boards would continue to decrease while processing power increased, and as the processing power doubled, the price would be cut in half at the same exponential rate. The price wars have been continuing over the last two years. In November 2016, Amazon cut its S3 pricing to US$0.026/GB while Microsoft Slashed its Microsoft Azure Virtual Machine price by 24%–61% in February 2017.[21]

Digital Natives and Their Entry into the Workforce

The term digital native was coined by Marc Prensky, a well-known U.S. educator and writer, in 2001 in an article titled "On the Horizon." As part of K-12 educational reforms, he used the concept of "digital immigrants" and "digital natives" to drive home the point that teachers employ an approach more attuned to the needs of the yesteryear students, who are "digital immigrants," and how they need to radically transform their approach to address the needs of the twenty-first century students, who are largely digital natives.

Digital immigrants leverage technology for informational purposes. They are more comfortable with "face-to-face" interactions with peers and friends, and wouldn't mind viewing textual representation as against audio–visual representation of information. They prefer the linear way of completing their tasks one after the other.

The digital immigrants prefer a clear separation between their real-life and their virtual life, and are more prone to guard their privacy online. They do not mind consuming information that is not "recent," and are fine with "deferred" rewards.

Digital natives live and breathe technology. They not only use technology for information consumption but also transacting with the world around them. They are users more comfortable with texting using mobile devices and sharing private information on social networking platforms. They are more comfortable with multitasking. They can text with their friend while having a Facebook chat. They do not mind making friends with total strangers. For the digital natives, there is no difference between the real world and the virtual world.

The digital natives prefer rich audio–visual information over purely textual information. They demand real-time information and seek immediate rewards.

More and more digital natives from the Gen Y generation (also known as millennials) are entering the banking and financial services workforce. They are demanding from their employers applications that provide the same experience as consumer applications. They are demanding access to enterprise information on their personal devices.[22,23]

Large banks and financial institutions have also taken note of this. Goldman Sachs has made available a mobile app called "Make an Impact" to help candidates through their job search and recruitment process. This app can be downloaded on Apple and Android devices. Through this mobile app, Gen Y candidates from university campuses who are potential employees are kept engaged with information on Goldman Sachs interview events. This also enables the candidates to view career feeds from social media channels like Twitter and LinkedIn, apart from career blogs, and keep themselves better prepared for their interview processes.[24]

Rise of the Digital Consumer, and Prosumer

"Digital consumer" is the term used to describe today's highly knowledgeable and constantly connected consumer. These consumers are very active and highly influential in social networking platforms, are critical of any shortcomings of any product they consume and vent out their frustrations with the product in the same social networking platforms. Any bad experience they may have with the company selling the product is quickly amplified or "goes viral" immediately and can damage the reputation of the product or the seller. They demand individual attention and personalization of products to cater to their preferences. They are quick to adopt self-service options provided by the product seller and are always keen to reduce their dependence on the enterprise making, selling, or marketing of the product. They prefer to research a product online on consumer forums and look at the feedback from online communities before buying a product. They trust the feedback about the product from their social networks rather than what the product seller or maker mentions about the product.

Digital consumers, too, are "digital natives," and mostly belong to the Gen Y generation. In order to introduce new products for their Gen Y customers like graduate students, banks and financial institutions need to engage with them more on social and mobile channels.

Social networking platforms enable these enterprises to harvest the network effect, a term used to describe the effect where the value of a service or a product is dependent on the number of its end users. One end user (of a service or product) can potentially impact all the other end users with whom they are networked or connected directly or indirectly, and this can have a compounding effect on the perception of the value provided by the service or product.[25]

The digital consumer is not always bad for the product or the maker or seller of the product. A wonderful experience they may have had with the product will also be shared by these digital consumers to their fans and followers, and thus become their brand ambassadors.

The products being discussed in social media need not just be electronic devices or items in a grocery store. They can also be credit cards, the annual fee charged for a credit card, or a housing loan and its annual percentage rate (APR).

The digital consumers are also "prosumers" or "producing consumers." They don't just consume content published by the enterprise about the product. They can instantly produce content about the product from any device from which they consume the content. Consumer- (user-) generated content about the product is as important as the content published by the enterprise.

The concept of self-service and reputation management, which is all about how to handle product feedback on social media and limit damages to the reputation of the product or the seller or maker of the product, is radically altering the way banking and financial institutions need to engage with the consumer. These enterprises would need advanced analytical tools to identify these influencers and cultivate them.

Race between Enterprization of the Consumer and
Consumerization of the Enterprise

Until the last century, enterprises were the ones with access to advanced technology for processing data and transactions. Due to the high cost of computing and technology, the enterprises used to dictate the services they offered to the customer. A consumer could not afford to own a high-end computer or a mainframe. But now with the advent of cloud and open source technology, democratization of technology and reduced cost of computing and technology, more consumers have access to smart digital computing devices. Reduction in the cost of advanced computing has significantly lowered entry barriers to new players (who need not necessarily be existing financial services players). The digital consumer has more choice. More and more new players in the financial services arena are intermediaries and aggregators and have managed to gain access to be the interface/gateway of choice for end users due to the enhanced experience they provide to their customers. Thus the consumer today has equal or more access to advanced enterprise technology than the enterprises themselves. More often we find consumers having first access to advanced technology thereby dictating the services which the financial services enterprises need to provide.

On the other hand, Gen Y employees themselves have access to advanced experiences as consumers and are asking their enterprises for similar consumer technology to access their internal systems. Enterprises cannot any more afford to play the role of a mute spectator in the race between the enterprization of the consumer and the consumerization of the enterprise anymore and need to adopt advanced SMAC technology to retain their consumers.

Rise of Open Source Technologies

Unlike the established banks and financial service enterprises, the new-age superstars like Facebook and Google have all built their software platforms based on open source technologies and commodity hardware rather than be dependent on proprietary software. Facebook, Google, LinkedIn, and Twitter have not only used open source software to build their platforms, but have also contributed back to the community many of the currently popular open source frameworks associated with development of social, mobile, and analytics software development.

Open source software, which are freely available and enable developers to download, customize, and also share the code with others, not only reduce the cost of IT and software development, but also have helped in improved speed, response time, and scalability of websites. JavaScript, which was earlier considered just a scripting language, is now becoming more the lingua franca of the Web and mobile app development world. Coupled with Bootstrap, another open source framework from Twitter, JavaScript can be used to make websites mobile-friendly. In order to increase speed of response as well as make websites scalable, Web applications are increasingly being migrated to MEAN stack, a short form for MongoDB, Express.js, AngularJS, and Node.js. It is not just the user interface that can be developed using JavaScript; server-side application servers, which were largely the turf of proprietary software, can also be coded using Node.js, and these can be several times faster than the proprietary application servers.

Hadoop, which is an open source framework for enabling distributed processing of large data sets across commodity hardware, is the fulcrum around which big data analytics revolves. Hadoop has an entire ecosystem of support libraries like Hive, PIG, and so on to make it friendlier for developers to leverage Hadoop.

Open source frameworks have reduced the entry barrier for the not so-wealthier financial technology (fintech) startups to challenge established banks and financial service enterprises in their core areas. Lending Club, the online lending platform that in December 2014 debuted to an initial public offering (IPO), taking its market valuation of over US$8 billion leverages open source frameworks like Hadoop, HBase, and Storm for its analytical needs.[26]

AlphaLinks, a fintech startup launched in 2013 focused on a peer-to-peer (P2P) platform for investment management, is using open source software to create a unique product. Similarly, MicroExchanges, a fintech startup focused on P2P trading platforms, is leveraging open source software for building their micro-trading platforms.[27]

Banks and financial institutions have also realized that adoption of open source software, apart from reducing costs, is also fostering co-creation of innovation through better collaboration. This is leading them to explore community-based software development models in this decade. In the latter half of 2012, Deutsche Bank launched the "Lodestone Foundation" to share markets and trading software for the financial markets.[28]

NYSE Technologies, the IT Division of NYSE Euronext (which operates the NYSE as well as other stock exchanges across the world), open sourced its middleware, called middleware agnostic messaging API (MAMA), and called it OpenMAMA. The objective to open source this middleware was to enable smaller financial institutions to adopt its market data services.[29]

Goldman Sachs has placed some of its proprietary software code on GitHub, which is an open online source code repository to allow developers outside Goldman Sachs to refine and improve the code.[30]

Zions Bancorporation, a premier financial services company based out of Salt Lake City, is leveraging Hadoop, the open source big data technology, for building a security data warehouse to enable analysis of security threats and proactive decision making for security-related aspects.[31]

API Economy

There is a growing shift in the servicing mindset of the enterprises from enabling customers to interact with them on their own channels to being of value to the customer when they need them and where they need them either through their own or third-party channels.

More and more, enterprises realize that innovations are happening outside the enterprise. Aggregators, who may or may not be from the banking and financial services sector, are able to engage the customers better today through their innovative products than the mainstream banks and financial institutions. At the end of the day, if there is one valuable thing that the banks and financial service enterprises own about the customer, it is the data about the customer. Not everything that may be useful for the customer can be built by the bank or financial institution (by themselves).

API, which was more of a software term used by developers to describe an entry point into an application module, is now being used more by the business to describe an entry point into a business process or a domain. More and more banks and financial institutions are exposing their valuable data, reusable code and intellectual assets securely to their partners and outside world through APIs, which support open standards for integration. These APIs can also be used internally to simplify integration between various applications, services, and business processes.

APIs enable an entire ecosystem around them and enable the "monetization" of valuable assets the enterprises hold with them while enabling innovative use of these assets by their partners. They enable third-party developers to build social, mobile, or cloud-based apps that may be of immense use to the customers, but which banks and financial institutions are themselves unable to build. In the process, the banks and financial institutions which own the API (and the data) can charge the third-party developers for data/API requests.

The API ecosystem has also been strengthened by availability of advanced commercial and open source API management software like CA Layer 7, WSO2 (open source), and Apigee. These API management software enable enterprises to securely manage their APIs and control access apart from metering the requests for these APIs by every third-party developer or partner.

The success of the non-traditional financial companies like PayPal, Tilt, and Bill Trust, which were the primary adopters of the API culture, influenced the mainstream banks and traditional financial institutions to explore API-fication of their business processes and applications.

Simon Redfern, the founder and CEO of TESOBE, a Berlin-based company, was instrumental in the conceptualization of the Open Bank Project, which enables an ecosystem of third-party apps and services for their customers. The Open Bank Project supports banks with an open source API to enable third-party developers and partners access to their data and assets to build secure applications and services for their customers apart from an app store to enable the bank's customers to discover third-party apps built leveraging the bank's assets. The aim of this project was to turn the concept of "bank as a platform" into reality. The Open Bank Project has a strong community of third-party developers to build innovative applications. Various personal finance management apps like Kinder Bank,

Momentum, Money Garden, and Spend Chart have been built using the Open Bank Project API.

Various German-based banks like Postbank-Berlin and GLS Gemeinschaftsbank-Bochum have leveraged the Open Bank Project for their needs.[32]

APP ECONOMY

The API economy is accelerating the growth of the app economy, an economic ecosystem around mobile and social apps. Millions of individual developers are able to develop mobile apps or social apps with their development tools, which are largely open source or available for free downloads, upload the app to public app stores (like Apple iTunes, Google Play Store, or Facebook App Store), and get paid for downloads of the apps by end users. This represents true democratization of technology. There are more than two million apps now in the iTunes App Store available for download by iPhone and iPad users and about 700,000 mobile apps available for download by Android devices from the Google Play store.

In 2014, Apple distributed US$10 billion in revenues to developers, more than the revenues of Hollywood from the U.S. box office.[33] By 2016, this revenue distribution to developers had increased to US$20 billion.[34]

Banking the Unbanked[35,36]

More than three-fourths of the adult population in developed economies has a formal bank account. In developing economies, however, fewer than half of their adult population has any kind of relationship with a formal bank or financial institution. Africa, a continent with more than a billion people spread across 56 countries, has less than a quarter of their adult population using formal banking channels. The higher cost of transacting with formal banks for people with lesser incomes as well as the lower density of banking channels like ATMs in rural pockets of African nations has driven the unbanked population to alternate channels like mobile money. The key driver for the growth of mobile money alternatives is the fact that there are far more adults owning mobile phones than having formal bank accounts.

Due to their reach, telecom operators (telcos) who own cellular networks have been more successful in addressing the needs of the unbanked population with their mobile transfer ventures than the formal banks. M-Pesa, a mobile money transfer service introduced by Safaricom, a Kenyan mobile network operator, has been successful in providing financial inclusion to the unbanked Kenyans. Vodafone group, which owned a large stake in Safaricom in early 2015, is now trying to introduce M-Pesa in various other developing economies across the world to replicate this success.

The success of the M-Pesa experiment has also encouraged many African banks to explore alternate channels as part of their strategy to acquire customers who have been left out of the banking system. One of the popular successes they have seen is with the deployment of mobile agents, who are banking agents employed to provide banking services to the financially excluded population, through a mobile device and mobile application.

Mobile wallets are increasingly being seen as successful tools for financial inclusion. These wallets, which store money and can also enable payments to vendors or peers, have gained in popularity by enabling customers (largely, the lower-income categories) to recharge their prepaid mobile services. Mobile wallets have also been popularized by telcos. We now see mobile wallets being introduced by various third parties, who are neither telcos nor financial institutions.

In India, the Reserve Bank of India, the equivalent of the Federal Reserve of the United States, has solicited applications for granting payment bank licenses for servicing the financially underserved. These payment banks may not offer an entire range of financial services like the formal banks, but is still of enormous value to the lower-income migrants to cities who do not own a formal bank account. Payment banks would help the migrants in transferring money to their immediate and extended families living in remote rural areas of India.

Most of the applicants for the payment bank licenses are largely telcos or e-commerce companies. Banks have looked to support these applicants more as supporting partners rather than taking a primary role.

Benefits of SMAC Adoption

Adopting SMAC technologies provides visible benefits both from an internal perspective as well as an external perspective for the banks and financial institutions.

Foundation for Digital Transformation

SMAC technologies, coupled with artificial intelligence and machine learning, form the pillars of any digital transformation initiative. Social technologies provides the base platform for collaboration and engagement initiatives leveraging the network effect, mobile technologies provides the base platform for "anywhere, anytime, any device" initiatives for employees as well as customer intimacy initiatives. Analytical tools serve as the enabling platform for analyzing voluminous customer data to identify fraud or provide personalized customer experiences. Cloud provides the technical infrastructure needed for any voluminous data analysis exercises for digital transformation needs. Omnichannel banking, or branchless banking, would all involve one or more of SMAC technologies coming together.

Productivity Gains, Operational Efficiency, and Automation

From an internal perspective, the gains that are most visible are productivity gains for their employees. Sales force automation and agent automation mobile apps can enable the sales force and the agents to plan their meeting with customers as well as their travel to the meeting sites, identify the customer profile, and have a guided questionnaire for the customer, all from their mobile devices from wherever they are.

Cloud-based infrastructure is enabling banks and financial services to enable their IT teams to do more with a lesser number of people. Cloud-based infrastructure services providers ensure high reliability and availability. Automated provisioning tools are available to nominated members of individual business units and line of businesses (LOB) for addressing any IT infrastructural needs on the cloud or virtualized infrastructure. This reduces dependency on internal IT as well as the delay for addressing the infrastructural needs of IT projects. The IT team can be leveraged for what they provide value; for example, consultation related to capacity planning and performance tuning rather than repetitive tasks involving environment setup.

Customer Intimacy and Entry to New Markets

From an external perspective, opening additional channels (mobile, social) for revenue generation and new customer acquisition offer clear benefits. SMAC technologies also enable banks and financial institutions to engage their customers better at cheaper costs. With huge amounts of customer data available to banks and financial institutions for analysis, more and more activities that used to be done by advisors or agents after discussions with customers can now be planned earlier. These sales activities are gradually moving into the pre-sales domain or the marketing domain, enabling the banks and financial institutions to target their products better through analytics.

Customers can be encouraged to login to banking websites through social channels. This process can help banks and financial institutions identify the demographics, likes, and preferences of their customers, analyze them, and target their products and offers accordingly. For example, a customer who is a millennial and a gadget freak can be offered financing for buying the gadgets at attractive interest rates. Providing the customer what they want when they want brings in more intimacy.

Engagement initiatives through games on social and mobile channels can enable the banks and financial institutions to target millennials as potential customers.

Mobile money initiatives or "bank-in-a-pocket" initiatives can help banks and financial institutions serve new market segments. In early 2015, ICICI Bank, a leading Indian bank, introduced a mobile app called "Pockets," which allows users to pay for movie tickets, utility bills, send money or gifts, and even share the expense between friends for a lunch or dinner at restaurants. This app can be used even by those who don't have an account with the bank. The bank believes that this will help them target the millennials as well as those who do not have accounts with the bank.

Challenges and Impact of SMAC Technologies on the Financial Sector

The growth of SMAC technologies has greatly reduced the entry barriers for innovation and thereby let new disruptive competitors into the financial sector.

The Rise of Fintechs

Popularly called fintech startups, these companies are disrupting the entire value chain of the banking and financial services segment through their innovative products and services in the areas of lending, personal finance, payments, and even equity financing. These startups can arise anywhere in the world and need not necessarily have a banking or financial services background. Given that regulations are nonexistent or minimally applied for the products and services offered by the fintech startups, there is a real threat of reduced profit margins, revenues, and loss of customers to established banks and financial institutions.

Goldman Sachs has predicted that fintechs are disrupting the financial domains being serviced by traditional Wall Street firms. Close to US$5 trillion of their revenues and close to US$500 billion of their profits (of traditional Wall street firms) will be under threat.[37]

Disintermediation of Financial Services

Increasingly there is no need to transact with a bank or an established financial service provider for a variety of financial services. Fintech startups, with their nimbleness and focus on SMAC and AI technology, are making financial services cheaper, faster, and more transparent for their customers. Financial advisory services, which were hitherto available only to the wealthy from banks and financial institutions, are being disrupted by these fintech startups and are now being made available in a cheaper and transparent form to the not-so-wealthy category of customers.

A study by Accenture indicates that investments in Fintech startups, which has started gaining traction after the global financial crisis of 2008, is just short of US$5.5 billion for the first quarter of 2016.[38]

Aggregators

As financial services become more and more data-driven and there is higher adoption of API technology, there are a host of fintech start-ups offering financial data aggregation services on the cloud. Xignite, a San Mateo-based fintech company, not only serves as a data provider for other fintech aggregators like Wealthfront and Personal Capital, but also established financial services players like TD Ameritrade and Charles Schwab, and non-financial services players like Starbucks and Zipcar. The established banks and financial institutions need to look at how their services can benefit from financial data aggregators as well as how they can monetize their data through such aggregators.

Culture and Mindset Change

In the name of security and regulatory compliance, the traditional banks and financial institutions have been bogged down in bureaucracy when it comes to new technology adoption as well as introduction of services. This has reduced their nimbleness and agility when it comes to addressing the threat of new-age competitors or providing new services to their customers. The IT processes in banks, and financial services in established banks and financial institutions, are more geared toward long implementation cycles. Customer service technology is designed for one-way communication from banks toward customers. On the contrary, adoption of SMAC technology adoption requires short release cycles for software applications and faster software upgrade cycles. Communication through social media requires humility, transparency, ability to handle negative feedback, and an intent to collaborate rather than assuming that customers will agree with whatever information a bank provides through questions or comments. How the customer experiences the services and products would need to take a higher priority when designing a new service or a product.

New Competitors

At the risk of repetition, SMAC technologies have facilitated the reduction of entry barriers for the financial services sector. The established banks and financial institutions need to be ready for the entry of new competitors from the non-financial services sector as well as startups, and these competitors can arise from anywhere across the globe. They would need to have a strategy to either partner with these players or start their own "lab-like" setup to incubate new services and products or even acquire them. We can see an example of this strategy being played out in the investments made by BBVA Compass, one of the big banks of Europe, which operates in the United States as a subsidiary. Through BBVA Ventures, they have invested in fintech startups or even acquired startups like Simple, an online-only bank based out of Portland. Coinbase, which is involved in setting up an exchange to trade virtual currencies like bitcoin, has attracted investments from BBVA Ventures, USAA as well as the New York Stock Exchange.[39]

Shift in Business Model

In the SMAC era, revenues are made from a large number of smaller-value transactions. Established banks and financial services are geared to a model where they generate revenues from a small number of high-value transactions.

Analytics combined with artificial intelligence and business process management tools is also taking automation to the next level and making various traditional bank branch services redundant. Online and mobile banking has resulted in fewer and fewer people needing to go to the bank branch for their transactions. This leads to job losses and reduction in the workforce. During the latter half of 2014, Lloyds Bank, a leading bank in the United Kingdom, announced that they plan to close 200 traditional branches, but would open 50 new branches equipped with iPads enabling customers to video chat with their employees through collaboration tools like Skype. These employees may or may not be present in the same branch and would be able to service more customers.[40]

Financial Technology Evolution

Figure 1.1 depicts how computing and software systems have evolved over a period of time and how these have impacted the evolution of new channels for banks to service the customer. With the maturity of SMAC technologies, the importance of the branch has been eroding continuously.

One of the other major challenges banks and financial service enterprises face is the growing complexity of their IT systems in order to support multiple channels. While the IT system landscape evolves, despite application portfolio rationalization exercises, these enterprises are unable to do away with their legacy applications and systems.

The next wave of evolution is seeing some of the future-focused banks and financial institutions combine artificial intelligence along with big data analytics to deploy self-service banking services like virtual agents, which are systems answering questions from customers without human intervention, and robo-advisors, which are automated online advisers for making investments for customer service. Fintech players like Wealthfront and Betterment have successfully deployed robo-advisors. Charles Schwab has also piloted robo-advisors for asset management.[41]

Conclusion

In 1994, Bill Gates said, "Banking is important, but banks are not." This statement is getting very close to reality now after a couple of decades with the frenetic pace of innovations in the financial sector enabled by SMAC technology. With the entry of millennials into the global financial system as well as the advent of nimbler competitors, a large number of whom are still unknown to the financial sector, the established banks and financial institutions need to be prepared for culture shifts, business model changes, and much faster technology refreshes in order to retain their customers and employees. Adoption of SMAC technologies, along with artificial intelligence technology, would help prevent the established banks and financial institutions from becoming irrelevant in today's world.

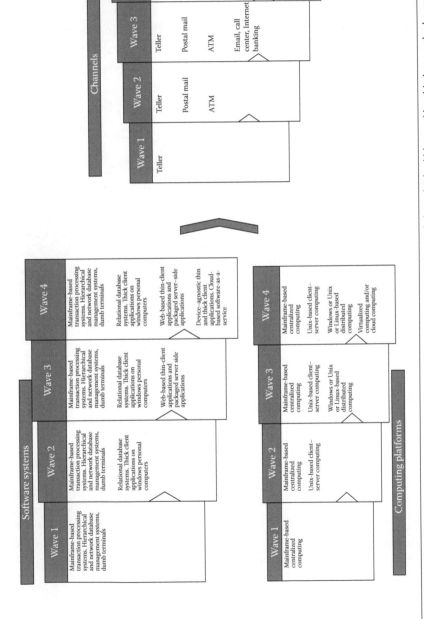

Figure 1.1   Banking systems evolution. The evolution of software systems, computing, and channels should be considered to have evolved over different periods of time and not necessarily at the same time.

Points to ponder:

- Shift of IT investments in banking and financial services sector
- Drivers behind the increased adoption of SMAC technologies by banks and financial institutions
- Benefits of SMAC adoption
- Challenges and impact of SMAC technologies on the financial sector
- Financial technology evolution

References

1. Connie Hui Ann Tan. 2015. Indian Billionaire Worries about Disruptive Technology. CNBC. May 20. http://www.cnbc.com/id/102677283
2. Tom Groenfeldt. 2014. American Express Opens Tech Lab in Palo Alto. *Forbes*. Dec 24. http://www.forbes.com/sites/tomgroenfeldt/2014/12/24/american-express-opens-tech-lab-in-palo-alto/1/
3. Tom Groenfeldt. 2014. American Express Opens Tech Lab in Palo Alto. *Forbes*. Dec 24. http://www.forbes.com/sites/tomgroenfeldt/2014/12/24/american-express-opens-tech-lab-in-palo-alto/2/
4. Elliott Holley. 2015. RBS Sees Future in Start-Up Partnerships. *Banking Technology*. Jan 19. http://www.bankingtech.com/273312/rbs-sees-future-in-start-up-partnerships/
5. Ulster Bank Hackathon. 2017. *Dogpatch LABS*. http://dogpatchlabs.com/ulsterbankhackathon/
6. Ivy Schmerken. 2014. Fidelity Labs Takes Innovation to the Next Level. *InformationWeek—Wall Street & Technology*. Oct 2. http://www.wallstreetandtech.com/asset-management/fidelity-labs-takes-innovation-to-the-next-level/d/d-id/1316288
7. *InformationWeek—Wall Street & Technology*. Fidelity Labs Launches Oculus Rift Investment Visualization App. http://www.wallstreetandtech.com/asset-management/fidelity-labs-launches-oculus-rift-investment-visualization-app/v/d-id/1317588
8. Jim Marous. 2015. Top 10 Retail Banking Trends and Predictions for 2016. *The Financial Brand*. Dec 21. https://thefinancialbrand.com/55952/2016-top-banking-trends-predictions-forecast-digital-fintech/
9. Jim Marous. 2016. Top 10 Strategic Priorities for Banking in 2017. *The Financial Brand*. Dec 7. https://thefinancialbrand.com/62711/top-10-strategic-priorities-for-banking-in-2017/
10. Wikipedia. Technological Singularity. http://en.wikipedia.org/wiki/Technological_singularity

11. Ray Kurzweil. 2005. *The Singularity Is Near: When Humans Transcend Biology*. New York: Penguin.
12. Gartner. IT Glossary: Consumerization. http://www.gartner.com/it-glossary/consumerization
13. Louis Columbus. 2014. How Enterprises Are Capitalizing on the Consumerization of IT. *Forbes*. Mar 24. http://www.forbes.com/sites/louiscolumbus/2014/03/24/how-enterprises-are-capitalizing-on-the-consumerization-of-it/
14. Vangie Beal. Webopedia. Consumerization of IT. http://www.webopedia.com/TERM/C/consumerization_of_it.html
15. Phil Wainewright. 2009. The Democratization of IT. *ZDNet*. Sep 18. http://www.zdnet.com/article/the-democratization-of-it/
16. Shel Waggener (CIO). 2009. The Democratization of IT: Cloud-Computing and the Berkeley Community. UC Berkeley (Technology @ Berkeley [news]). May 1. https://technology.berkeley.edu/news/democratization-it-cloud-computing-and-berkeley-community
17. Paul Willmott and Bill McIntosh. 2014. Digital Strategy. McKinsey. May. http://www.mckinsey.com/insights/business_technology/digital_strategy
18. Frederic Lardinois. 2015. Google Drops Cloud Computing Prices by up to 30 Percent, Launches Preemptible Instances. *TechCrunch*. May 18. http://techcrunch.com/2015/05/18/google-drops-cloud-computing-prices-by-up-to-30-percent-launches-preemptible-instances/#.2be5ae: G96s
19. Wikipedia. Moore's Law. https://en.wikipedia.org/wiki/Moore%27s_law
20. Daniel Burrus. 2015. Moore's Law Continues to Drive Change. *Burrus Blog*. Sep 23. http://www.burrus.com/2015/09/moores-law-continues-to-drive-change/
21. Shankar Narayanan. 2017. Cloud Computing Price Cuts Move from Virtual Machines to Object Storage: New Research. *1redDrop*. April 23. https://1reddrop.com/2017/04/23/cloud-computing-price-cuts-move-from-virtual-machines-to-object-storage-new-research/
22. Wikipedia. Digital Native. https://en.wikipedia.org/wiki/Digital_native
23. Ofer Zur and Azzia Walker. 2016. On Digital Immigrants and Digital Natives: How the Digital Divide Affects Families, Educational Institutions, and the Workplace. *Zur Institute—Online Publication.*. http://www.zurinstitute.com/digital_divide.html
24. YouTube. 2013. Goldman Sachs Careers iPhone (Make an Impact) App Demo. May 9. https://www.youtube.com/watch?v=SL9OP3WixBY
25. Wikipedia. Network Effect. https://en.wikipedia.org/wiki/Network_effect
26. Nav Athwal. 2014. LendingClub and Billion-Dollar Valuations Are Just the Beginning for Online Lending. *Forbes*. Dec 18. http://www.forbes.com/sites/navathwal/2014/12/18/lendingclub-ondeck-ipos-billion-dollar-valuations-are-just-the-beginning-for-the-online-lending-market/
27. Jonny Kay. 2014. 15 FinTech Start-Ups to Watch Out for in 2015. *Harrington Starr*. Dec 19. http://www.harringtonstarr.com/15-fintech-start-ups-watch-2015/

28. Tracy Alloway. 2012. Deutsche Bank Urges Rivals to Share IT. *Financial Times*. Sep 14. https://www.ft.com/content/6ee1921c-f14f-11e1-a553-00144feabdc0?mhq5j=e1
29. Cade Metz. 2011. Wall Street Won't Share the Wealth but Will Share the Code. *Wired*. Oct 31. http://www.wired.com/2011/10/nyse-open-mama/
30. Accenture. 2015. The Future of FinTech and Banking. https://www.accenture.com/_acnmedia/Accenture/Conversion-Assets/DotCom/Documents/Global/PDF/Dualpub_11/Accenture-Future-Fintech-Banking.pdf
31. Anne Rawland Gabriel. 2012. Banks Push Hadoop Envelope to Open Big Data's Secrets. *Information Week—Bank Systems & Technology*. Feb 3. http://www.banktech.com/data-and-analytics/banks-push-hadoop-envelope-to-open-big-datas-secrets/d/d-id/1295116
32. OpenBankProject. FAQ. https://www.openbankproject.com/faq/
33. Robinson Meyer. 2015. The App Economy Is Now "Bigger Than Hollywood." *The Atlantic*. Jan 27. http://www.theatlantic.com/technology/archive/2015/01/the-app-economy-is-now-bigger-than-hollywood/384842/
34. YourStory. 2017. Apple App Developers, Many of Them Indians, Earned over $70B. Jun 2. https://yourstory.com/2017/06/apple-app-developers-earned-70b/
35. iVeri (Research compiled by Calleo). 2014. Accessing the Unbanked. Branchless Banking for Africa. http://www.iveri.com/papers/Accessing%20the%20Unbanked%20English.pdf
36. Anne Bouverot. 2014. Banking the Unbanked: The Mobile Money Revolution. CNN. Nov 6. http://edition.cnn.com/2014/11/06/opinion/banking-the-unbanked-mobile-money/
37. Ritika Trikha. 2015. FinTech Ushers Banks into the 21st Century. Hackerrank. Jun 8. http://blog.hackerrank.com/fintech-ushers-banks-into-the-21st-century/
38. Shoshanna Delventhal. 2016. Global Fintech Investments Hit Record High in 2016. Investopedia. Jun 13. http://www.investopedia.com/articles/markets/061316/global-fintech-investment-hits-record-high-2016.asp
39. Michael Corkery. 2015. Big Banks Embrace Disruptive "Fin Tech" Startups. *The Seattle Times*. Apr 5. http://www.seattletimes.com/business/insights-not-profits-draw-banks-to-tech-startups-big-banks-court-tech-startups-for-insights-more-than-profits/
40. Business News. 2014. Lloyds Bank Confirms 9000 Job Losses and Branch Closures. BBC. Oct 28. http://www.bbc.com/news/business-29798532
41. Wikipedia. Robo-Advisor. https://en.wikipedia.org/wiki/Robo-advisor

2

SMAC PRIMER

It's amazing how quickly people on the Internet can pick something up, but it's also amazing how quickly they can drop it.

Sir Tim Berners Lee

inventor of the World Wide Web and one of Time Magazine's *"100 Most Important People of the 20th Century"*[1,2]

Social media, mobility, analytics (information, big data), and cloud computing form the fulcrum around which the "nexus of forces," conceptualized by Gartner Inc. (a leading information technology research and advisory company), and the "third platform," conceptualized by the International Data Corporation (IDC, a leading market intelligence and advisory services provider for information technology, telecom, and consumer technology industry), revolve.

The nexus of forces describes the interplay of the SMAC forces and how they mutually reinforce each other. This nexus of forces enables creation of new opportunities for businesses. The size of their businesses does not matter for them to take advantage of these opportunities.[3,4]

The third platform refers to the dawn of the era where billions of users and trillions of things are serviced by millions of applications. Big data, mobile devices, cloud services, and social technologies form the four pillars of the third platform. The third platform builds on the first platform (mainframe era) and second platform (client–server era) and makes the IT solutions of enterprises available through the cloud and accessible over a variety of mobile devices.[5]

SMAC Era: the "Coming of Age" of Web 2.0

The rise of the SMAC technologies we see today can be attributed to the application (coming of age) of practices and principles outlined as part of the Web 2.0 paradigm.

Web 2.0, a term invented by Tim O'Reilly, visualized "Web as the platform," leveraging the core competencies of "architecture of participation," "cost-effective scalability," and "harnessing collective intelligence" to serve the needs of the long tail. Web 2.0 goes on to describe "software above the level of single device," "data being the intel inside," "rich user experiences," and the "perpetual beta" (or the "end of the software release cycle")[6] (Figure 2.1).

As shown in Figure 2.1, while "Web as platform," "servicing the long tail," and "lightweight software programming model" are the underlying principles driving the growth of SMAC adoption, leveraging the benefits of "architecture of participation" and "harnessing collective intelligence" serve as the drivers for the adoption of social platforms and applications. "Data is the next intel inside" serves as the basis for the growth of analytics, "software above the level of a single device," and "rich user experience" serve as the drivers for mobility adoption, and "cost-effective scalability" and "perpetual beta-end of the software release cycle" serve as the drivers for cloud technology adoption.

Social Primer

Social technologies provide a platform for enterprises to collaborate or "socialize" with their stakeholders, within the enterprise as well as outside. These platforms enable the enterprises to engage, share content, and build relationships with their employees, partners, and customers, analyze their feedback, and improve their businesses by capitalizing on the power of the network effect.

Power of Social Networks

When the value of a product or service increases as more and more users use the product or service, we are then experiencing "network effect." Here, the value experienced by each user is dependent on

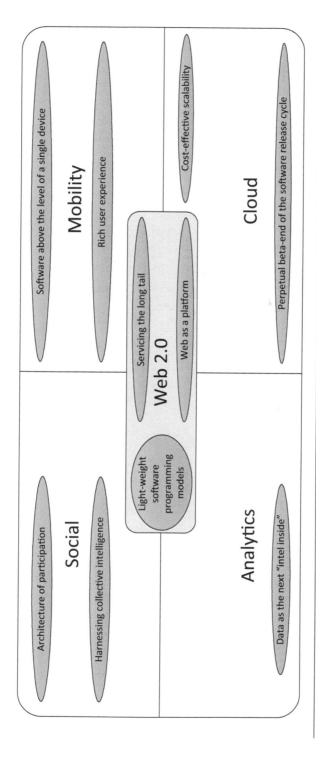

Figure 2.1 Web 2.0 in action.

the number of other users of the product. The addition of a new user significantly increases the value of the network. Conversely, the exit of an influential user from the network can result in drastic reductions in the value of the group

One of the laws often used to evaluate the value of a social network is Metcalfe's law. This law was propounded by Robert Metcalfe, the co-inventor of Ethernet and founder of 3Com Corporation, a digital electronics manufacturer started in 1979 that became more popular in the 1990s when it was used to assess the value of telecommunication networks. In the last few years, the valuations of social networking companies have been based on Metcalfe's law.

Metcalfe's law states that the value of a network is proportional to the square of the number of nodes of the network.

Let's assume that a bank wants to popularize the launch of its new product, say, a flexible savings account for graduate students in Boston, through a social network. Assuming that the user (student) has close to 100 friends or contacts in the network, the bank has the potential to foment up to 10,201 (i.e., 101^2) conversations about the product (in other words, make the conversation go viral) through the use of the social network within a few seconds.

This explains why accessing the power of social networks is a must for today's enterprises.

Metcalfe's law provides a basis for calculating the estimated value of a network. However, not every user in the network would generate the same value, thereby increasing or decreasing the overall value of the network.[7,8]

Socially Mature Enterprises

The popular myth in banking circles remains that social media is only relevant to the marketing department, and in order to handle the social media needs of its customers, it is sufficient if the marketing department has accounts in social networking sites and a representative from the bank's marketing department or creative agencies announces events or run campaigns on social media. Contrary to this myth, social media can be leveraged as more than just a marketing channel.

Socially mature enterprises (SMEs) are equipped with the right set of people, processes, tools, and infrastructure to support the entire **social media management** needs of all the stakeholders of their organizations. These enterprises realize that social media can be useful in not just creating marketing buzz or **word of mouth**, but also in keeping the customer engaged and loyal to the brand through **crowdsourcing** and co-creation, improving customer experiences and services by **listening** to their feedback on social media, and incorporating these back into the product or service.

By leveraging **social communities**, enterprises improve customer service and enable customers to help other customers, not only reducing the cost of servicing their customers but also creating brand advocates.

SMEs realize that not all content is meant to be used in the same way across different social media channels and know when to use YouTube, when to leverage Facebook, when to use Twitter, and when to use Pinterest. For example, Twitter is leveraged for situations that merit an urgent response, while Facebook can be leveraged more for content that has a longer life. Sometimes, a YouTube video link can be announced through the use of Twitter.

SMEs have realized that social media is a double-edged sword. Despite their initial assessment of return on investment (ROI) being uncertain, they have invested in a dedicated 24/7 **social media command center** with a dedicated team to handle social media feeds in real time, and have realized significant benefits. This dedicated team listens to social media channels through use of **social analytics** and big data analytics tools and **responds** immediately in case negative conversations have the potential to go out of hand and bring disrepute to the brand (**social reputation management**). The sentiments expressed by customers are monitored and analyzed by these enterprises to identify **brand advocates** and **influencers**. Popular blogs, discussion forums, and product review sites are also monitored through the social analytics tools for any discussion related to their brands.

SMEs invest in **social customer relationship management** (social CRM) systems to identify leads from social media. They design special campaigns for encouraging and engaging brand advocates and influencers. They also leverage social media to influence customers at various stages of their buying decision journey, right from the time they are identified as leads, and this continues even after they have become customers. Experts, who can be brand advocates, are encouraged to blog about their experiences in the blogosphere. They have an integrated content strategy for **paid media, owned media**, and **earned media**.

Having leveraged social media sites like LinkedIn for recruitment and realizing the benefits of leveraging social media, many of the SMEs are taking up "no email" initiatives and replacing email with **social collaboration platforms** to benefit employees, enable access to experts within and outside the organization, foster knowledge management, and improve their productivity. **Gamified** user interfaces enable employee engagement. SMEs also engage and collaborate with their partners using social media.

SMEs go beyond leveraging just the social networking sites as part of their social media strategy. Given the enormous amount of public data available on social media, they look at custom solutions to integrate feeds from social networking sites into their internal systems to service innovative use cases like competitor analysis, assessing credit worthiness of a lead or customer based on the credit worthiness of people they are immediately connected to (as part of social networks; some of these use cases stretch the boundaries of regulatory compliance), and crowdfunding.

Broadly, the SMEs are moving from social engagement to social insights and lead generation, from a marketing-only participation to enterprise-wide participation in their social media strategy. For these enterprises, user-generated content (UGC) is as important as enterprise-generated content.

Retail-focused companies have looked at various contextual use cases leveraging social media (Facebook check-in, Foursquare). Across various industry segments, there are more companies in the retail industry that come under the SMEs as compared to other industries. Retail companies are exploring or have already implemented **social shopping, social currency**, and **social sharing** as part of their next steps in leveraging social media.

Banks and financial services have not been as proactive as retail companies in adopting social media in a big way due to security, privacy, and regulatory compliance concerns.

Social Media Management

In the world of social media, the consumers hold more power than the enterprises. The reality is that content, once published by the enterprise, cannot be controlled and can be used anytime immediately or later by anybody for positive or negative or downright evil intentions. Similarly, negative comments, posts or rumors about a brand, a product, or a service by the social media community of users, even if uncalled for, cannot be controlled by the enterprises. These comments can emanate from a genuine customer or publicity seekers who pose themselves as customers at no cost to themselves. There is a high potential of the comments or posts going viral or generating a buzz within a few seconds through social networking channels.

Given the high potential of positive word of mouth through social media channels, social media can also be leveraged by enterprises to generate favorable reviews for their new or refurbished products.

Efficient social media management, as outlined in Figure 2.2, is all about bringing some semblance of order to social media content generated about the enterprise or the brands, products, services, assets, and resources it owns and deriving benefit from this through a closed-loop process.

Publishing: The process of publishing involves identification of the social media sites or platforms relevant to communicate with the targeted consumer, creation of appropriate social media real estate or assets in these platforms, generating relevant content appropriate to the social media platform, and publishing this content as part of a campaign, communication, or collaboration with their targeted users.

The aim of such content is largely to create a positive buzz encouraging the users to share the content with others they have influence over. Content can also be aimed to solicit

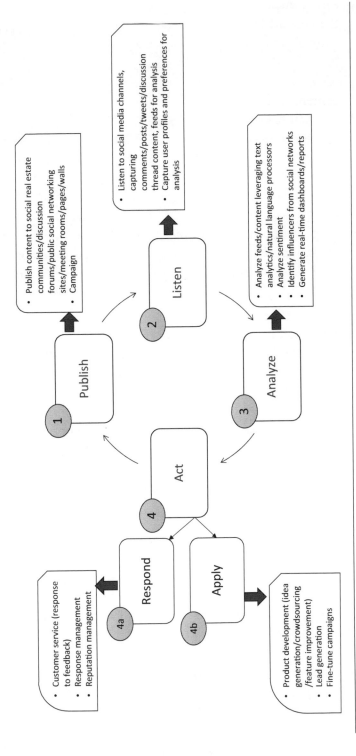

Figure 2.2 Social media management.

early feedback about the product. In such cases, consumers of the content may have to be encouraged to share the content through rewards. Content is also published in social media to engage users. Gamification (covered in later chapters) is often used to engage users as well as encourage them to share content with their network.

In an enterprise, there can be more than one user posting content to multiple social media channels. The tools used for publishing content must support multiple social logins.

Social listening: This is the ability to monitor conversations, posts, comments, and feeds about a brand, a product, or a service across multiple social channels (and Internet websites), perform keyword searches, and analyze the right set of conversations and the sentiment associated with these conversations. Social listening and social media monitoring are used synonymously.

A rudimentary version of social listening can be achieved by the act of manually searching on Google, Bing, or Yahoo for specific key words. However, this manual search can generate an enormous amount of search results and can include content from spamming sites. This is where social listening tools come into play with their ability to filter out spam.

These tools allow the users (who are largely digital marketers) to identify the social media websites and channels for listening through the ability to construct complex search queries from key words (Boolean operators help in forming complex queries for specific mentions of brand, product, and terms associated with the product or service, etc.). Queries help in defining what data is picked up by the tool from social media for further analysis. Ability of the tool to support complex queries and advanced Boolean operators decides the ability to filter out unwanted noise data.[9]

These tools support multiple languages as well as geographies and allow the user to specify the channels (where conversations are happening about the product, brand, or service). The identified channels are crawled periodically or at real time; the data cleaned, aggregated, and fed to analytical tools for identifying trends, buzz, sentiments about the brand, product, or service; and determining their influencers and detractors.

Social analytics: The data sourced from social media channels is unstructured in nature. Analysis of this data is facilitated through text analytics and natural language processing (NLP) algorithms. These algorithms extract the entities from sentences and aid in identifying the positive and negative sentiments around the extracted entities, which may be brands, products, or services. Today's algorithms also have the ability to analyze emojis (icons that convey emotions) to assess the intensity level of likes as part of sentiment analysis.

Buzz around a brand, product, or service can also be analyzed. The higher the number of posts about the brand, product, or service, the higher the buzz.

Social analytics tools can also include algorithms to perform social network analytics and identify the influencers who have the ability to elicit a higher number of responses for their posts. Some of these tools leverage services from websites like Klout to show the relative influence by means of an influence score. The "Klout Score" uses various social media channels to arrive at a value between one and 100 based on a combination of social media metrics like reach (number of people who actively engage with the user's post), amplification (the possibility of the social media post generating a response and the rate at which the followers of the user share the content with their network), and network impact (the computed value of the influence of the audience engaged with the user). The higher this score, the better the influence.

There are hundreds of tools available for social listening and analytics. Most listening tools also have the capability for social analytics but vary in the degree of customization and configurability needed to support the needs of the enterprise. The whole process from listening to social media to providing trend analysis and sentiment analysis around a brand, product, or service can be potentially automated with the aid of these tools.

Acting on social media posts: Social media posts can be ignored or acted upon by either responding to posts or being leveraged by the enterprise for application in marketing, sales, customer service, research, product development, and risk management activities.

Responding to social media may involve answering queries of users on various social media channels about their brand, products, or services; providing tips to users; addressing specific customer problems; or countering targeted posts designed to tarnish the reputation of a brand, product, service, or the entire company itself.

Social listening tools are used for social media response management. These tools listen to negative sentiments in addition to a sudden surge in the frequency of social media conversations about a brand, product, or service; treat them as indicators of an impending reputation crisis; and alert their end users. The end users monitoring social media through these social listening tools can then look at these posts, assess the influence of the person posting the comment, and take appropriate actions, which can include connecting back to the poster on the appropriate social media channel, tendering an apology if required or ignoring the comments of the poster of the negative comments based on their influence score. The value of these tools lies in their ability to filter out the posts they need not respond to, as well as their ability to not miss out on posts that need response.

Many social listening tools also support responding to social media posts across different channels through an interface. The more advanced social listening tools also aid automation of the reputation management activities through a workflow and thus standardize the process of online reputation management.

The terms "social media reputation management" and "social media response management" are explained in the Appendix as part of the "More Social" section.

Integration of Social Media with Enterprise Systems

Beyond serving as an engagement channel, social media can be leveraged by enterprises as an input channel to marketing, sales, and customer service to better target customers and increase loyalty. Product research and development teams can co-create better products and services along with their customers as well as leverage social media for crowdsourcing ideas. Enterprise risk departments can identify risks from social media content.

Many enterprises have a dedicated team to generate insights from social media. These teams periodically create reports from the insights they derive from social analytics tools and send them over to stakeholders cutting across various departments in the enterprise for further action. Many of them have also taken a more automated route for this by investing in building systems to integrate and correlate data from social media with their enterprise data and generate leads and plan loyalty programs. Social CRM systems are typical examples of these.

Mature enterprises have taken a combination of both of the approaches and operate a 24/7 centralized social media command center operating out of multiple countries to disseminate insights from social data across the enterprise.

Mastercard has a social media command center with cross-functional teams (largely from public relations [PR], marketing, and customer service functions) operating out of their U.S.-based center and collaborating with teams in Dubai, Australia, and Singapore to derive insights out of social media, leveraging advanced tools and diffusing them across the organization for further action. This has helped them transform the way they do business, with their processes accommodating insights from social media. For example, one of their business units leveraged the social media command center to identify the typical areas where mobile wallet users experienced issues from tens of thousands of social media conversations and ensured that most of these experience-based issues were addressed when they launched Masterpass, a digital wallet.[10]

SOCIAL CRM

The traditional customer relationship management systems (CRMs) receive inputs from enterprise data and content sources to help the enterprise sales, marketing, and customer service departments communicate with the customer through Internet, interactive voice response (IVR), direct mailing, and print media as channels. Social CRM enhances CRMs with the capability to handle content from social media and engage with their customers using social media as an additional channel.

With social CRM, enterprises are in a position to engage customers much earlier in the sales cycle and leverage user-generated content to better target content and gain their loyalty. By listening to social media, they gain capability to understand what potential customers and leads are looking for before buying any product or service, engage them with the content they need, influence their buying during the sales cycle, understand their post-buying behavior, and get feedback about their products and services. The vital cog in the wheel for social CRM initiatives to succeed lies in encouraging customers and leads to share their social identity with the enterprise. CRMs typically hold the postal, telephonic, and email contact information of the customer, but not the social identity of their customers. Until they have a mapping of their social identity, it becomes difficult to separate comments from genuine customers from the typical groaners (whose comments in social media channels are sizable in number) about their brand, product, or service.

Unlike many of the earlier trends in the industry, customers have adopted social media earlier than enterprises, and enterprises in turn began adopting social media before their CRM vendors. As a result, many of the enterprises have already developed custom applications for handling social media and integrated these with their CRM systems. Only later have CRM vendors come in with their own add-on modules for social media.

Either way, given the diversity and speedy evolution as well as fast changes in the popularity ratings of social media channels, most enterprises still do not have advanced capabilities to engage with their customers across social media. The capabilities they lack include mapping of the social identities across social media channels, identifying if customer feedback has been consistent across social media channels, and engaging their customers in different channels based on their influence level in that channel.

Figure 2.3 provides an overview of the capabilities provided by a social CRM and highlights the difference with what a traditional CRM provides.

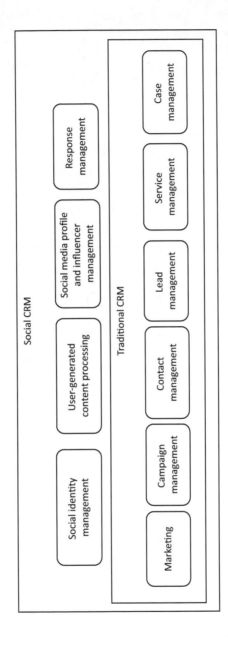

Figure 2.3 Social CRM capabilities.

User-Generated Content and Collaborative Tagging

Discussion forums are one of the oldest forms of social media (channel type). For a discussion forum, the social media conversation or user-generated content would adhere to a hierarchical structure as shown in Figure 2.4.

Each forum can have different categories. Each category can have multiple sub-forums, and each sub-forum can contain multiple topics of conversation. There can be multiple posts made by different users within a topic. Topics can be either non-threaded, that is, posts without replies or comments; semi-threaded, that is, posts having replies or comments; or fully-threaded, that is, posts containing replies to replies to replies (and so on).

The conversation structure of user-generated content in other types of social media channels would also be in the form of topics, posts, and comments. These topics may be pre-classified or dynamically classified through user-generated tags. The content type of the posts can be text or emoticon, or can include audio, video, or a mixture of all types of content. The content can be real-time textual or audio–video feeds.

Apart from feedback analysis, the primary value derived from user-generated content lies in the area of collaborative tagging. Collaborative tagging, or the process of users classifying content collaboratively through tags, helps in ground-up classification of content, aids the generation of folksonomies, and can be considered to be the reverse of taxonomies, which is more of a top-down classification of content. Collaborative tagging helps build rich metadata for content and helps understand the way users think about any

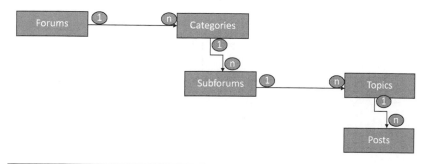

Figure 2.4 Structure of conversations in a discussion forum.

domain object at any point of time. The flipside of collaborative tagging is that these are not bound by rules and can be more representative of a trend than reality. For example, an image depicting the Leaning Tower of Pisa can be tagged by several users as "Wonders of the World." It can also be tagged as "tourist attractions," or as "Italy."

Twitter hashtags are an effective implementation of collaborative tagging.

WHAT KIND OF CONTENT IS USUALLY SHARED BY PEOPLE WITH OTHERS IN THEIR NETWORK? CAN WE PLAN FOR CONTENT GOING VIRAL IN SOCIAL MEDIA? IS THERE A METHOD TO THE MADNESS?

Going by Professor Jonah Berger's decade-long research on what makes things go viral, we can safely assume that the probability of content going viral is high if the content makes the targeted user look good in front of their network (social currency), if the content relates to a subject that is on top of their minds (triggers), if the content is about something they care about (emotion), if the content enables the user to imitate what they see people around them doing (public), if they feel that the content can be of practical value to others in their network (practical value), or if the content narrates a story rather than just being informative (stories). Social currency, triggers, emotion, public, practical value, and stories, together called STEPPS, constitute the six principles of virality.

One of the other popular tactics used by marketers for making content viral is to foster a sense of exclusivity to their end users. The by-invite-only method of getting people to use or buy their products is a popular application of the exclusivity technique.[11]

Social currency has been explained in the "More Social" section of the Appendix.

How are Banks and Financial Services
Organizations Leveraging Social Media?

Banks and financial services are leveraging social media to analyze credit history of their potential customers as well as to trap defaulters of their loans, crowdsourcing (soliciting ideas from the public), and even funding them.

Danske bank launched Idebank, a crowdsourcing app on Facebook. Payments facilitated by social networking platforms like WeChat (China) are making banks think about tying up with these platforms for facilitating payments. Hashtag banking, a Twitter-based initiative of Kotak Bank, a leading Indian bank, is an example of banks teaming up with Twitter for payments.

From an internal perspective, banks and financial institutions are trying to foster a more non-hierarchical culture. More and more financial enterprises have begun to feel email to be very hierarchical and not matching up to the collaboration experience their employees need. Increasingly, they are adopting social enterprise collaboration software (also called enterprise social) like Jive, Microsoft Yammer, and Facebook Workplace. Royal Bank of Scotland has rolled out Facebook Workplace for 100,000 employees across the world. Yes Bank (a leading Indian private bank) is also leveraging Facebook Workplace to foster better communication between their employees. Most of the enterprise social software are cloud-based.[12]

Quite often, enterprises use multiple tools to achieve their complete collaboration needs. Factors influencing collaboration tool selection include the immediacy needs for communication for specific scenarios, the amount of control the enterprise would like to provide their users when it comes to creating and sharing content and stakeholder communication dynamics (like individual, group, and enterprise communication needs).[13]

Figure 2.5 depicts a view of the typical capabilities with which enterprise social software equips enterprises.

Features in enterprise social like searching for specific topics, the ability to create (and join) focused groups, the ability to share content, and the ability to reach out to named experts and communicate with them real time foster better knowledge management practices as well as enhance productivity. In fact, most enterprises are seeing tangible

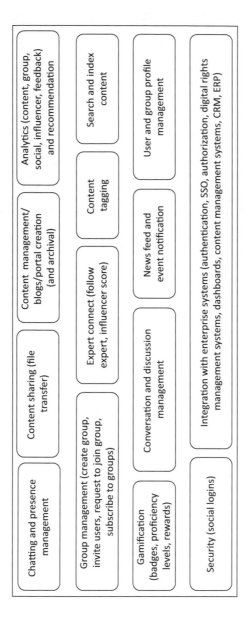

Figure 2.5   Enterprise social capabilities.

ROI when it comes to enterprise social with gains visible in productivity improvements.

GAMIFICATION

Gamification most often is confused with gaming, and both are not the same. Gamification is the application of "game-like" techniques, mechanics, and dynamics for non-game scenarios to motivate an end user to contribute to the achievement of an outcome. It is also used as an engagement technique to encourage end users to participate in initiatives.[14]

Gamification involves the deployment of popular gaming concepts of badges, points, levels, and rewards as motivation factors. For example, if the need is for technology experts or domain experts to contribute more to a company website in terms of thought leadership, the expert contributors can accumulate points for each of the articles they contribute. The points per article can vary based on the level (say, for each contribution at a simple level (problem/topic complexity), the contributor can be allowed to gather two points, for medium-level complexity topic contribution, they can be allowed to gather four points, and for complex-level topic contributions, they can be allowed to gather 10 points). Based on the points they accumulate, the contributors can be tagged with different badges. For example, silver badges can be awarded to those having 25–50 points, golden badges can be provided to those with 50–75 points, and diamond badges given to those with 75–100 points. Once a contributor accumulates more than 100 points, they can convert them into cash rewards, virtual rewards, or, say, a coffee meeting with the CEO. Enterprise social software can have its own built-in-gamification module or can be integrated with third-party gamification software like Bunchball, Badgeville, and so on.

Social is thus enabling banks and financial service institutions to foster better collaboration between customer-to-customer, employee-to-employee, partner-to-partner, customer-to-employee, and partner-to-employee.

Social Shopping and Social Sharing[11,12]

Every social media channel wants its consumers to spend more and more time on its channel and is exploring ways to serve the business beyond engagement and influence. These channels are trying to get into business transactional spaces, too.

Before, social shopping was limited to enable connected people to collaboratively make a buying decision by sharing photos and comments about the item they intended to purchase, but for the actual buying transaction, the consumer had to leave the channel and transact through e-commerce websites or business-owned websites.

Many social networking channels are now piloting "buy" buttons to enable social shopping without leaving their mobile app or website.

Banks are foraying into social commerce (e-commerce through social channels) as an enabler for commercial transactions. Kotak Mahindra Bank, a leading retail bank in India, has enabled its customers registered as part of its Hashtag Banking initiative to order movie tickets through Twitter.

Social Technology Ecosystem for the Enterprise

The core characteristics of social networking platforms include user-centricity as against content-centricity, existence of a mechanism for users to generate content, focus on the common preferences between a group of people to form communities, and building and leveraging relationships and social networks.

Thus a website can be considered to be social if it provides its users Web space for uploading content, if each user is given a unique (Web) address to post and share their content, and if it helps the user to build their profile by entering their personal information with the objective to mine this information. This mined profile information helps users build relationships with other users (with similar preferences and interests) and connect with friends. The website must enable the friends of the users to comment and reply for each post, photo, audio, or video uploaded. Each post (and content uploaded) has a timestamp, and the website sorts the posts and content by reversing the timestamp to ensure that fresh posts or content appear first.

A mobile app can be considered to be social if it provides its users an interface to upload content, view content, share content, provide their profile information, view their relationships and network connections, share information with their network, and view information from the ones they follow.[15–17]

As Gartner describes, "Social technology can be defined as any technology that enables social interactions over an underlying communication infrastructure like the Internet and is accessible from computing devices that can also be mobile devices."[18]

Here are some of the technology ecosystem foundational capabilities required for socially enabling the enterprise:

Social logins[19,20]: One of the main frustrations of an end user in transacting with a multiplicity of websites and mobile apps is the need to remember their logins and passwords. Today's SMAC world needs enterprises to simplify their processes for accessing their systems without compromises on their security. With users spending more time on social networking platforms and not shying away from providing these platforms their real identity information, these platforms realized that they can serve as "outsourced" identity providers to third-party websites and apps. The latter half of the first decade of the twenty-first century saw a lot of work related to standards and frameworks for social logins like OpenID, OAuth, OpenID Connect, and Facebook Connect, which enable users to login to third-party websites and apps by just providing their email IDs or social platform logins without having to provide their passwords to the third-party websites and apps. These standards and frameworks differ in the amount of profile and network connection information they share with third-party websites and apps.

As part of the OpenID Connect protocol, a few GSMA providers have also collaborated with social networking platforms to enable users of third-party websites and apps to login using their cell phone numbers. Short messaging services (SMS) and one-time passwords (OTP) sent to the registered cell phone numbers also enhance security by enabling two-factor authentication.

With the explosion in the number of websites and apps requiring user registration before access to their resources, open standards like OpenID and OAuth have provided much-needed relief to both developers and end users. These frameworks enabled users to leverage their social identities for access to resources protected by applications (mobile and Web) without having to register again with these applications.

Facebook supports Facebook Connect to enable third-party websites and mobile apps to login.

Despite PayPal demonstrating the benefits of leveraging OAuth, and the Open Bank Project leveraging OAuth, banks and financial institutions have been very reluctant to adopt OpenID and OAuth given their concerns on regulatory compliance, as well as the perception that these frameworks are inferior in security when compared to their own authentication and authorization implementations. Some of the German banks that have started adopting Open Bank Project initiatives have made a small start though.

OPENID, OAUTH, AND OPENID CONNECT

OpenID enables users to use a single set of credentials to log on to multiple websites and apps with the OpenID provider, where the users would need to register their credentials, serving as the authentication provider. OpenID provides a standard to enable third-party websites (called relying parties) to communicate with the OpenID providers. LiveJournal, Google, Yahoo, and WordPress serve as popular OpenID providers.

OAuth enables third-party sites and apps to leverage the OAuth providers to grant access to their resources. When a mobile app or a website seeks access to resources from a server API, the server API can ask the client app (or website) to fetch an authorization token from the OAuth provider before they can grant access. The OAuth provider requires the user to permit sharing of the required profile information to the third-party client app (or website). Google, Yahoo, Microsoft, and Twitter are popular examples of OAuth providers. OAuth has evolved into OAuth 2.0. Figure 2.6 depicts the difference between OpenID authentication and OAuth pseudo-authentication.

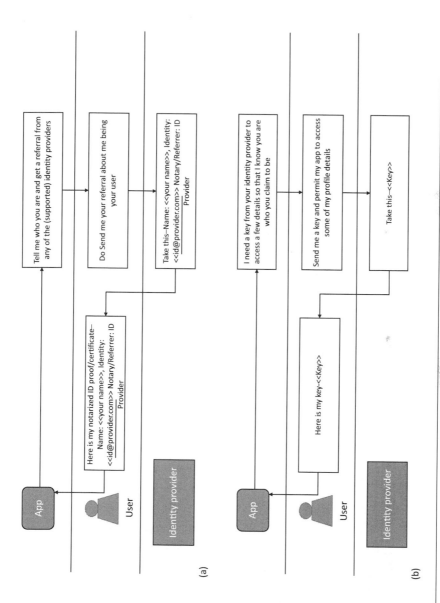

Figure 2.6 (a) How OpenID works (From https://en.wikipedia.org/wiki/OpenID); (b) How oAuth works (From https://en.wikipedia.org/wiki/OpenID).

OAuth was meant to be only an authorization framework, but more and more clients began using OAuth as a pseudo-authentication framework and ended up with their own implementations for authentication over OAuth. To standardize this, OpenID Connect framework was built over OAuth 2.0. Unlike OpenID, which was complex to implement and only facilitated users to authenticate, OpenID Connect provides the client application with both the identity token as well as an access token to gather user profile information in addition to authentication information.

Social apps and developer platforms: The successful social networking platforms have been those that haven't just enabled people to collaborate using their networks, but have also enabled a thriving developer ecosystem enabling developers to use their APIs to gain access to the user's profile, their connections as well as their activities. They enable two-way integration with third-party websites (and mobile apps).

Any app or website that integrates with social networking platforms by leveraging its developer platform can be termed a social app.

In the below section, third-party websites and apps can also be considered to be synonymous with the banking websites, and apps and developers of third-party websites and apps can be considered to be synonymous with the bank's application development and IT teams.

As shown in Figure 2.7, most developer platforms supported by popular social networking sites largely include a software development kit (SDK) to be used by client developers for their apps, application programming interfaces (APIs) to leverage social data stored by the social networking sites, provisioning infrastructure for social apps, and an infrastructure for app monetization and ad management as their key components.

SDKs and social plugins enable developers of third-party websites and apps to provide application features that make it easier for their users to login with their social identity, share the content of the app or website with their networks, or even view specific activity feeds from

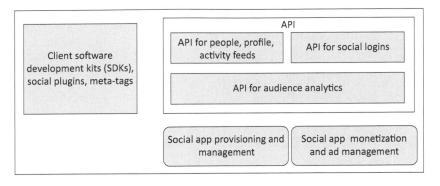

Figure 2.7 Developer platform components.

these social networking platforms. SDKs can also enable third-party websites and apps to post content and feeds onto the social networking platform.

The social app provisioning infrastructure enables the social networking platforms to ensure that all requests to their platform services are secure and traceable. Before leveraging their APIs and SDKs, most social networking sites require developers of social apps to register their apps with their platform. A unique app ID and app key is generated for each of the apps, and the developers are required to use the app key along with any request to their APIs. The app provisioning infrastructure may also need users to register the URL of their website.

The developer platforms also allow third-party apps to monetize themselves through their social networking platforms and enable the developers to advertise using their apps.

For example, Facebook facilitates viral distribution of apps by allowing them to appear as feeds in the user's personal pages. Facebook also allows the developers of social apps to retain a large share of the ad revenues generated from the app.

Most of the popular social networking platforms also provide audience analytics, which enable the developers of the apps to look at who accessed the app from what location and device. This effectively serves as feedback for developers to improve their apps and refine their app monetization strategy.

For example, Twitter's mobile app development framework (called Fabric), enables developers to build mobile apps to capture logs of crashes (when users experience them) and help resolve these issues and improve the user experience of the app. This is in addition to the standard social features they enable the developer to build (like social logins, ability to share content and view feeds).

SDKs thus serve as the enablers for more apps for the users and more users for the apps.[21]

Social networking platforms either host third-party (social) apps within a social container or support virtual hosting. Facebook supports virtual hosting; that is, they give the user an impression that the app is hosted by the social networking platform, while actually they are hosted by the developer on their own server infrastructure. The end user needs to only go to their Facebook page to view the social app. Facebook intercepts the user request, renders the third-party social app, and enriches the user experience of the app (with people, profile, and activity information) as shown in Figure 2.8. The social app would invoke Facebook APIs to gain access to the user's people, profile, and activity information.

Many banks are leveraging social apps to target millennials. CaixaBank, a leading bank in Spain, has a Facebook app that allows users to make banking transactions as well as view account balances from Facebook itself. One of the challenges with social apps is the need to watch out for any changes to APIs of the social networking platform that can break the app.[22]

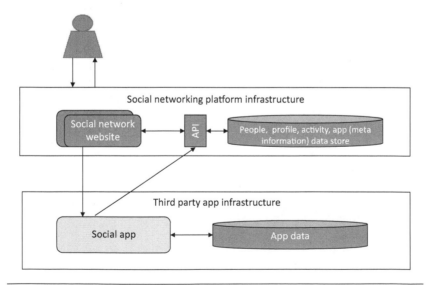

Figure 2.8   Virtually-hosted social app architecture.[23]

Social app review process has been explained in the "More Social" section of the Appendix.

Activity streams: Social networking platforms can largely be envisioned as a list of social activities performed by the end users (or actors). The list of activities performed on the site by these actors represented as a timeline (ordered from recent present to past) together forms an activity stream (imagine Twitter streams or Facebook newsfeeds).

Given the evolution of social networking from largely infrequent publishing of content to streams of frequent updates, and the necessity of standardizing the format to share the social activities to third-party apps and websites, popular social networking platforms agreed on the activity stream protocol as the standard for syndication of activities on the social Web. This protocol leverages the activity stream as the standardized open format specification for representing an activity (on the social networking platform).

In the activity stream world, actors (users of a social networking platform) connect with each other through shared social objects and their associated verbs. The social objects can be articles, images, videos, or any content the user uploads. This content elicits a response from other actors through social objects like comments, replies, likes, or shares. Updates, following, playing a game, joining a group, tagging, and sharing are verbs associated with social objects. If an actor, say Ram Pothineni, added Hotel Royal Bhutan to his list of places to eat out in the social networking platform, the activity stream can be used to represent this activity (in ATOM or JSON format) as actor: Ram Pothineni, verb: add, object: Hotel Royal Bhutan, target: list of places to eat out.

Activity streams are supported not just by social networking platforms like Facebook and Twitter, but also social data providers like Gnip (which has now been acquired by Twitter and is a product from Twitter), and enterprise collaboration (and social networking) platforms like Jive. Frameworks like GetStream.io help third-party apps syndicate or integrate with feeds from Twitter, Facebook, and anybody who supports activity stream.

Social data providers have been described in the "More Social" section of the Appendix.

OpenSocial containers also expose activity streams as a collection of actions a user has taken. They support activity templates to allow application developers to define messages with placeholders.[23,24]

URL shortening: URL shortening services, which often have domain names owned by less-known or exotic countries like Libya, Samoa, and Liechtenstein, provide the convenience of shortening, customizing, sharing, and tracking long links. Typically most URL shorteners provide an interface to allow the users to specify the base URL and make available the shortened URL. Instead of a URL like http://abc.de.fgh.com/Link1/Sublink1/Sublink11/the-cost-of-dgtal-dvde.htm, the user can share a shortened URL like http://bit.ly.com/DigitalDivideCost, which is easier to type and carries the reduced risk of mistyping. URL-shortening services also provide the user with link analytics related to location and referrer sites, the number of hits, and so on.

URL shortening comes with a security risk of spam sites hidden in the guise of shortened URLs. It also carries the risk of link rot (nonavailability of the link due to closing of the service or expiry of the short link). As a result, some sites disallow usage of shortened URLs or require their users to leverage their own shortening service. From among the close to a hundred URL shortening services that sprang up in the last decade, the popular URL shortening services that have survived include goo.gl (from Google), t.co (from Twitter), bit.ly, TinyURL, ow.ly, and ow.li (from Hootsuite).[25,26]

Social Network Analysis

Online social networks largely mimic real-world social behavior. The more frequent the conversations, the greater the relationship strength, and conversely the fewer the conversations, the weaker the relationship. The stronger the network, the better is the performance of the individual and the company.

Social network analysis (SNA) is a perspective that relies heavily on graph theory to aid understanding the flow of information between two or more people (represented as nodes) in the network. The focus is on relationships and networks rather than on individual attributes. SNA helps in representing social networks, identifying the strength of the relationship between people (nodes) within the same network, identifying the critical players of a social network (key influencers, those who are central to the network, those who help connect the network with other social networks) as well as studying the characteristics and structure of the network.

SNA was already being used in social sciences several decades ago. The advent of social networking platforms renewed interest in this field during the latter half of the last decade, with various books and papers being published in this area. Ever since, more and more tools for network visualization (pattern maps) as well as for calculation of relationship strength metrics and node centrality like NodeXL, Gephi, UCINET, and igraph R packages (language) have gained popularity.

SNA is not just useful for analyzing social media conversations and identifying key influencers, but also for understanding how information flow and collaboration between various teams within and outside an organization can be improved. This analysis can help in measuring and improving the performance of knowledge networks. SNA can also be used for personal network analysis (ego network, alter ego network) as well as organizational network analysis.

Let's face it: banks and financial institutions analyze social media conversations of their customers not because they are interested in the customer, but rather in the social network of their customers, and this is where SNA has a big role. Banks and financial institutions are increasingly leveraging SNA to identify their customers who are at risk of defaulting on their loan repayments based on not just their credit worthiness but also the creditworthiness of the social network they belong to. They also leverage SNA to identify the brand influencers and advocates.

SNA TERMINOLOGIES[27–30]

A network serves as the way to represent a group of individuals or groups communicating with each other. A network consists of nodes and ties as shown in Figure 2.9.

A node (or a vertex) can represent a group or an individual person and can be linked to another node through an edge, tie, or link. Tie strength serves as a measure of the strength of the relationship between nodes. Ties may be homophilic (nodes having tendency to relate to other nodes with similar characteristics) or heterophilic (nodes having tendency to relate to other nodes with dissimilar characteristics). The sequence of intermediate nodes and ties between any two nodes of a network represents the path of the network. The number of such nodes and ties between any two nodes represents the distance or the path length between any two nodes.

A node that serves as a link between the network it is part of and another network, serves as a bridge node. A node that is not connected to another node is an isolated node. The network can be an undirected graph (which only depicts which node is connected to which other node) or a directed graph (which depicts the direction in which nodes communicate with each other).

An undirected graph provides a visualization of who knows whom (appropriate for Facebook analysis) whereas a directed graph provides a visualization of who contacts whom (appropriate for Twitter analysis). Figure 2.10 provides a directed-graph representation of Figure 2.9.

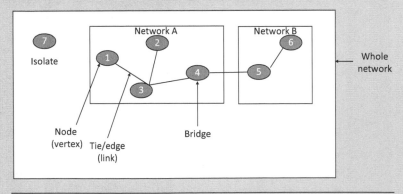

Figure 2.9   Undirected graph.

The number of incoming links to the node is the in-degree of the node. The number of outgoing links from the node is the out-degree of the node. In Figure 2.10, node three has an in-degree of three, and node six has an in-degree of one and an out-degree of one.

In Figure 2.10, the path between nodes one and four is two; that is, node one to node three and node three to node four. There can be multiple paths between the same nodes. One or more of these paths can be the shortest path between the two nodes.

Broadly, the metrics aided by SNA can be classified into structural metrics (which provide a perspective about the network as a whole as well as its components) and centrality metrics (which provide a perspective on individual nodes based on their position within their network) as shown in Figure 2.11.

Structural metrics are relevant for comparing networks within the whole network as well as changes in the network over time.

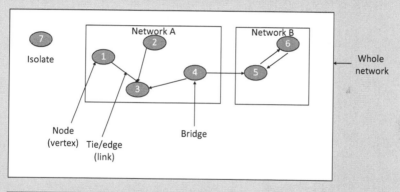

Figure 2.10   Directed graph.

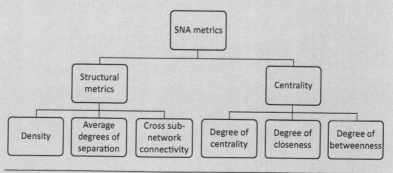

Figure 2.11   SNA metrics.

SNA RULES OF THUMB[31-35]

High levels of homogenization can limit innovation and inhibit the generation of new ideas. An influencer with connections to diverse networks has a higher probability of generating new ideas.

The presence of bridge nodes in a network is essential to foster communication and improve the flow of information between different groups of the whole network.

The degree of centrality/in-degrees and out-degrees indicate how well-connected the node is and thereby how vital the node is to the network for fostering communication (and transmitting information) within the network. The higher the degree (in/out), the better connected and more vital the node is for the network. In-degree and out-degree are valid measures only for directed graphs. For undirected graphs, the measure is degree centrality. Degree centrality provides a view on "how many other nodes can this node reach directly" and can indicate the local popularity.

Closeness centrality provides a measure of reach or how close a node is to other nodes and thereby which node has capacity to communicate faster with other nodes within the network.

Betweenness centrality provides a view of the nodes that serve as an intermediary between other nodes in the network. This measure identifies the nodes that have a high probability of being the broker when two nodes communicate with each other in the network.

Eigenvector centrality provides a perspective on which nodes are well-connected with most-connected nodes. The shorter the path between two nodes, the faster the communication between them.

The usage application capability (UAC) framework for social has been explained in the "More Social" section of the Appendix.

Reference Architecture (for Leveraging Social Media for Enterprise Benefits)

Figure 2.12 depicts a reference architecture for enterprises to benefit from social media analytics.

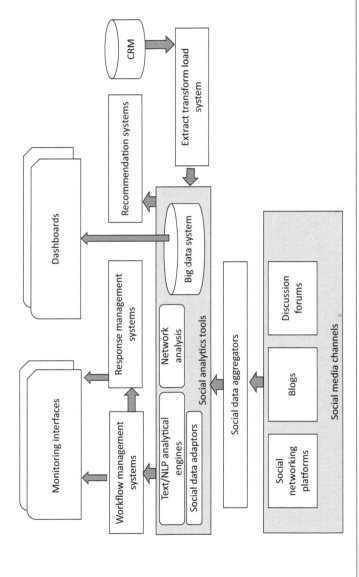

Figure 2.12 Reference architecture for financial enterprises to benefit from social media.

At the foundation lies the list of social channels that need to be monitored. Instead of individually listening to each of the channels, social data aggregators can be leveraged to listen to multiple channels. This would shield the developers from having to frequently change their code whenever the social channel changes its API (which they do very frequently). Data from social data aggregators typically arrives in the form of activity streams. These activity streams can be analyzed leveraging text analytics engines (and natural language processing algorithms). Social network analysis can also be performed to identify influencers.

Data from customer relationship management systems can also be used as an input for fine-tuning analysis. (Enterprise data when combined with social data can act as a powerful source of input for planning and response management. Social data when combined with CRM data can benefit enterprises in identifying customers who are satisfied and dissatisfied and help provide inputs to retain their loyalty). Given the enormous volume of data, big data platforms are typically needed.

The big data analytics help in generating recommendations, triggering alerts (or initiating workflows), and can warn the enterprise users whenever scenarios that can potentially damage the reputation of their brand arise. The response management systems aid the enterprise users in deploying the appropriate response.

Best practices for social media management have been explained in the "More Social" section of the Appendix.

Mobility Primer

The word "mobility" has different connotations. It can denote the movement of personnel from one location to another in the human resources world, or it can just denote the ability of people to move around. In this book, however, mobility will be used to refer to enterprise mobility technology or the technology associated with mobile devices.

Mobile technology has served as the gateway for access to anywhere, anytime, and on-demand services, and has enabled the banks to deliver their services straight to the pockets of their customers. The ability of smartphones to be context-aware and location-aware enable the banks to provide contextually relevant experiences to the customer.

With various surveys pointing to the fact that most customers would avoid going to banks as much as possible, apart from the mobile banking apps of established banks, we see more and more mobile-only banks and digital-only banks like Moven, Atom Bank, Fidor Bank, Osper, GoBank, Simple, and BankMobile servicing the market. These mobile- and digital-only banks physically have no branches but have still managed to attract a sizable number of customers (each has been able to attract 25,000–100,000 customers within two years of operation, and some are aiming to target more than a million customers within five years of operation).[36]

The pervasive influence of mobile devices has also given rise to more and more employees in the financial services sector demanding access to enterprise information and systems through their mobile devices. Thus mobile technology has been a boon to banking and financial service enterprises, enabling them to increase the productivity of their employees as well as to reduce the cost of operation by servicing more customers with a reduced number of branches.

Mobility Challenges

Lightweight engagement mobile apps (providing a rich experience to customers) do not need any integration with enterprise systems and can be developed within a short duration. However, the success of enterprise mobility initiatives, which need to provide data and content from enterprise systems, needs a detailed strategy for integration. In the rush to introduce mobile banking apps to retain the loyalty of their existing customers (as well as partners and employees), most often banks and financial institutions forget the extent of change required internally to mobile-enable their enterprise as well as underestimate the technology diversity and process challenges the introduction of mobile technology has resulted in.

> *Technology diversity challenges*: Figure 2.13 provides a schematic overview of what happens when a user transacts with enterprise systems using an app on his/her mobile device.
>
> The data or the content that the user wishes to view has to travel all the way between the enterprise system (on-premise or cloud-based) and the device through mobile towers and wireless networks; that is, they have to pass through the network layer all the way up to the OS layer (on the device), to the application layer and back. The challenges arise because

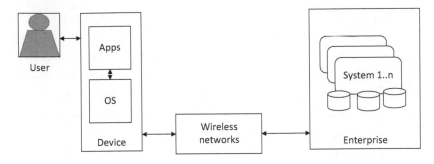

Figure 2.13 How does a user transact with enterprise systems through a mobile device?

of the various possibilities and options before the user consumes the services exposed by the enterprise. Table 2.1 lists the diverse choices that need to be addressed for providing a seamless experience to the user.

Handling mobile device extensions: Extensions and accessories to mobile devices are growing. Different types of wearables (smartwatches, health-trackers) and virtual reality sets are gaining popularity, and these are largely tethered to

Table 2.1 Diversity Table for Mobile Transactions

LAYER/LEVEL	DIVERSITY/OPTIONS POSSIBLE	DECISIONS TO BE TAKEN
Network (wireless)	Can be 2.5 G or GPRS (in developing world), 3 G, 4 G, or 5 G in developed nations	Where will the users tend to use the app? In areas of high-speed networks or spotty networks?
Network type	Wi-Fi or data network	Where will the app be used? In the user's residences, office premises, or on field?
Device make	The device can be of any make (Samsung, Sony, Apple, Microsoft, Lenovo, Micromax, Xiaomi, etc.)	On which devices would the users use the app?
Device type	Tablets, smartphones, or laptops; screen resolution can be different within each device type	Would the users view the app on tablets, smartphones, laptops, or all?
Device OS	The operating system can be Android, iOS, or Windows (or possibly BlackBerry, Tizen, or Firefox OS)	What is the device profile of the users? Which are the operating systems that the app should support?
App type	Native app, browser-based (Web) app or hybrid app	How should the app be delivered to the user? Through the app store or through the browser? Should any device features like camera, GPS, accelerometer be leveraged?

smartphones and do not work independently. Mobility programs need to identify use cases that can extend to wearables in advance rather than as an afterthought.

Business process tweaks: Often, the same functionality that is available online is made available on the mobile devices without any thought to the difference in experience (touch against click). Processes that require heavy data entry still continue in mobile apps as business managers hesitate to tweak or skip steps in the workflow leading to less-than-expected adoption of mobile programs. Existing processes and workflows may need to be simplified, or new processes may need to be built for supporting mobile devices.

Enterprise integration challenges: The more the data exchanged between enterprise systems and mobile devices, the higher are the chances of mobile apps with performance issues. Mobile devices cannot have the same payload as Web applications, and most option existing APIs would have to be rebuilt for enabling mobile consumption. More than half the effort in developing mobile apps lies in the integration effort. Ignoring this aspect leads to heavy costs, time over-runs, suboptimal performance, and thereby suboptimal adoption of these apps by the intended end users.

Security challenges: Mobile devices put more power into the hands of the user than into the enterprise, and the enterprise needs to be cautious of the potential vulnerabilities any mobility introduces. Mobility infrastructure and strategies to enable security of data at rest as well as in motion needs to be available with the enterprise before enabling mobile access. Procedures and policies for handling scenarios related to lost or stolen devices of users need to be in place. Decisions related to whether the enterprise should restrict the choice of their employees by providing corporate-owned devices or permitting a "bring your own device" strategy will also have an impact on the security.

Mobility Strategy

Figure 2.14 depicts what goes into defining the mobility strategy for the enterprise, or in other words, the components of the mobile strategy.

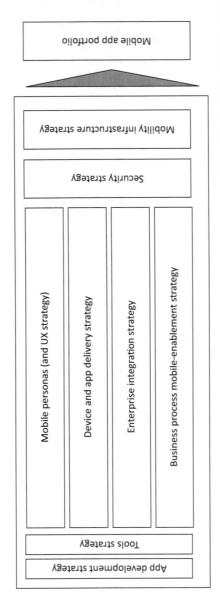

Figure 2.14 What should an enterprise mobility strategy focus on?

At a broad-level, the mobility strategy for an enterprise looks at mobile enablement from both the user and enterprise readiness perspective.

From the user perspective, this strategy identifies the target users (consumers, employees, and partners) for mobile enablement and categorizes them based on what, when, where, and how they will consume data and content on their mobile devices.

From the enterprise perspective, the strategy identifies the processes and applications within the enterprise that should be mobile-enabled, the tweaks that are required for these processes and applications for mobile enablement, and the infrastructure and tools required for integrating and delivering these processes and applications.

The strategy would also identify the threats that mobile enablement brings in for the users as well as the enterprise and outline the approach, infrastructure, and tools to address these security challenges.

As with all other strategies, the mobility strategy would provide a roadmap for addressing the mobile-enablement gaps along with a governance model for implementing this strategy.

User experience (UX) strategy: Any mobility strategy should start with identifying who are the mobile personas targeted for mobile enablement. A persona describes more than just the user (for whom the mobile apps are targeted) and can be a customer, a partner, or an employee. A persona captures the role the user performs, how they perform the role, when, how, and where they execute the tasks associated with their role, a description of the scenarios when they could potentially use a mobile device for performing the tasks associated with the role, the typical places where they would potentially use the mobile device for performing their role-specific tasks, and how they would potentially use the mobile device (and app) for performing their role-specific tasks. Identification of the mobile personas forms the crux of the user experience strategy, and this is kicked-off by observing the day in the life of the persona. Personas can broadly be classified into enterprise personas and consumer personas as shown in Figure 2.15.

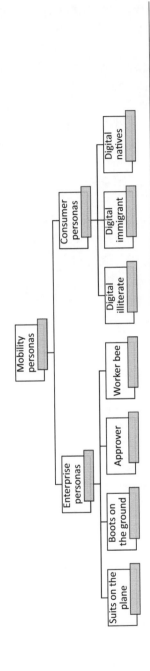

Figure 2.15 Mobility personas.

Enterprise personas can be divided into four categories: "suits on the plane," "boots on the ground," "approver," and "worker bee," as described in Table 2.2.

Based on how comfortable the consumer is with respect to using mobile devices and technology as well as sharing content and personal information, the consumer personas can be divided into digital illiterates, digital immigrants, and digital natives. Figure 2.16 provides a comparison of the different digital consumer personas.

Hyper digital natives, who live and breathe technology, can further be categorized into a new "ultra-digital native" persona.

Most often, mobility initiatives are targeted toward the consumers who are millennials. These consumers largely have the persona of a digital native or an ultra-digital native. The impatient, constantly connected, real-time information-seeking, quick-to-praise but quick-to-complain, instant action-oriented digital natives or ultra-digital natives are as comfortable with mobile apps as fish are with water. These personas need apps that will help them complete their tasks within a few seconds

Table 2.2 Enterprise Mobility Persona Comparison

PERSONA	PERSONA DESCRIPTION	EXAMPLES
Suits on the plane	These are the typical executives who are always on the move. These profiles typically require reporting and dashboard-like apps, and approval and workflow apps on their mobile devices.	Senior management profiles of an enterprise
Boots on the ground	These are the service representatives, collection agents and entry-level sales personnel who spend the larger part of their daily work-life on the field. This persona gets to work in areas with spotty network connectivity (especially in developing countries) and quite often needs applications that work offline and also support offline synchronization.	Field service and sales representatives, collection agents
Approver	These are typically the "middle management" employee cadre, the ones who need to approve expense, travel, resource, purchase, and payment requests from subordinates. These are also the ones who would need to trigger the approval processes.	Resource managers, IT managers, branch managers, middle managers
Worker bee	These are the hard-working employees who may need to raise requests or trigger workflows to get their job done when they are on the move.	Bank tellers, IT employees, Software developers

	Digital illiterate	Digital immigrant	Digital native
Security and privacy	• Highly concerned about sharing personal information with strangers • Not comfortable with using technology	• Concerned about sharing personal information	• More open to share personal information if required
Immediacy of information	• Not worried about immediacy of information as long as it is accurate	• Doesn't demand real-time information	• Demands real-time information

Sharing information with social networks	• Not aware of or not comfortable with mechanisms to share bad experiences
	• Not willing to share information with strangers
		• May not complain unless they have a really bad experience	• Plays the role of a vocal consumer
			  • Will immediately share bad experiences across social networks
			• Can also be a brand advocate
			  • Will immediately share good experiences across social networks

Preferred content type for consumption	• Text	• Does not mind textual content	• Multimedia content preferred • Video against audio and audio against text
Tendency to multi-task	• Concentrated on completing a single task	• Single tasking preferred for better focus	• Multitasking preferred • Demands self-service • Shorter attention span

Figure 2.16   Digital consumer persona comparison.

while allowing them to share any information they find useful with their social networks. Thus simplicity, rich user experience, contextual capability, performance, and ability to share with social networks or login through social networking platforms are the key parameters that decide the success and speed of adoption of these apps (mobility initiatives).

Device and app delivery strategy: Once it is established "who" the personas are that should be mobile-enabled, we get on to identifying which device platforms should be supported and what the delivery mechanisms should be for mobile-enabling the users.

1. *What device platforms should be supported?*

For enterprise personas, there is a need to look at whether the enterprise should provide corporate devices to their employees or allow them to bring devices of their choice and loosen control. Bring your own device (BYOD) strategy will be discussed more in the *enterprise device strategy* and *mobility infrastructure strategy* sections. In the first decade of this century, mobility platform for the enterprise user (especially the executives) was synonymous with secure BlackBerry devices. However, after their rapid decline, banking and financial service enterprises, especially in the developed world, seemed to prefer Apple's iOS devices as the corporate device platform for their enterprise personas.

While the enterprises can control what device platforms their employees need to use if they need access to enterprise information, this cannot be done for their consumers (and partners). Most financial service enterprises tend to ascertain this information based on the analysis of what mobile browsers (and thereby device platforms) their consumers have used to access their website. If their customer-facing website is not optimized for mobile devices, this analysis is erroneous to determine what device platforms should be supported. Hence market research data related to the region/country/geography-specific mobile device shipment is also used as an input to decide on the device platforms they should support for their consumers.

2. *What should the delivery mechanism for mobile-enabling the user be?*

Different personas will have different kinds of needs. For some of the enterprise users, security and anytime, anywhere, any device access may be a priority, while for some of them, especially the sales force as well as those on-field, offline access may be of equal importance. From a consumer perspective, it is important to consider if users would feel it worthwhile to download another app on their device given that they already have so many apps on their mobile device, or they would only use the mobile browser to view the application. Typically, if the need is to serve disparate users spread across different types of devices (Android devices, iOS devices, Windows devices) with no offline synchronization requirement, mobile websites, or mobile Web apps accessible through mobile browsers are the way to go and this should be sufficient for anytime, anywhere access. However, if the demand is for an app with a game-like, rich user interface with split-second performance and offline synchronization needs, it is better to consider apps that will be delivered through public or enterprise app stores.

Mobility use cases related to dashboards and reports, apps that enable agents or wealth advisors to open accounts, are usually made available on tablets, as these can display more data (on higher-resolution screens). Workflow applications or consumer applications like mobile banking applications are more suitable for smartphones.

Enterprise integration strategy: How will the systems of record (SOR) in the enterprise be accessed by mobile channels? Can the existing integration mechanisms used by Web channels also be reused by mobile channels? These are the questions addressed by the enterprise integration strategy.

One of the key challenges when it comes to reusing the integration interfaces meant for Web channels for mobile channels is the amount of payload. Mobile channels are meant to handle lighter payloads, and if the payloads are heavier, there can be a significant performance impact. Hence the key decisions of enterprise integration strategy are also to focus on how to optimize the data and content from the enterprise back-end (system of records) for mobile devices. More and more enterprises are investing in API management tools like Layer 7 and Apigee for accelerating the development of Web services that expose the data (and content) from enterprise back-end. The API management tools also support management, monitoring (as well as monetizing), and securing the APIs/Web services exposing the system of records. Popular enterprise integration strategies rely on lightweight RESTful (representational state transfer) services and a microservice architecture.

Business process mobile-enablement strategy: Not all business processes need to be mobile-enabled. For example, a few static business processes may require the user to access the process only at a specific location and not when on the move. These are the processes that can be ignored for mobile enablement initiatives. The ones that matter for mobile enablement can be classified into mobile-only processes, mobile-first processes, and mobile-also processes (Figure 2.17).

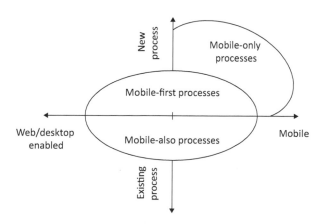

Figure 2.17 Categorizing business processes for mobile enablement.

As shown in Figure 2.17, mobile-also processes usually tend to be existing processes that are already available for access on the desktop/Web browser and need to be enabled for access on mobile devices, whereas mobile-first and mobile-only processes usually tend to be new processes that need to be created from scratch. Mobile-also and mobile-first processes are targeted to be available both on desktop/Web browsers as well as mobile devices.

When dealing with mobile-also processes, the strategy will need to outline how much the existing integration interfaces can be reused from a mobile-enablement perspective. Some processes, which are meant for Web browser/desktop, need a lot of data input (which is not suitable for mobile use). In order to optimize such processes for mobile, we need to look at ways for skipping these processes or having the data pre-loaded for as many fields as possible. Thus the success of adoption of mobile-also processes lies in the rejuvenation and renewal of the existing business process rather than just the reuse of the existing business process. Employee travel expense claims can be considered as an example of mobile-also processes.

While in a mobile-also process, the existing process accessible by Web/desktop needs to be extended to mobile devices. In mobile-first processes, we end up creating a new process for mobile devices and ensuring that the process optimized for mobile is also accessible through Web browser/desktop (either partially or fully). Thus to some extent, mobile-first processes can be considered to be the reverse of mobile-also processes, with the exception that we will have to create a new process and not reuse the existing process. Sales force mobility and agent mobility can be considered to be good examples of mobile-first processes.

Mobile-only processes are where there is tremendous room for innovation. These are new process that are designed only for mobile devices and thus "contextual" parameters (location, gesture) that leverage the native mobile device features to be used to enrich the experience for the end user. Payment using mobile devices can be considered to be a good example of mobile-only processes.

The categorization of business processes into mobile-also, mobile-first, and mobile-only is only to help identify the activities (and comparatively assess the effort) that are needed for mobile enablement. For example, given that mobile-first and mobile-only processes are new processes, the training effort of internal stakeholders would be significant as compared to a mobile-also process.

DO MOBILE BANKING APPS BELONG TO MOBILE-ALSO, MOBILE-FIRST, OR MOBILE-ONLY PROCESSES?

Mobile banking is a classic example of where banks go wrong when dealing with mobile enablement of their business processes. Given that banking has existed on Web-based channels, many banks assume their mobile banking app to be a mobile-also process and have the mobile bank app as a reflection of their Internet (Web) banking site. Completing a transaction on these mobile banking apps often requires the same number of steps to be completed by the end-user customer, leading to customers continuing to use only their Internet banking site and not wanting to use their mobile banking app.

Mobile banking apps have succeeded (have higher adoption) when they are treated as mobile-only processes rather than as mobile-also processes. Top-rated mobile banking apps like Capital One mobile banking app and Simple Bank app have features and experiences more unique to mobile devices. Simplified and mobile-optimized experience and mobile-only features like better mobile deposit capture and SureSwipe (of the Capital One app; simplified login to mobile apps using pattern-matching as against typing passwords) turned out to be the key differentiators when separating the leaders from the laggards in the mobile banking space.[37]

App development strategy: The first of all questions when it comes to mobile app development is: "What is the type of app that needs to be built?"

App types are broadly classified into mobile Web (site), hybrid, and native. Mobile Web (site) is essentially Web code (HTML5, cascaded style sheets [CSS], JavaScript) getting executed within the mobile browser without access to native device capabilities while native apps use platform-specific code (Android-Java or iOS Objective-C code) with full access to native device capabilities. Hybrid apps lie somewhere in-between mobile Web apps and native apps when it comes to native device-access capabilities and can be considered to be Web code (HTML5, CSS, JavaScript) running within a native shell. The "equalizer chart" provides a comparison of the mobile app types (Figure 2.18).

There is no one-size-fits-all strategy that can be used across the enterprise, and different use cases (and constraints) merit different app type strategies. Strategies can only loosely recommend which type of use cases merit which type of app strategies. From Figure 2.18, it is clear that we should go for native app development when there is a need for access to device features, rich user experience needs, when we need offline data synchronization capability for the mobile app, fast performance, and only to support a few device platforms. Increasingly though, newer JavaScript frameworks (coupled with RWD frameworks) are becoming more and more rich (and powerful) when it comes to creating rich user experiences and are tilting app development decisions in favor of mobile Web development (responsive Web design) in case the drive toward native app development is only from a rich user experience perspective.

APP TYPES FOR CONSUMER MOBILITY AND EMPLOYEE MOBILITY

Different banks have been trying different approaches for their retail-specific mobility initiatives. Customer/retail mobility initiatives usually begin with native app strategy given their better experience capability and native device-access capability. However, with the diversity and rapid evolution of mobile devices among their customer base, banks, and financial institutions need to keep supporting enhancements to their retail-facing mobile apps, and this increases their costs. In order to keep the costs lower,

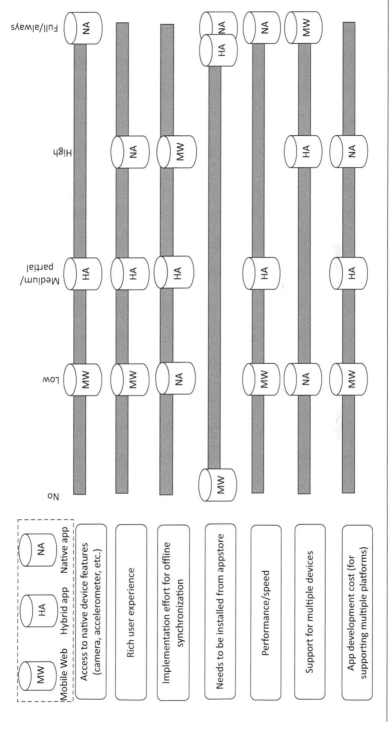

Figure 2.18 Mobile app-type equalizer chart.

some banks jump onto the hybrid app bandwagon but then find the experience quotient an obstacle and go back to their native app strategy for customers. Given the potential of wearables for customer engagement and extensibility of native apps to support wearables, native apps still seem to be a better fit for retail mobility.

For employee initiatives, banks prefer to go with hybrid app development, especially when it comes to enterprise approvals and workflow-based scenarios, given the ability of hybrid apps to support multiple device platforms at an economical price. Only when disconnected-network scenarios (like mobile sales force enablement and mobile field force enablement) arise, is native app development preferred.

Another way of looking at mobile-enablement delivery is to look at it from a business-to-employee (B2E), business-to-business, or business-to-partner (B2B), and business-to-consumer (B2C) lens. When it comes to spending on mobile-enablement initiatives, most banks and financial institutions usually focus on their customers, then move their focus to the sales and marketing team. The rest of the employees come in only later.

RESPONSIVE WEB DESIGN

When it comes to actual development of mobile-friendly websites, one of the key decision points is whether to have separate websites for different devices or have the same website render as per their device resolution. Quite often, enterprises go down the path of having separate websites for different devices only to realize that it is an expensive route to maintain multiple sites although the experience is better.

Increasingly they are adopting responsive Web design (RWD) techniques to build a single website to cater to desktop browsers and smartphone browsers as well as tablet browsers (and if necessary, even large-screen TV browsers). RWD is a Web design technique that separates the presentation, styling, and behavior of the websites based on the resolution of the consuming devices. Various open source RWD frameworks like Twitter Bootstrap and Zurb Foundation, apart from HTML5, CSS3, and JavaScript technologies, have made it easier to develop RWD sites and have accelerated adoption of this technique by enterprises.

Thus the chances of finding a http://m.abcbank.com and http://www.abcbank.com are increasingly remote, and we'll only find that http://www.abcbank.com itself is optimized for smartphones and desktops as well as tablets.

MADP VERSUS MBAAS VERSUS CUSTOM APP DEVELOPMENT

When it comes to enterprise mobility, some of the common requirements include security of data at rest as well as in motion, ability to generate push notifications to different device platforms, and connectivity to enterprise systems like Web services, ERP, CRM, and supply chain management packages, apart from the ability to synchronize data between the local app and a back-end data store. These capabilities are available through popular mobile application development platforms (MADP) or cloud-based mobile backend as a service software (MBaaS). MADPs also provide app templates and pre-built workflow accelerators to speed up cross-platform as well as native mobile app development. Given the relative financial stability of MADP vendors as well as their on-premise capability, most banks and financial institutions prefer MADP-based development against MBaaS-based development.

While MADP is definitely useful from a mobile app development time to market perspective when compared to a non-MADP-greenfield-custom app development-based-approach, banks and financial institutions do face challenges related to vendor lock-in, high costs, customization challenges, and also slower response to device platform (operating system) upgrades when taking the MADP way.

Cloud-based platforms like Amazon Web Services (AWS), Microsoft Azure, and IBM Bluemix also provide backend-as-a-service features.

Tools strategy: Mobile app development is considerably different when compared to building and deploying Web-based
or desktop application. The tools strategy encompasses the
tools needed for rapid prototyping (user experience tools), app
development (integrated development editors (IDEs)), and
testing, or in other words, the tools required across the enterprise for mobile app lifecycle management.

Rapid prototyping UX tools (like iRise, Axure) help capture the usability requirements of the end user.

When it comes to app development, the tools strategy
would decide whether MADP (like SAP mobile platform
(SMP), IBM Worklight/MobileFirst, Kony, etc.), or MBaaS
(like Kinvey) need to be looked at for mobile app development
and, if yes, prescribe the options for their evaluation. This
tools strategy (for app development) also recommends the
use of any cross-platform app development frameworks like
Cordova/PhoneGap, Appcelerator, and so on, mobile Web
development JavaScript frameworks like Sencha, AngularJS,
React, Backbone.js, JavaScript pre-processors, and responsive Web design frameworks (like Twitter Bootstrap, Zurb
Foundation), and so on.

The behavior and look and feel of mobile apps can vary based
on the device on which they are used, (wireless) network coverage and speed of the network and conditions of stress. The
mobile testing space is not fully mature as compared to Web
application and desktop application testing space, and hence
in addition to unit, performance, and regression testing tools,
there is a need to evaluate and use multiple sets of testing tools
like cloud-based device testing tools like DeviceAnywhere
(which remotely tests the app across multiple devices), network variability testing tools (for testing a mobile app for its
behavior when offline or when there is a spotty network),
behavioral, and stress testing tools (to test behavior of the app,
when multiple keys are pressed—also called monkey testing
i.e., how the app would behave if a monkey were to use it).
The additional testing activities like device testing, network
variability testing, behavioral, and stress testing especially are
mandatory for consumer-facing apps.

Given that mobile is all about experience, there is a need to ensure that the app doesn't crash in a stressful environment, and even if it crashes, the developer is able to figure out when (where and how) the app crashed. Mobile app analytics tools (like Crashlytics, Flurry Analytics, and Localytics) as well as mobile application performance management tools (like Aternity) are also increasingly becoming part of the standard mobile app lifecycle management toolset.

Security strategy: The security strategy for consumer or partner mobile enablement varies when compared to employee mobile enablement. From a consumer or partner mobile-enablement perspective, the scope of enterprise data and content available for their consumption is much less than what needs to be available for employees. The security and privacy imperatives are largely to protect (and encrypt) data at rest and motion and to prevent jailbroken devices from accessing their apps; thus, the security measures would be largely limited to authentication and authorization strategy, use of Secure Sockets Layer for data transmission, and data encryption on the device to specific application policies (like preventing jailbroken devices from accessing the app). These measures are in addition to the standard enterprise measures related to protection of customer/consumer data security and privacy.

When it comes to security strategy for employee mobile enablement, the risk of leakage of strategic and confidential data and content is very high. The strategy includes (mobile) device-level, app-level, and content-level security.

Enterprise device strategy: begins with deciding whether to go in for corporate-owned devices (COD) or permit employees to bring their own device (BYOD) for accessing their work content and data. Though the basic policies that prevent unauthorized access of data and content remain similar for COD and BYOD strategies, the areas where the enterprise control differs is in dealing with unmanaged apps, data, or content on the user's device. In case of BYOD, when the user leaves the organization/enterprise, only the enterprise data is wiped off and not the entire data on the device.

Device security strategy typically is fulfilled by implementing mobile device management (MDM). MDM software helps enterprises commission and decommission devices apart from enforcing policies related to protection of data (and content) on devices as well as protection of devices from access and use of data and content from unauthorized or illegal sources that can compromise enterprise security. These include policies around accessing public Wi-Fi networks, detecting if the device is jailbroken or somebody is trying to tamper with the root, Bluetooth connectivity, password protection, device locking, app download, content download, and website access restrictions. The policies also include remote device wipe in case the device is stolen, lost, or compromised. MDM also includes email management (and configuration) on the device. It also ensures that the appropriate software (and updates) are pushed to the user for installation.

CORPORATE-OWNED DEVICES (COD) VERSUS BRING YOUR OWN DEVICE (BYOD)

When it comes to device strategy, especially for the employees, the first step is to decide on whether to provide COD to the employees to enable access to enterprise data and content. COD has its own benefits, like tighter control on the device and the external data and content it accesses.

BlackBerry is to date the best known COD, and with the decline of BlackBerry, COD also seems to be losing out against BYOD. The rapid evolution of MDM software and enterprise EMM software has enabled enterprises to have a fair level of control even on employee-owned devices. Features like app containerization and app wrapping, introduced by MDM/EMM vendors, are enabling enterprises to separate out the enterprise data and personal data on employee devices while enabling employees to use the same device for both the enterprise use as well as personal use. One of the advantages of BYOD over COD also lies in the fact that enterprises need not invest in procuring mobile devices (as well as upgrading the devices already procured), and this has helped increase the number of employees who can be provided secure access to enterprise data and content (on their own preferred device) and thereby also improve employee engagement. The challenge with BYOD lies in ensuring that enterprise controls (device policies) don't end up suffocating the employees so much that they opt out of the BYOD program. BYOD does not mean that enterprises will support all devices. In order to keep BYOD programs manageable, most enterprises limit this to iOS, a few Android phone vendors, Windows, and BlackBerry. Even from the device platform perspective, access is limited only to the current OS version and earlier two versions.

App security strategy: This revolves around provisioning (and upgrading) the necessary enterprise (and third-party) apps on the devices, deploying policies (on devices) that protect the data (and content) accessed by the app, and prevent the app from performing unauthorized actions or accessing data or content from unauthorized sources and is typically fulfilled by mobile application management (MAM) software. These include authentication and authorization policies, deploying configurations, and profiles for single sign-on login for the (enterprise) apps on the device. MAM software allows enterprises to have their own app store for distributing their enterprise mobile apps, support app containerization or app wrapping, and sometimes both.

APP CONTAINERIZATION VERSUS APP WRAPPING

Both app containerization and app wrapping are leveraged in BYOD scenarios to help the device user in separating enterprise apps (and data) from personal apps (and data).

App containerization requires the app developer to invoke the client-side SDK (software development kit) (of the MAM provider) from the app code, and this enables the app to execute within a separate container or communicate with other apps within the same container.

In comparison, app wrapping is a lighter and easier option for enhancing app security and control. This does not need any code tweaks. The MAM administrator can instead wrap the (already compiled) app with the security libraries provided by the MAM vendor through the management console.[38]

MAM software initially was separate from MDM software, and the distinguishing factor between MAM and MDM was the level of granularity of control possible. MAM was largely used to cater to management of BYOD employee devices and was able to ensure that control need not be enforced on the whole device if the device user needs to only use specific enterprise mobile apps. MAM ensures that only the managed apps (i.e., apps pushed by the enterprise) will be wiped off the device. Those apps that were downloaded by the user will remain on the device and will not be wiped off.

BEST PRACTICES FOR APP SECURITY

Other than implementing MAM, some of the best practices for enterprises to ensure security of the app include:

Enterprise data classification: The first step toward protection of data privacy begins with classification of data (and content) owned by enterprises into what is publicly shareable, shareable within the enterprise, confidential, and secretive. Those apps that handle confidential and secretive data must provide a higher level of data protection.

App security certification process: Procedurally, some of the large banking and financial services enterprises have an internal app security certification process as part of the mobile app development process. This security certification process is integrated with the IT security process as well as the risk and compliance process. This process prevents the app from being made available to end users if they handle confidential and secretive data without adequate controls.

Leveraging development and testing security tools and guidelines: Apart from adhering to open Web application security project (OWASP) mobile security guidelines for development, testing, and app risk mitigation, threat modeling for the app can be performed when developing the requirements for the app. The app code can be run through security tools like IBM AppScan to identify security vulnerabilities as part of the app code. Penetration testing (popularly called pen testing) can be performed on the apps.

Content security strategy: This is all about securing enterprise content (largely documents) the users may have access to. Figure 2.19 depicts a day in the life of an enterprise mobile user, a view of how enterprise users work with documents on their mobile devices.

For an enterprise mobile user, the source of an enterprise document could be either an email attachment, network file share systems, enterprise document management systems, or even cloud-storage providers. The mobile user can receive the document through an email attachment; can directly download this document from network file storage, enterprise document management systems, or cloud-storage providers; can open this document; and can save it on their device. They may want to edit this document or share it (collaborate) with other users for editing and upload this document back to enterprise or cloud storage or save it locally on their device. Especially in BYOD scenarios, these actions of the mobile user represent immense possibilities for leakage of enterprise content for the enterprise IT department. The department's

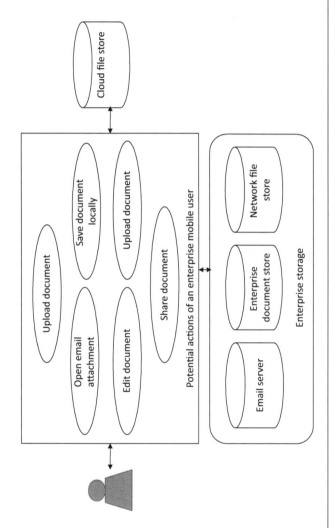

Figure 2.19   A day in the life of an enterprise mobile user.

key concerns would be how to ensure that enterprise documents on the device are secure, how to ensure that mobile users don't upload the enterprise document to unauthorized external (cloud) storage providers or share it with unauthorized users. This is where mobile content management (MCM) software supports the enterprise IT department.

MCM software comes with secure file storage (server) for enabling mobile users to collaborate, mobile apps for mobile users to open the documents securely on the device, components for file-locking, versioning of documents, synchronizing the documents between the device and the file storage (server), and identity management components to ensure that the mobile user is an authenticated user and doesn't have to enter their login credentials for each and every action on the enterprise document. In addition, MCM also provides the enterprise IT with a set of content leakage prevention capabilities like ability to configure policies for control of the enterprise document, the ability to wipe off the enterprise documents from the device in case of the mobile user leaving the organization or loss of device. MCM satisfies the "control" needs of enterprises by enabling them to protect their documents from leakage while at the same time enabling the enterprise mobile users to meet their natural experience expectations with regards to document collaboration.

MCM software too differs from MDM and MAM software in terms of the granularity of control. There is no need for restrictive device management of personal devices if the employee's primary needs are to access enterprise documents and collaborate with other employees.

MDM VERSUS EMM

Given the overlapping capabilities of MDM, MAM, and MCM as well as the fragmented nature of this market, there has been a consolidation drive by major vendors. Suddenly MDM has evolved into enterprise mobility management (EMM). EMM includes MDM, MAM, and MCM and provides enterprises a near-complete package for secure control of employee mobile devices. Most EMM and MDM also provide customizable and pre-configured management reports related to the number of devices and users enrolled, the type of devices, device platform distribution ratio, and so on. EMM is geared toward enabling employees to be almost as productive with their mobile devices as their desktops and laptops. Many of the EMMs also come with a billing module enabling enterprises to track the employee mobile data usage. They also come with geofencing capabilities for tracking employees within a perimeter of the enterprise locations or providing them additional access to their enterprise systems, data, and content within the perimeter. Popular EMM vendors include VMware AirWatch, IBM MaaS360, SAP Mobile Secure, Citrix XenMobile, Microsoft Intune, MobileIron, and so on.

Mobility infrastructure strategy: Mobility infrastructure serves as the backbone for the enterprise mobility strategy of the enterprise. Broadly, the mobility infrastructure needs can be classified into networking, software and tooling, and virtualization enablers. Figure 2.20 depicts a view of what an enterprise would need to cater to their enterprise mobility needs.

The need for each of these enablers is driven by the strategy of the enterprise. If the enterprise plans a retail customer-focused mobility strategy, the infrastructure needs would include wireless access points and routers along with location-detection sensors and beacons. Decisions related to the support for various network protocols like NFC (near-field communication protocol), Bluetooth LE protocol, messaging protocols like MQTT (message queueing telemetry transport), WebSockets, and so on would also have to be considered.

The app development strategy would impact the decision on whether to go in for MADP or MBaaS or stay with non-platform-based development tools. Device platform strategy and app type strategy

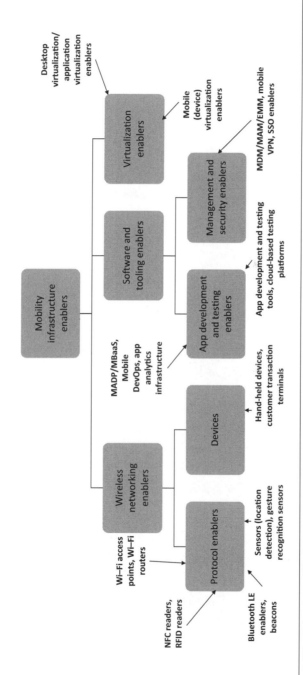

Figure 2.20 Enterprise mobility infrastructure enablers.

would also impact the need for cloud-based testing tools, app monitoring, performance management, and analytical tools to be used.

The level of data security permitted by the enterprise decides the virtualization infrastructure needs. For many enterprises, rewriting all the important existing applications for mobile device consumption may prove to be too expensive. This results in the need for desktop and/or application virtualization infrastructure to enable the employees to access their (Windows) desktop applications on their mobile devices. This virtualization infrastructure supports protocols for making these applications mobile- (touch-) friendly.

In many cases, the enterprise security strategy would necessitate the requirement that enterprise apps leave no footprint on the end users' (employees') devices. In these cases, a virtual mobile infrastructure (Android OS) would ensure that end users only access the apps remotely (virtually) and don't have to install the enterprise apps on their personal devices.

Device strategy (on whether to go in for a corporate-owned device or permit BYOD) for their employees has a large say in whether to go in for MDM or EMM for management of mobile devices. Other decisions like single sign-on requirements for enterprise apps, adherence to Federal Information Processing Standards (FIPS) for regulatory compliance needs (if cryptographic modules need to be used), and strategy for employee devices to connect to enterprise (need for mobile virtual private networks) are also based on the enterprise mobility security strategy of the enterprise.

The usage application capability (UAC) framework for mobile technology has been explained in the "More Mobility" section of the Appendix.

Mobile Payments and Wallets

Mobile wallets and payment through mobile devices have enabled financial institutions to reach out to the underbanked segment of the population. The rapid rise in adoption of mobile wallets and payments through mobile devices can be directly attributed to the widespread growth of consumer mobility due to the drastically reducing costs of owning a mobile device.

As per the 2015 World Bank's Global Financial Inclusion Database, more than 60 million people in Sub-Saharan Africa have mobile money accounts or mobile wallets. More than half of the adult population in Kenya accesses their money through a mobile device.[39]

In India, where higher denomination currency notes of 500 and 1,000 rupees were demonetized in November 2016, transactions through mobile wallets have seen an exponential increase after demonetization. During November 2016, while the growth of credit and debit cards has been less than 3% month-on-month, mobile wallets have grown by more than 9% during the same period.[40]

> *Mobile payment mechanisms:*[41] Broadly, any payment mechanism that needs a mobile device can be termed as mobile payment. This can either involve only the customer using a mobile device to pay, a retailer using a mobile device to collect payments, or both.
>
> Mobile point-of-sale (mPOS) mechanism involves a card reader that is attached to a mobile device. This card reader connects wirelessly to a payment network. A customer can use their credit or debit card to swipe and pay. Thus, mPOS is a mobile payment mechanism where the customer can continue to use their existing plastic (credit or debit) card for payment, but do not have to walk to a specific location at the retail store to make the payment. But a retailer would need a mobile device to connect a card reader. Square is a good example of an mPOS mechanism.
>
> Quick Response (QR) code scanning mechanisms are those in which the account details of the retailer are displayed as a QR code. The app on the customer's mobile device can read this code to make payment.
>
> Near-field communication (NFC) mechanism involves the use of contactless payments using NFC readers. The customer will have to open their mobile app and tap (or wave) on the retailer's POS terminal, which has an NFC reader to make the payment.
>
> *In-app payment:* This requires the user to open their mobile wallet, select the card they would want to use, search for the retailer, or scan the QR code of the retailer to make their payment. PayPal, Apple Pay, Samsung Pay, and Android Pay, or mobile wallets can all be considered in-app payment mechanisms.

Mobile wallets:[42] These can be considered virtual money pre-
loaded onto mobile apps that can be used for both offline payments (involving POS devices) and online payments. Online
payments include peer-to-peer transfer of money, payment
of utility bills, and recharge of prepaid mobiles. Some of the
mobile wallets also support storing (and using) loyalty coupons
and loyalty program points. In the United States alone in 2015,
there were more than 200 mobile wallet providers (with banks,
telcos, fintechs, and retailers being the wallet providers apart
from the tech companies like Apple Pay, Android Pay, and
Samsung Pay).

Mobile wallets may be open (launched with bank support), which
can be used for making payments to multiple merchants who have
agreements with the wallet service provider or withdraw pre-loaded
amounts (or the amount remaining in the wallet) as cash from
ATMs; semi-open or semi-closed wallets (telco-provided or third-
party-/fintech-provided wallets that can be used across multiple
merchants, but from which cash cannot be withdrawn); or closed
(a retailer-provided wallet that can be used only for buying goods or
services from the same retailer and cannot be used for transacting
with other merchants).

Transactions using mobile wallets are made secure by ensuring that card information is securely stored on the device SIM or
on the cloud (host controlled emulator, HCE) in an encrypted or
tokenized form. Thus there is no actual transfer of sensitive card
information between the consumer and the merchant. Wallets like
Apple Pay (which can be used on wearables like Apple iWatch)
ensure additional security by requiring the user to authorize payments through the use of their touch ID (fingerprint). The channel
for transfer of payment information is also through secure mechanisms like NFC.[43]

Mobility Reference Architecture

Systems of record can be exposed as Web services through
the integration layer for consumption by mobile devices
(Figure 2.21). The integration layer can be API or REST (or

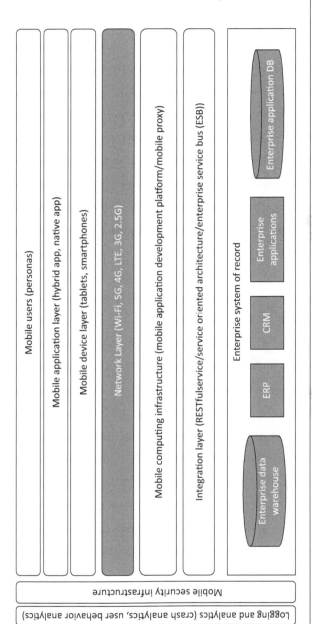

Figure 2.21   Reference architecture for financial enterprises to benefit from mobile technology.

SOAP) Web services exposed through an enterprise service bus (ESB). Mobility computing infrastructure like a mobile application development platform (MADP) can help isolate the enterprise network from the wireless network. An MADP or mobile backend as a service (MBaaS) can also serve as a proxy to connect to the enterprise backend (or systems of record) securely as well as support the generation of push notifications. The mobile apps residing on the mobile devices connect to the mobile computing infrastructure layer through a wireless network. Any crashes on the device as well as user behavior can be logged for further analysis.

Analytics Primer

We are today at the cusp of the "smart and intelligent" era. Intelligent enterprise, data-driven organizations, smart management, and smart decision making all have a common thread running among them, namely, their ability to intelligently use data and analytics for performing their tasks better and faster.

Traditionally, banks and financial institutions have been collecting enormous amounts of transactional data of their customers in a structured format. This data was largely used for "**informational**" and "**descriptive**" purposes like **reporting** and measurement against key performance indicators (KPIs) to senior management on "what is happening currently." The data management processes were tailored toward **converting structured data to information through a pipeline** process of **extracting** data from multiple transactional systems, **cleaning** data, and removing duplicates and **transforming** them into the format needed by a large, enterprise-wide **data warehouse** (which stores historical data in a query-friendly, de-normalized structure).

Figure 2.22 depicts the architecture used for descriptive analytical use cases. Operational data stores were also used in most large enterprises as an additional step before the creation of a data warehouse. Data marts specific to different functions and departments were carved out of the enterprise data warehouse. Online analytical processing engines were also used for modeling what-if scenarios.

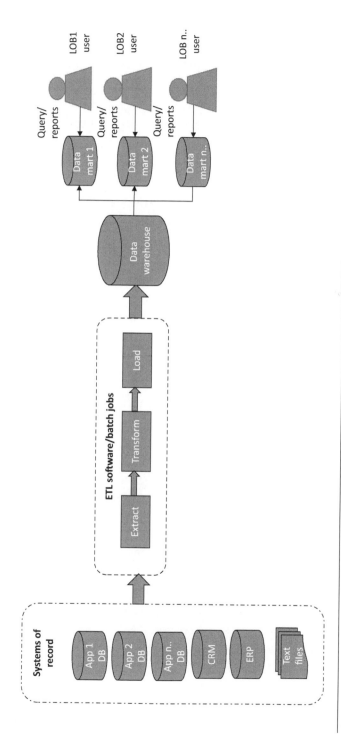

Figure 2.22 Architecture for descriptive analytics.

The explosive growth of social content and user-generated content in the last decade has resulted in more information about customer preferences and feedback lying outside the enterprise than inside. To understand their customers better (from this external unstructured data), some of the financial enterprises ended up investing in **natural language processing** (NLP) and **text analytical** capabilities to extract information from unstructured content as an add-on capability.

The analytical process was executed largely on-premise, and the cost of hardware infrastructure and (expensive) storage was still a key factor driving data management initiatives. By the end of the last decade, banks and financial institutions had thus gained the capability to not only understand "what happened" but also to extract patterns out of their historical data and predict "what can happen," and to a reasonable extent, "why did it happen." Investment in NLP and text analytics helped banks and financial enterprises in understanding the customer better through sentiment analysis of social media content (and content from product review sites) and customer analytics.

But the exploding data from apps on mobile devices, data from sensor (and wearable) devices, and data from server logs apart from social and transactional data meant that banks and financial enterprises had to think of other ways to generate insights from this data without driving up the hardware infrastructure and storage costs. With Internet companies like Amazon, Google, and Facebook having already solved this problem by leveraging big data analytics running on networked commodity hardware, banks, and financial enterprises have begun to adopt big data analytics.

Big data analytics is all about the generation of insights from both structured and unstructured data. The four Vs, namely volume, velocity, variety, and veracity, define the dimensions of big data. When we are talking big data, we are talking about **petabytes** (one petabyte = 1,000 terabytes), **exabytes** (one exabyte = 1,000 petabytes), **zettabytes** (one zettabyte = 1,000 exabytes), and **yottabytes** (one yottabyte = 1,000 zettabytes). Big data analytics can involve both batch analytics leveraging the Hadoop ecosystem, as well as analyzing streams of high-velocity data involving Apache Spark and complex event processing frameworks. The sudden spike in **artificial**

intelligence solutions can be directly attributed to the growing maturity of big data analytics.

FOUR VS OF BIG DATA ANALYTICS[44]

Traditional analytics involves extraction of patterns and information from only structured data in a batch mode. The data size is typically in terabytes (one terabyte = 1 million gigabytes) or lesser amounts. However, big data analytics can handle huge volumes of diverse data arriving at rapid velocity in real time or in batch mode. The below statistics provide the extent of what big data analytics involves and why there is a huge focus on big data analytics across industries:

Volume: More than 2 trillion gigabytes are estimated to be generated daily. By 2020, 40 zettabytes of data are expected to be generated daily (which is a 300-time increase from 2005). Thus, enterprises are staring at a volume of data that is beyond what traditional analytical approaches can address.

Velocity: In 2016, about 6,000 tweets per second or 350,000 tweets per/minute were generated on average on Twitter, the social networking platform. Analyzing data with this speed presents a huge challenge for enterprises with traditional approaches and tools.

Variety: Over 80% of data is unstructured. The format of data generated from sensors is different from data from server logs. And so is data from social networking platforms. Traditional analytical approaches require a standardized format for analytics.

Veracity: The quality and accuracy of data have always been a challenge, even in the traditional analytics world, but with a lot of tools to standardize master data, remove duplicate data, and solutions like master data management, there is now a reasonably accurate single source of truth for enterprises. With big data analytics involving multiple sources of data (external and internal), maintaining the authenticity and accuracy of data is a challenge.

BIG DATA INFRASTRUCTURE: HADOOP[45,46]

Multiple tools and technologies revolving around Hadoop framework form the ecosystem of big data analytics. These tools and technologies support applications that need high-throughput access to large data sets. At its core, Hadoop includes HDFS (Hadoop file system), a data storage system on a cluster of commodity server machines, along with MapReduce, a software framework coded in Java for managing resources, managing the distributed processing of data (in parallel), and scheduling jobs (and tasks) for transformation and analysis of this data in a distributed manner.

HDFS enables a highly fault-tolerant architecture that can be deployed on any platform. The master-slave architecture supported by HDFS enables quick detection (of faults) and automatic recovery from faults. A master name node (for managing file operations and mapping blocks to data nodes) and a set of data nodes constitute the HDFS cluster. HDFS stores user data in files. These files are split into different blocks and distributed across the data nodes. The data blocks are further replicated across the cluster, enabling fault tolerance. HDFS architecture works on the assumption that it is more economical to move computation to where the data resides than vice versa and provides interfaces for applications to move themselves to where the data resides.

BIG DATA INFRASTRUCTURE: THE HADOOP ECOSYSTEM

Other tools that form the ecosystem of Hadoop include HBase (a column-oriented data store and Hadoop database for random read/write access), Hive (a query language interface similar to SQL for querying Hadoop; Hive enables performing SQL-like queries on large data sets), Pig (a dataflow language and compiler that also serves as a high-level query language for large-scale data processing), ZooKeeper (a coordination service for distributed applications), Sqoop (enables integration of Hadoop with enterprise databases and data warehouses), Flume[47] (a distributed, reliable, and available service for efficiently collecting, aggregating, and moving large amounts of log data; its main goal is to deliver data from applications to Apache Hadoop's HDFS), and so on.

The multiple toolsets associated with big data infrastructure are largely open source. However, the multiplicity (and often duplicate functionality) of these toolsets complicates the infrastructure setup and adoption for enterprises. This has spawned a lot of players in the market who simplify, refine, and customize the open source Hadoop stack and distribute them for enterprise adoption as well as provide any required support. Cloudera, Hortonworks, and MapR are the popular Hadoop distributors.

Traditionally the data management needs of banks and financial institutions have been centered around consistency of structured data (i.e., database management systems that support ACID (atomicity, consistency, isolation, and durability) transactions) along with a friendly interface for querying (structure query language interface or SQL) this data. In other words, they have been focused on waterfall mode of application development, managing data for internal users to access and development, maintenance, and support of systems of record.

Today's systems of engagement need data management systems that can handle huge volumes of structured and unstructured data at an economical cost, inherently support elasticity of computing and storage needs, enable high-throughput, low-latency reads for millions of external users (and not just internal users), and support flexibility of data structures over consistency to support the agile needs of the organization. This is where NoSQL databases fit the bill, especially for use cases like high-volume trading data feeds, social media analytics, personalizing ads, real-time dashboards, biometric analysis, and real-time fraud analytics.

NoSQL databases are databases that store entire documents (in XML or JSON format) or can store data in key-value pairs or as graphs. Querying of the data is exposed through APIs or through scaled-down SQLs. These databases represent a relaxation in the design (and constraints) of relational databases. NoSQL databases can be on-premise or reside in the cloud and may also use Hadoop underneath for storage and processing. MongoDB, Cassandra, HBase, and Amazon DynamoDB can all be considered NoSQL databases. They can integrate with in-memory computing engines like Apache Spark (used for real-time analytics).[48]

Artificial intelligence (AI) is all about computer systems (and machines) that can perform tasks that typically require human intelligence.[49]

Passing the Turing test is the benchmark for a system to be considered artificially intelligent. The Turing test was designed by Alan Turing, an English mathematician who was one of the earliest (during the 1940s and 1950s) pioneers in the field of artificial intelligence. As part of this test, if a human being is not able to consistently determine which answers were provided by the computer system and which were answered by human beings, then the computer system is said to have passed the Turing test and is considered to be intelligent.[50]

AI has been around for the last few decades in different forms. Earlier expert systems and rules engines were considered AI. Later it was NLP and text analytics. Now, AI means **machine learning, robotics, facial recognition, speech recognition, voice recognition,** and **natural language generation**.

Leveraging cloud infrastructure has brought down the cost of storage and computing infrastructure required for big data analytics. This has also provided elasticity for the growing storage and computing needs of big data analytics. Combining artificial intelligence with big data analytics, banks, and financial institutions have been able to move toward a **predictive** and **prescriptive** mode of operations from a **descriptive** mode. The combination of big data analytics and AI is helping financial institutions make contextual recommendations, identify fraud real-time and alert customers, personalize, and optimize the online as well as offline experience for the customer.

COGNITIVE COMPUTING, MACHINE LEARNING, AND DEEP LEARNING

This is the era of cognitive computing, where computers and machines can be taught to learn, reason, and perform tasks that were earlier possible only by human beings. Going forward in this book, cognitive computing and AI will be used synonymously.

DBS Bank, a bank headquartered in Singapore, has partnered with IBM (leveraging the IBM Watson cognitive computing platform) for providing next-generation client experience for its wealth management customers using cognitive computing. Cognitive computing will help its client relationship managers analyze large volumes of research reports and financial product information and match this with their customer profiles and needs to recommend the best financial options for their customers.[51]

Machine learning can be considered a part of AI, where the computer (or machine) automatically discovers patterns from data and the relationship between different data points without executing any explicit programming logic (instructions). Machine learning can be supervised, unsupervised, or reinforced.

Deep learning can be considered to be a part of machine learning used for computer vision-based use cases. Deep learning models itself on how the human brain (and the interconnection of neurons) works and leverages artificial neural network algorithms. Image recognition, driverless cars, and so on are examples of deep learning applications.

SUPERVISED LEARNING

Supervised learning involves providing the computer system with input data sets and example training data sets or labeled data. Both the input data and the training data (which is actually a corresponding output) are provided in pairs. As more and more input data and training data are provided, the computer system automatically learns the pattern and provides the corresponding output for inputs (even those input data that it has not been provided) using algorithms like random forest, linear regression, and support vector machines. Supervised learning is used when data needs to be classified (use cases like classifying text) as well as to detect fraud. Supervised learning is also widely used for regression use cases like forecasting of product sales. Predictive analytics applications largely use supervised learning.

Figure 2.23 depicts a view of how supervised machine learning is applied, features (or attributes) are mathematical representation of the input data while models can be considered as the mathematical summary of features.

UNSUPERVISED LEARNING

Unsupervised learning involves providing the computer system with only input data sets and allowing the computer system to automatically cluster the data or group the data based on the concept of distance between the points in the data set. The data points close to each other are clustered together using algorithms like k-means, hierarchical clustering, and Apriori algorithms. Unsupervised learning is used for customer segmentation, targeted marketing, and recommendation systems.

Figure 2.24 depicts a view of how unsupervised machine learning is applied.

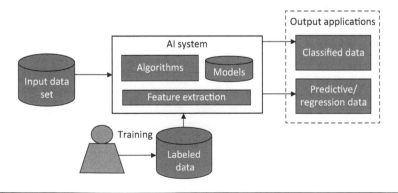

Figure 2.23   Supervised machine learning applications.

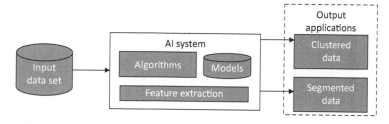

Figure 2.24 Unsupervised machine learning applications.

In today's world, machine learning applications largely involve semi-supervised learning, which involves a mix of both labeled and unlabeled data. In semi-supervised learning, techniques involving both supervised and unsupervised learning are used.[52]

Apart from supervised and unsupervised learning, reinforcement learning is another category of machine learning popular in the field of robotics and real-time coordination. Here, input data is provided to the computer system, and the system learns the right way to move forward (right action) on a trial and error basis through the feedback provided. Right actions are typically rewarded while wrong actions may be punished. Reinforcement learning is used for scenarios where the environment is unknown, physical control is desired, and feedback can be provided in real time. We are seeing many banks acquire robots for specialized and secure tasks like locker and smart vault facility.

ICICI Bank, a leading Indian bank, is piloting robotic lockers to enable their high net worth clients to use their high-end lounge facility to try out their jewel ornaments (stored in safe vaults and lockers) securely with minimal human intervention by involving robots. These robots leverage reinforcement learning to perform their tasks.[53]

DEMOCRATIZING MACHINE LEARNING

Package software like MATLAB®, SAS, and IBM SPSS were already being used by large financial enterprises for the statistical and mathematical modeling of data. However, adopting machine learning to fine-tune their business processes was always a challenge for most enterprises due to the enormous computing power and storage required and the complexity of algorithms involved, apart from the need for high-end talent.

Advancement in big data technology, cloud infrastructure providing elasticity and open sourcing of machine learning algorithms and frameworks (like Apache Mahout and Google TensorFlow), apart from the amount of data currently available for analysis are powering "machine learning as a service" (MLaaS) platforms. These platforms are enabling not just scientists but also software programmers and even business analysts to use machine learning for their needs.

Amazon, Microsoft Azure, Google, and IBM, apart from a host of other niche vendors like DataScience, Domino, CrowdFlower, and so on, are positioning themselves as MLaaS providers and widening the application of machine learning across industries. MLaaS providers support R, Python, and Scala (many of the popular machine learning frameworks are available in these programming languages). Most of these platforms also provide tools for feature engineering and data modeling and are accessible through simple REST-based APIs.[54]

Adoption of machine learning techniques has enabled various banks in Europe to experience a double-digit increase in new product sales apart from a double-digit increase in cash collection and double-digit decrease in customer churn. Machine learning is enabling these banks to build better recommendations for their customers apart from helping predict potential defaulters.[55]

Challenges Faced by Chief Data Officers

The deluge of data presents a formidable challenge for today's enterprises to manage and the role of a chief data officer has never been as important as it is today. Traditionally the efforts of the chief data officer have been expended more on managing data security, ensuring data integrity, ensuring data governance, and satisfying the needs of the internal users (mostly the executives) with the available data warehouse. The decision points were more regarding creating a separate data mart for the line of business or leveraging the existing data warehouse and customizing it, if necessary. Increasingly, the chief data officers are being asked by enterprises to also take over a lead role in devising the data analytics strategy for the enterprise and owning up the execution, maintenance, and support of this strategy.

Thus, in today's world the chief data officer's concerns are more proactive in nature. How to proactively make a difference to the business through insights from the data available internally and externally, what tools they should go in for, where they should execute their analytics (on-premise or cloud), where they should store new data that would be generated, how they should integrate their existing data management systems into future analytics strategy, and the kind of roles and skills they should acquire all represent the key concerns of a chief data officer today. Generating insights out of both internal and humongous external data (from sources that may not even exist today) that are of different formats presents a severe challenge to today's chief data officer.

Democratizing insights is the foundation on which an efficiently performing, data-driven organization is built. The chief data officer plays an important role in ensuring that not just executives but even lower-level employees have the information they need for performing their duties efficiently.

Developing an Enterprise-Wide Integrated Analytics Strategy

Most financial enterprises have a strategy for managing their data. Evolving this into a strategy for analytics is where many enterprises fall short. Business analytics initiatives run as siloed initiatives from forward-looking business units rather than an integrated enterprise initiative. This results in multiple proof of concepts (developed as part of these initiatives), especially related to big data analytics and artificial intelligence not scaling up to provide the intended business benefits. Increasingly there is a talk of "big data fatigue" among leading enterprises referring to the more-than-expected efforts spent by individual teams on big data analytics leading to less-than-satisfactory outcomes. Figure 2.25 depicts the approach for developing and deploying an enterprise-wide integrated analytics strategy.

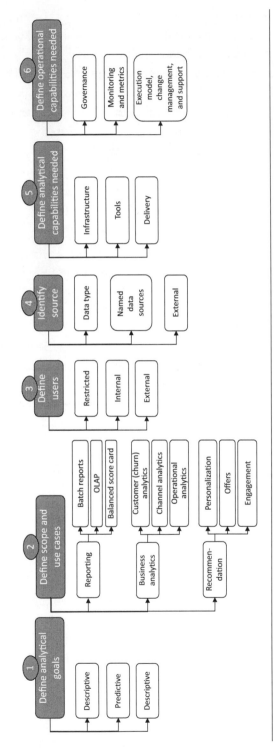

Figure 2.25 Strategy for enterprise-wide integrated analytics.

Defining the analytical goals: The first step in defining the enterprise-wide integrated analytics strategy involves defining the purpose for which the organization needs analytics and what is the business value expected out of the investment in analytics. The analytical goals have a deep impact on the analytical capabilities needed by the organization. Having the goal of only descriptive analytics implies that data would need to be analyzed only from a perspective of reporting, balanced score card, and what-if analysis (OLAP). This implies that traditional business intelligence tools like extract transform load (ETL), apart from reporting and data visualization tools, are sufficient. Predictive and prescriptive analytics goals implies that there would be a need for analyzing huge amounts of data and thereby a potential need for big data analytics and even artificial intelligence.

Defining the scope and the analytical use cases: The scope of analytics and the high-level use cases envisioned are a direct offshoot of the analytical goals of the enterprise.

A roadmap of only descriptive analytics implies that the scope of analytics will largely be around reporting. Use cases like batch reports, "what-if" analysis and balanced score card use cases focused on internal executive and operational users (providing them information on "what happened") would be the priority.

Those enterprises whose analytical goals also include predictive use cases would focus on business analytics as scope. Analytical use cases would revolve around customer analytics (focusing on churn as well as understanding the high-value customers and customer life-time value), channel analytics (Web analytics, social analytics, mobile analytics) to understand the customer behavior, fraud analytics, and operational analytics (crash analytics, log analytics for understanding where the customers (as well as enterprises) are facing issues).

Enterprises with futuristic goals of prescriptive analytics would need to focus on generating recommendations as part of their scope. Analytical use cases include targeted

personalization, generating contextual offers based on preferences of the user as well as engaging users.

Identifying the type of users/consumers: The type of users targeted
for analytics plays a role in the infrastructure needed for
analytics.

If internal as well as external users are involved, and the
scope of analytics is business analytics and recommendations,
it is implicit that structured as well as unstructured data
would be required for analytics.

Identify the source of data for analytics: The source of data may be
internal or external. Typically descriptive analytics need only
internal sources of data (from systems of record), and the type
of data is structured data. Predictive and prescriptive analytics would need to analyze both structured and unstructured
data from internal and external sources.

Define the analytical capabilities required: Descriptive analytics
would require on-premise business intelligence (BI) infrastructure. Here the structured data from systems of record
would need to be extracted, transformed into the format
required by a data warehouse and loaded into the data warehouse. Individual lines of businesses may have their own data
marts created out of the data warehouse for their reporting
purposes.

Predictive and prescriptive analytics would require big data
analytics infrastructure (Hadoop-based as well as real-time
complex event processing) and machine learning infrastructure. This infrastructure is mostly cloud-based. Predictive
and prescriptive use cases evolve over a period of time, and
hence any new data structure addition should not result in
a long time to implement the necessary changes. Given that
the consumers of analytical data may be all kinds of users
(internal and external) and data types may be structured and
unstructured, data warehouses may not be sufficient, and we
may need **data lakes**, which can be considered warehouses
storing massive amounts of data running into petabytes and
yottabytes. Data lakes store both structured and unstructured data. Apart from storing data from external sources,
documents, photos, audio, and video files, data lakes can also

source data from existing data warehouses and data marts for further analytics. Data lakes are meant for all types of users (internal and external) where data is stored in its native format (and structure) on Hadoop file system (HDFS). Consumers of this data can transform the data to the format they need on demand (when used). This "schema-by-read" design of data lakes ensures that any changes to data structure format do not require a long time to implement. As data lakes use commodity hardware for storing data, the cost of storage is not a concern when designing data lakes and all (historical) data is retained for analysis. Hadoop-based infrastructure ensures that queries from data lakes respond fast.

Define operational capabilities needed: Most financial enterprises already have the capabilities required for descriptive analytics. For prescriptive and predictive analytics, they can look at an external partner (from IT services companies) in case they lack internal execution capability. Before adoption across multiple business units and LOBs, banks and financial institutions typically explore specific big data analytics and machine learning use cases through a centralized analytics center of excellence (CoE) execution model.

Coming to the skills needed by enterprises, in addition to traditional business intelligence roles, banks and financial institutions may need additional roles like data scientists and data engineers for their big data analytics and machine learning implementation needs for predictive and prescriptive analytical needs.

Figure 2.26 provides a comparison of what is needed for implementing an enterprise-wide integrated analytics strategy for different analytical goals (descriptive, predictive, prescriptive).

Reference Architecture for Analytical Applications

Figure 2.27 depicts the reference architecture for financial enterprises planning for a multitude of analytical applications leveraging descriptive to predictive to prescriptive analytics. It needs to be noted that traditional BI software may continue to coexist along with big data infrastructure. A data lake stores all types of data (historical structured data,

	Descriptive			Predictive			Prescriptive		
Scope for analytics	Reporting			Business analytics			Recommendations		
Use cases for analytics	Batch reports	OLAP	Balanced score card	Customer churn analytics	Channel analytics	Operational analytics	Personalization	Offers	Engagement
Users	Restricted internal			Internal and external			External		
Source data type	Structured			Structured and unstructured			Structured and unstructured		
Source of data	(Internal) systems of record			(Internal) systems of record, social, third-party data, documents, audio, image, video			(Internal) systems of record, social, third-party data, documents, audio, image, video		
Analytical infrastructure capabilities needed	Business intelligence (BI) infrastructure			BI tools + big data (Hadoop) analytics + real time analytics + machine learning infrastructure			BITools + big data (Hadoop) analytics + real time analytics + machine learning infrastructure		
Analytical tools needed	Business intelligence (BI) tools like data warehouse, ETL tools, reporting software, OLAP, data marts, and structured analytics packages like SAS/IBM SPSS			BI tools + data lakes, structured analytics packages like SAS/IBM SPSS + big data analytics (Hadoop) infrastructure, real-time analytics (apache spark/storm/Kafka) and complex event processing), machine learning infrastructure, high-end data visualization tools			BI tools + data lakes, structured analytics packages like SAS/IBM SPSS + big data analytics (Hadoop) infrastructure, real-time analytics (Apache Spark/Storm/Kafka) and complex event processing), machine learning infrastructure, high-end data visualization tools		
Analytics infrastructure hosted on	On-premise			On-premise + cloud			On-premise + cloud		
Delivery mode	Batch mode + online mode for OLAP			Batch mode + online mode			Batch mode + online mode		
Roles (type of resources needed)	Traditional BI roles skilled in BI tools, SQL, and relational database concepts			Traditional BI roles+ data scientists would be needed to develop features and models and choosing the right algorithms for implementation+ big data engineers			Traditional BI roles and data scientists would be needed to develop features and models and choosing the right algorithms for implementation + big data engineers		

Figure 2.26 Comparison of what is needed for implementing an enterprise-wide integrated analytics strategy for different analytical goals (Descriptive, Predictive, and Prescriptive).

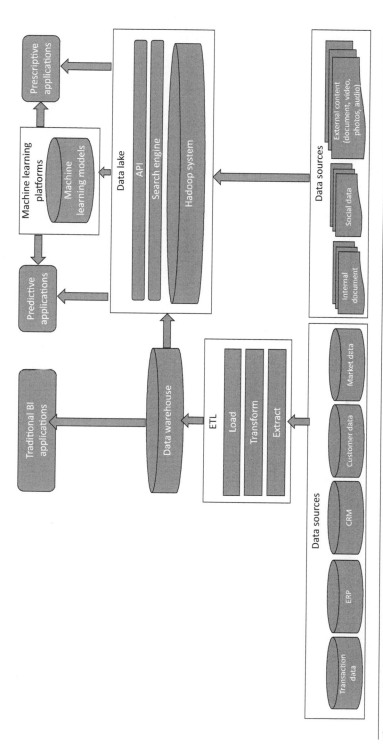

Figure 2.27 Analytics reference architecture for financial enterprises.

new structured data as well as unstructured data) and provides access to data to predictive and prescriptive applications through an API.

Cloud Primer

Cloud computing can be considered as a model for delivery of computing from a remote location accessible over the Internet. In a cloud computing scenario, computing resources (compute, storage and network) are all shared. The location from which the software is delivered is often not known or is unimportant to the enterprise signing up with the cloud provider. For the traditional enterprise IT team, which is accustomed to having a data center on-premise stacked with infrastructure (hardware, storage, software, and network), the cloud has been a major impact in the way they work.

In this book, cloud and cloud computing are used synonymously.

Ignoring Cloud Computing, the Prescription for Shadow IT

The statement "first they ignore you, then they laugh at you, then they fight you, then you win,"[56] made by Mohandas Karamchand Gandhi (also known as Mahatma Gandhi), known as the father of India, seems apt when referring to the way many chief information officers (CIOs), especially in the financial services industry, have gone about adopting cloud technologies for their enterprise. The ease with which IT infrastructure can be provisioned, within minutes, at very economical prices, has led to many departments and functions within the financial enterprise bypassing the CIO's organization and adopting the cloud, leading to the formation of "shadow IT," a dangerous development (considering IT security aspects) in which the IT department is unaware of the infrastructure where the enterprise users store and process data and execute their software. Thus data security concerns, which were the prime reason why CIOs in the financial industry were reluctant to adopt cloud computing, were leading to potential IT security concerns for the IT departments.

Cloud computing models have been evolving rapidly over the last few years, making it difficult for the enterprise IT to ignore. "Private cloud" options provide almost a nearly equal level of control for the IT department. Beneficial factors like the growth of the "hybrid cloud," the elasticity supported by the cloud for additional storage and computing needs, the drastically reduced time needed for solutioning, and the more advanced capabilities like machine learning available as a service on the "public cloud." Most important of all, the cloud enabling the CIO to move to an opex (operational expenditure) model and a variable-cost model based on usage from a capex (capital expenditure) model and a fixed capital cost (for infrastructure they may not use all the time) have shown how much adopting cloud computing can benefit an enterprise. CIOs and IT departments are now working with the lines of businesses and enterprise functions within their organizations to enable the cloud as an option for their software needs.

Capital One, World Bank, Goldman Sachs, and Bank of America are examples of leading banks that are using cloud-based infrastructure. Apart from innovations leveraging big data analytics and machine learning, examples of applications that are being used from cloud-based infrastructure include email applications, customer relationship management (CRM), document and file storage (and collaboration), apart from cloud-based environments for development and testing of custom applications.[57]

Engaging Cloud Computing Infrastructure Providers

With different industries needing different levels of control on IT assets on data, cloud computing providers support different models of engagement, namely private cloud, hybrid cloud, and public cloud.

> *Private cloud:* This model provides the highest amount of control for the enterprise IT team though the administration and management of the computing infrastructure would lie with the cloud computing provider. The enterprise can lease or own the computing infrastructure from the provider and can have their own controls and security policies enforced while still retaining benefits of the (on-demand provisioning and) consumption model of the cloud. The computing infrastructure is dedicated to the enterprise. Only the units and departments within the enterprise share the cloud computing infrastructure, and this is not shared with any other non-enterprise user. This infrastructure can be hosted internally

or externally. Given the higher levels of data security and controls achievable, most CIOs in financial enterprises find the private cloud model the most acceptable option among the cloud engagement models.

Public cloud: This model provides the highest benefits of cloud computing in terms of elasticity of computing resources, pricing, and infrastructure for innovation, but the lowest level of control. The computing infrastructure is multitenant; that is, the same infrastructure can also service other customers. All the customers would have to go with the same set of backup, restore, and security policies as enforced by the cloud provider and each enterprise cannot have their own security policies for their systems (and data) hosted on the cloud.

Public cloud is also enabling newer service models and democratizing access to advanced software capabilities through their on-demand access and pay-as-you-go models. Cognitive computing, machine learning, big data analytics, and high-performance computing are all available on public clouds, enabling even smaller companies and startups to research, explore and come out with innovations quickly.

It needs to be noted that if any application needs a high level of data security and has to comply with regulations on having data stored internally, the public cloud is not an option.

Hybrid cloud: Most IT heads prefer a cost-effective, highly secure (and non-shareable) infrastructure for hosting their core applications while at the same time wanting an option to provide elastic storage and computing infrastructure for research and innovation purposes. This is where hybrid cloud fits in the bill. Hybrid cloud computing blurs the boundary between public cloud and private cloud and provides the best of both worlds.

It needs to be mentioned that when provisioning the computing infrastructure, even public cloud providers try to provision the infrastructure at a data center closer to the region of consumption. Redundancy as per the extent desired is also supported although at a higher but still reasonable cost.

Consuming Cloud Computing

Cloud computing can be consumed at an infrastructure level (over which operating system and other required application software can be installed), a platform level (over which application software can be installed), or at the level of software (which can be customized to an extent for the needs of the user).

Infrastructure-as-a-service (IaaS): Here, the computing, storage, and networking resources needed by an enterprise are made available through the Internet as a service on a pay-per-use basis, thus saving capital expenditure for the enterprise. The backup, recovery, management, monitoring, and administration of the infrastructure are all managed by the cloud provider. The consumer can provision infrastructure through an automated and self-service mechanism. Amazon (Amazon Web Services), Microsoft (Azure), Google (Compute Engine), and IBM (SoftLayer) are the leading IaaS vendors. Open source platform OpenStack is also deployed as an IaaS. Popular use case where IaaS is used include provisioning infrastructure for developing a new application or product.

Platform-as-a-service (PaaS): Here, in addition to the underlying hardware, software is also provided as a service on a pay-per-use basis by the cloud provider. Say, for example, if we need to use Microsoft Visual Studio tools for developing a Microsoft .NET application and deploying it onto a Windows environment, the PaaS provider can make available the Visual Studio tools apart from Windows OS and SQL server, along with the hardware required. The end user (enterprise) need not worry about upgrading the operating system with patches as well as upgrading the version of Visual Studio tools as these would be typically done by the PaaS provider (as per contract). Microsoft (Azure), Salesforce (SalesForce.com), and Google App Engine can be considered examples of PaaS providers. Cloud Foundry serves as a PaaS.

Software-as-a-service (SaaS): In this service model, the infrastructure, the application platform as well as the application are hosted on the cloud and managed by the service provider (they may internally leverage an IaaS or PaaS provider, though).

One of the biggest challenges faced by the enterprises consuming packaged software is access to latest upgrades and versions of the packaged software. Based on the licensing terms, the enterprise may or may not be denied access to future upgrades (and versions) of the packaged software. Even if the later versions of the packaged software are made available to the enterprise IT, the actual upgrade on-premise takes a long time for the enterprise to rollout, as it needs to be installed and tested. Most often, the upgrades themselves are separate projects for the enterprises. This is where SaaS products like Salesforce SFDC CRM and cloud ERP providers like Workday are gaining huge acceptance from enterprises. The SaaS products are automatically upgraded to the latest version by the SaaS provider, and enterprises need not spend their effort on installing the upgrades and testing them. The only effort the enterprise needs to spend is on testing any on-premise integrations with the SaaS product.

It needs to be noted that most SaaS products (and hence any upgrades) are multitenant, and therefore all upgrades (and features) are available to all the enterprise (and individual) consumers. So using a SaaS product (without customization) should only be looked at by the enterprise for cost and efficiency benefits and not for deriving competitive benefits. The customization of the SaaS product may still need third-party service providers if the enterprise does not have competency in this product. Most of the leading software vendors like Adobe, Microsoft, IBM, SAP, Oracle, and so on have their SaaS version of their products too.

The boundary between IaaS, PaaS, and SaaS vendors is increasingly becoming thin. Most of the cloud vendors now provide a mix of service models. We are seeing the aaS model being applied to more innovative use cases like machine learning as a service (MLaaS) and identity as a service (IDaaS).

Underneath the Cloud

Cloud computing runs on virtualization technology. In fact, if the service aspects of the cloud (i.e., on-demand, metering, automated provisioning, and self-service aspects) are taken away, there is not much of a difference between a private cloud and virtualized infrastructure. Cloud computing can be considered to be a service running on virtualized infrastructure. Virtualization is essentially running a software to abstract hardware, desktop, application, or even storage and creating a virtual version of them.

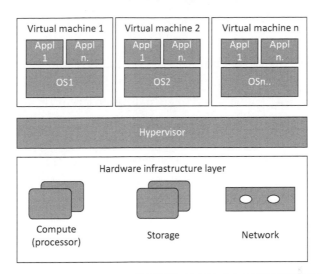

Figure 2.28   Server virtualization.

Server Virtualization: involves running hypervisor software over physical servers to create a set of virtual machines that are isolated from each other, but share the hardware infrastructure. Each virtual machine can have different operating systems installed. Hypervisor layer, which serves as a bridge between the operating system and hardware, enables virtual machines to share hardware infrastructure (storage, computing, and network). For the IT team, virtualized servers have solved an important problem of ensuring that server resources are optimally used and have reduced the number of servers needed to run the IT operations of the enterprise.

From Figure 2.28, it is clear that multiple virtual machines can run on one server and thus increase efficiency. VMware (vSphere), Microsoft (Hypervisor), and Citrix (XenServer) can be considered the leading vendors for server virtualization products.

Desktop Virtualization: involves running software to create a virtualized desktop that is accessible securely and remotely on any other device anywhere. When a desktop is virtualized, all the applications and the data installed on the desktop or specific applications can be made available securely and remotely to the authorized user on their devices.

Desktop virtualization enables the optimized high-definition delivery of applications to the end user on their devices while centralizing the control and management of desktops and applications. Thus the versions and upgrades of the operating system versions and applications on the desktop can be managed centrally. The same set of vendors, namely VMware (View), Citrix (XenDesktop), and Microsoft are popular providers of desktop virtualization products.

Application Virtualization: enables windows applications to be deployed (and managed) centrally at the data center while the application screen images can be streamed to client devices (mobile devices and desktops and laptops running other operating systems) over the cloud. As the execution of the virtualized application does not happen at the device, only the delta differences in the screen are shared with the client devices. Application virtualization also enhances productivity of the employee by enabling anywhere, anytime, any device access to the application. The same set of vendors, namely VMware (ThinApp), Citrix (XenApp), and Microsoft (App-V) are popular providers of application virtualization products. Many enterprises leverage application virtualization as an option to make available legacy windows applications on mobile devices instead of having to rewrite them as mobile apps. Some of the application virtualization products also have add-ons that enable the user to use touch instead of mouse pointer.

Storage Virtualization: enables the creation of a virtualized pool of storage resources spanning across local file storage (host-based) systems as well as network file systems. This pool of storage is available to all the servers and supports parallel (read-write) operations, thus enhancing the system performance drastically.

Containerization

Containerization is to operating systems as virtualization is to hardware: Each application can be packaged within a container and remain isolated from each other. Different containers share the same operating system. Containers thus are lightweight when compared to a virtual machine (because they do not contain the operating system) and are a way to standardize application delivery. Containers can be hosted on-premise or on the cloud. Given the environment in which the application is hosted is the same for every container, the time to deploy is also drastically reduced (Figure 2.29).

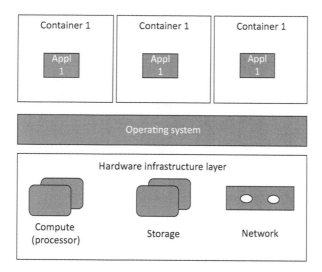

Figure 2.29   Application containerization.

The most popular container today is Docker, which is largely Linux-based and is open source. VMware vApp and Chef are other popular application containers.

Application containers find huge adoption in the world of DevOps and microservice architectures. With more container management tools like Kubernetes getting open sourced from Google, containerization is gaining popularity in the financial services world. Goldman Sachs is known in the financial services world for adopting Docker for the portability it provides.[58]

However, containers are not applicable yet in as many scenarios as virtual machines. Public clouds (especially Amazon Web Services) do support containers, but for an end user, creating a virtual machine is a lot simpler than creating containers. Virtual machines also provide a higher level of isolation than containerization. Containers are more suitable when the organization has a standardized operating system across their enterprise and is thus preferred for a private cloud environment for applications that are not monolithic.[59]

Cloud Strategy

Given the perceived data security and compliance risks involved in moving to a cloud, defining a cloud strategy plays an important part

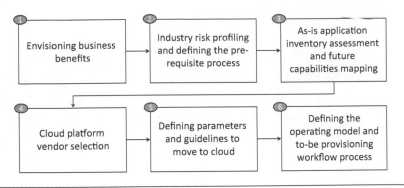

Figure 2.30   Cloud strategy for the enterprise.

in addressing security concerns when adopting the cloud. Figure 2.30 provides a view of the steps involved in defining a strategy for cloud computing adoption.

> *Envisioning the business benefits*: The first step in adopting the cloud goes back to defining the reasons for adoption of the cloud. The questions related to whether cloud adoption is required for improving IT flexibility and agility or whether it is to move from a capex to opex model is understood as part of this step.
>
> *Industry risk profiling and defining the prerequisite process workflow*: The next step is to identify the risk of regulatory noncompliance in moving to the cloud. Highly regulated industries require the enterprise (or the data custodian) to ensure that data is stored within their own premise or within the country. Thus whether to go for private cloud, hybrid cloud, or public cloud and what kind of applications should go into different cloud models is based on the risk profile of the industry. Approval processes, guidelines, and prerequisites for moving applications and data to the cloud are based on the risk profile of the industry in which the enterprise operates. The guidelines elaborate what kind of applications and data can be moved to the public cloud, when to go for public cloud and hybrid cloud, and how data should be secured on the cloud. Best practices define who in the organization should be involved in the approval process as well as the stage when the legal department should be consulted.

As-is application inventory assessment and future capabilities mapping: The list of existing capabilities that can move to the cloud is also identified. In addition, this step involves the future capabilities that the enterprise needs to acquire and mapping what is available or will be built on the cloud.

Cloud-platform vendor selection: Based on the future capabilities required and the as-is capability planned for movement to the cloud, cloud vendors are identified. If capabilities are readily available, typically a SaaS option is preferred. Otherwise, based on the risk profile of the existing application, the migration to a PaaS or IaaS cloud platform is tested out in pilot mode. One of the important steps here is to look at the fine print of the contractual terms and conditions of the vendor and bring the legal team to agree with the terms. Often where data is stored, compliance of the vendor to enterprise security standards (who from the cloud vendor team will have access to enterprise data), the rights of the cloud vendor to change terms of contractual agreement and acceptable usage policy (policy wherein cloud vendors can shut down access to the computing infrastructure instance in case of violation of its terms by the enterprise) take a lot of time for the legal teams to agree on.[57]

Complexity of integration of these cloud platforms with the enterprise IT systems and on-premise applications also plays a critical role in selection of vendors. Migration strategy for the existing applications to cloud is also defined as part of this step.

Defining the operating model and provisioning workflow process: Cloud computing has a transformational impact on IT departments, and the old way of provisioning IT environments for applications will not work for cloud-based models. Business users have a higher level of access and flexibility than what they used to have, and these are factored into the operating model post-cloud adoption.

Cloud Reference Architecture (Figure 2.31)

We foresee that a typical large financial enterprise would use a mix of on-premise infrastructure for running their legacy systems,

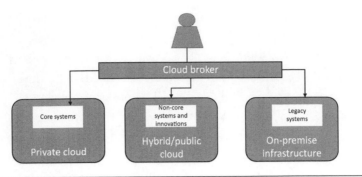

Figure 2.31   Cloud reference architecture.

private cloud for running their core systems, and public or hybrid cloud for running innovations and non-core systems. The economics behind cloud adoption will force the financial enterprises to move most of their core systems from on-premise to private cloud. An intermediary cloud broker would enable cloud interoperability, enable cloud integration, and manage the delivery of multiple cloud services.

Applicability of SMAC across Various Banking Businesses

Banking businesses can be classified into retail banking, private banking, small and medium enterprise (SM&E) banking, corporate banking, agricultural banking, and microfinancing. Let us take a high-level look at different types of banking before looking at how relevant SMAC is to these banking businesses.

BANKING BUSINESS CATEGORIES

Microfinancing: Microfinancing entities have sprung up in many developing economies such as South Asia, Africa, and Southeast Asia to cater to the needs of the unbanked and the underbanked segments of the population (these categories of people aren't served by the formal banking sector). Countries like the Philippines have more than 70% of their population unbanked, and similar percentages are true for Indonesia, Bangladesh, Myanmar, and many African countries. The basic banking features offered by microfinance institutions vary from small amount financing that falls in the range of less than US$100 to group lending, agency-based banking, and business correspondents-based banking.

Retail Banking: The world over, more than 40% of banking business in terms of the revenue mix is contributed by the retail business of the banks. Retail banking aims to serve individuals, families. and sole proprietors. This type of banking includes a wide range of products such as savings, deposits, personal lending, student lending, mortgages, auto finance, remittances, funds transfer. and other simple investment products depending on the regulatory nature of the region or country where such banks are operating. Globally, regulators are focused on protecting the interests of customers of retail banks and their policies are thus aimed at ensuring the safety and security of the funds contributed by such customers to the retail banks in the form of deposits, savings, or investments.

Private banking: This is a niche banking category that specializes in offering exclusive, personalized banking services to high net worth individuals globally. When compared to other categories of banking, private banking is high value and low volume in nature. It is also one of the most sophisticated and involves innovative ways of attracting and retaining customers. This category of banking deals with structured products, buying and selling of bullion, semiprecious stones, antiques, real estate, currency, and other exotic products. Private banks also manage the finances of royal families (and typically manage them for generations). Private banks are more prevalent in Europe. Typically, any individual or family with a net worth of more than US$2 million is eligible to have such a relationship with banks. There are more than 200 private banks around the world who manage a total of US$14.9 trillion of client assets.

SM&E banking: Globally, SM&Es constitute more than 90% of all enterprise in many countries. They constitute almost

95% in the United Kingdom and South Korea. SM&Es also constitute more than 50% of global employment opportunities and also contribute to more than 40% of gross domestic product (GDP) in many countries. SM&E banking is a category of bank that finances the needs of SM&E businesses. In many countries, regulatory agencies mandate financing the SM&E segment (as they are among the most neglected category of business). Typically, the size of the lending varies from US$100 to US$5,000.

Corporate banking: Lending to big corporate and commercial establishments is the main business of corporate banks. Globally, this business is growing at around 7%–8% annually, and it is the most profitable business for banks. It is expected to grow 6% in North America until 2020, 4% in Western Europe, 7% in Central and Eastern Europe, 8% in Latin America, 8% in the Middle East and Africa, and 9% in Asia Pacific. Commercial lending, trade finance, international remittances, infrastructure financing, and project financing activities are all part of corporate banking.

Agricultural banking: For the 70% of the world's poor who live in rural areas, agriculture is the main source of income and employment. But globally, this segment gets the least financing from the organized sector. Agricultural financing deals with funding the basic agricultural needs of crop financing, agro-based industries, cattle financing, and agricultural equipment. The nature and the seasonality of this business also makes it riskier for banks. There are legislations in many countries to ensure that agriculture gets the right kind of financing at the right time and also at subsidized interest rates.

As seen in Table 2.3, SMAC technologies are highly relevant to banking industry businesses and have varying degrees of applicability. Table 2.3 summarizes the varying degrees of relevancy. The indicator "L" signifies low impact, "M" signifies medium impact, and "H" signifies high impact of SMAC.

Table 2.3 Degree of Relevancy of SMAC Technologies across Banking Businesses

LINE OF BANKING BUSINESS	SUB GROUP/BUSINESS	RELEVANCY				
		SOCIAL	MOBILITY	ANALYTICS	CLOUD	
Retail banking	Deposits	L	H	H	H	
	Retail lending	M	H	H	H	
	Mortgages	L	H	H	H	
	Student lending	M	H	H	H	
	Personal lending	M	H	H	H	
	Auto lending	M	H	H	H	
	Credit cards	M	H	H	H	
Corporate banking	Deposits	L	M	H	H	
	Corporate lending	L	M	H	H	
	Syndication	L	M	H	H	
	Debt financing	L	L	H	H	
	Transaction banking	L	H	H	H	
	Trade finance	L	H	H	H	
	Payments	L	H	H	H	
	Cash management	L	H	H	H	
	Origination	L	H	H	H	
	Capital financing	L	L	H	H	
	Forex	L	H	H	H	
Investment and port folio banking	Investment banking	L	M	H	M	

(Continued)

Table 2.3 (Continued)   Degree of Relevancy of SMAC Technologies across Banking Businesses

LINE OF BANKING BUSINESS	SUB GROUP/BUSINESS	RELEVANCY			
		SOCIAL	MOBILITY	ANALYTICS	CLOUD
	Securities trading	L	H	H	H
	Bonds	L	H	H	H
	Mutual funds	L	H	H	H
	Insurance	L	H	H	H
	Equities	L	H	H	H
	Derivatives	L	H	H	H
SM&E banking	Deposits	L	H	H	H
	SM&E lending	H	H	H	H
	Working capital financing	H	H	H	H
Agency banking	Agency deposits	L	H	H	H
	Agency-led microfinancing	L	H	H	H
	Microinsurance	L	H	H	H
	Microlending	L	H	H	H

Conclusion

Social media, mobility, analytics, and cloud technologies are the four pillars that are transforming the way banks and financial services are doing business. Social media is enabling collaboration. Mobility is providing anytime, anywhere access to enterprise information to the user. The contextual capabilities of mobile devices are enabling financial enterprises to engage with their customers in a targeted manner. The journey from descriptive analytics to prescriptive and predictive analytics with the aid of big data analytics and machine learning is enabling banks to gradually turn into data-driven enterprises democratizing decision making. Delivery of software through the cloud has transformed the way IT works. The combination of SMAC is thus impacting the way the financial enterprise is interacting with its employees, partners, and customers in ways hitherto unseen and resulting in new models of business.

Points to ponder:

- What are the popular terminologies in the domain of social technology?
- What are the popular terminologies in the domain of enterprise mobility technology?
- What are the popular terminologies in the domain of analytical technology?
- What are the popular terminologies in the domain of cloud technology?
- How are SMAC technologies relevant to the banking industry?

References

1. BrainyQuote. Tim Berners-Lee Quotes. http://www.brainyquote.com/qeuotes/quotes/t/timberners444503.html
2 Quotery. Tim Berners-Lee. http://www.quotery.com/quotes/its-amazing-how-quickly-people-on-the-internet-can-pick/
3. Chris Howard, Daryl C. Plummer, Yvonne Genovese, Jeffrey Mann, David. A. Willis, David Mitchell Smith. 2012. The Nexus of Forces: Social, Mobile, Cloud and Information. Gartner (currently archived). Jun 14. https://www.gartner.com/doc/2049315/nexus-forces-social-mobile-cloud

4. TechTarget (SearchCIO). Nexus of Forces (Definition). http://search-cio.techtarget.com/definition/nexus-of-forces

5. *Commander*. 2013. What Is the Third Platform? Oct 30. http://blog.commander.com/platform/

6. O'Reilly. What Is Web 2.0? http://www.oreilly.com/pub/a/web2/archive/what-is-web-20.html?page=5

7. Sprinklr. 2011. (The Getsatisfaction blog URL has been archived and redirects to Sprinklr blog site.) http://blog.getsatisfaction.com/2011/05/25/network-effect/?view=socialstudies

8. Pascal-Emmanuel Gobry. 2011. How Strong Are Network Effects Online, REALLY? *Business Insider* (Tech Insider). May 19. http://www.businessinsider.com/network-effects-2011-5?IR=T

9. Jasmine Jaume. 2013. What IS Social Media Monitoring? Answers to Common Questions and Misconceptions. Brandwatch. Feb 20. https://www.brandwatch.com/2013/02/what-is-social-media-monitoring-answers-to-common-questions-and-misconceptions/

10. Giselle Abramovich. 2013. Inside Mastercard's Social Command Center. DigiDay. May 9. http://digiday.com/brands/inside-master-cards-social-command-center/

11. Samuel Hum. 2015. Example of Social Currency Used in Marketing. Referral Candy. Feb 6. http://www.referralcandy.com/blog/15-examples-of-social-currency-used-in-marketing/

12. Crowdsourcing. http://www.crowdsourcing.org

13. Microsoft. 2015. Align Enterprise Social Tools with Business Needs. https://www.microsoft.com/itshowcase/Article/Content/506/Align-Enterprise-Social-Tools-with-Business-Needs

14. Wikipedia. Gamification. https://en.wikipedia.org/wiki/Gamification

15. Ryan Dube. Characteristics of Social Networks. LoveToKnow. http://socialnetworking.lovetoknow.com/Characteristics_of_Social_Networks

16. Sprinklr. 2011. (The Getsatisfaction blog URL has been archived and redirects to Sprinklr blog site.) http://blog.getsatisfaction.com/2011/05/25/network-effect/?view=socialstudies

17. Sunil Saxena. 2013. 7 Key Characteristics of Social Media. Easymedia. Aug 11. http://www.easymedia.in/7-key-characteristics-of-social-media/

18. Chris Howard, Daryl C. Plummer, Yvonne Genovese, Jeffrey Mann, David. A. Willis, David Mitchell Smith. 2012. The Nexus of Forces: Social, Mobile, Cloud and Information. Gartner (currently archived). Jun 14. https://www.gartner.com/doc/2049315/nexus-forces-social-mobile-cloud

19. Ryan Dube. Characteristics of Social Networks. LoveToKnow. http://socialnetworking.lovetoknow.com/Characteristics_of_Social_Networks

20. Sprinklr. 2011. (The Getsatisfaction blog URL has been archived and redirects to Sprinklr blog site.) http://blog.getsatisfaction.com/2011/05/25/network-effect/?view=socialstudies

21. Patrick Chanezon. 2008. How Do We Socialize Object Online without Having to Create Yet Another Social Network? SlideShare. Mar 4. http://www.slideshare.net/chanezon/open-social-presentation-gsp-west-2008/15-Integrating_Community_Feedback
22. Karl Flinders. 2014. CaixaBank Facebook App Unites Social Media with Banking. Computer Weekly. May 7. http://www.computerweekly.com/news/2240220234/CaixaBank-Facebook-app-a-further-blurring-between-social-media-and-banking
23. David Nattriss. 2010. Facebook Platform. SlideShare. May 11. http://www.slideshare.net/davenatts/facebook-platform
24. Wikipedia. Activity Streams (Format). https://en.wikipedia.org/wiki/Activity_Streams_(format)
25. Wikipedia. Activity Stream. https://en.wikipedia.org/wiki/Activity_stream
26. Dave Olson. 2011. #HootSuite Offers Choice of URL Shorteners ~ From Libya to Liechtenstein. Hootsuite. Apr 27. https://blog.hootsuite.com/li-ly-url-shortener/
27. Wikipedia. URL Shortening. https://en.wikipedia.org/wiki/URL_shortening
28. Olivier Serrat. 2013. A Guide to Social Network Analysis. SlideShare. May 26. http://www.slideshare.net/Celcius233/a-guide-to-social-network-analysis
29. Georgos Cheliotis. 2010. Social Network Analysis. SlideShare. Feb 25. http://www.slideshare.net/gcheliotis/social-network-analysis-3273045
30. Guillaume Ereteo. 2010. Social Network Analysis Course 2010 – 2011. SlideShare. Nov 16. http://www.slideshare.net/ereteog/social-network-analysis-5800120
31. Patti Anklam. 2013. Social Network Analysis & an Introduction to Tools. SlideShare. Jul 15. http://www.slideshare.net/panklam/ikns-4305-unit-3-patti-anklam
32. Olivier Serrat. 2013. A Guide to Social Network Analysis. SlideShare. May 26. http://www.slideshare.net/Celcius233/a-guide-to-social-network-analysis
33. Georgos Cheliotis. 2010. Social Network Analysis. SlideShare. Feb 25. http://www.slideshare.net/gcheliotis/social-network-analysis-3273045
34. Guillaume Ereteo. 2010. Social Network Analysis Course 2010 – 2011. SlideShare. Nov 16. http://www.slideshare.net/ereteog/social-network-analysis-5800120
35. Patti Anklam. 2013. Social Network Analysis & an Introduction to Tools. SlideShare. Jul 15. http://www.slideshare.net/panklam/ikns-4305-unit-3-patti-anklam
36. Tim Green. Who Needs Branches? 10 Mobile-Only Banks Doing It All from the App. Hottopics. https://www.hottopics.ht/stories/finance/needs-branches-10-mobile-banks-app/

37. Brian Karimzad. 2014. Best and Worst Mobile Banking Apps: From 100+ Banks and Credit. *MagnifyMoney*. Dec 9. http://www.magnifymoney.com/blog/consumer-watchdog/best-worst-mobile-banking-apps-100-banks-credit-unions/

38. Robert Sheldon. 2014. Mobile Application Management Comparison: App Wrapping vs. Containerization. *TechTarget-SearchMobileComputing*. Dec. http://searchmobilecomputing.techtarget.com/tip/Mobile-application-management-comparison-App-wrapping-vs-containerization

39. Mariella Moon. 2015. Mobile Wallets More Popular in Sub-Saharan Africa Than Anywhere Else. Engadget. Apr 16. https://www.engadget.com/2015/04/16/mobile-wallet-sub-saharan-africa/

40. Virendra Pandit. 2016. India Skips Plastic Money, Leapfrogs into Mobile Wallet Payments. *The Hindu Business Line*. Dec 2. http://www.thehindubusinessline.com/economy/india-skips-plastic-money-leapfrogs-into-mobile-wallet-payments/article9407059.ece

41. Robin Arnfield. 2015. Mobile Wallets 101. Mobile Payments Today. Oct. https://lists.w3.org/Archives/Public/public-webpayments-ig/2015Oct/att-0026/cardlinx_guide_final.pdf

42. Kumar Saurav. 2015. Here Is a Guide to Mobile Wallet Services. *The Economic Times*. Aug 24. http://economictimes.indiatimes.com/slideshows/consumer-legal/here-is-a-guide-to-mobile-wallet-services/types-of-wallets/slideshow/48649647.cms

43. Sunaina. 50 Disrupting Fintech Facts about Mobile Wallets & Payments (Fintech Infographic). Coupon Hippo. https://www.couponhippo.in/blog/fintech-mobile-wallets

44. IBM Big Data and Analytics Hub. The Four V's of Big Data (Infographics & Animations). http://www.ibmbigdatahub.com/infographic/four-vs-big-data

45. Ravi Kalakota. 2011. What Is a "Hadoop"? Explaining Big Data to the C-Suite. Practical Analytics. Nov 6. https://practicalanalytics.co/2011/11/06/explaining-hadoop-to-management-whats-the-big-data-deal/

46. Hadoop. HDFS Architecture Guide. https://hadoop.apache.org/docs/r1.2.1/hdfs_design.html

47. Confluence. Apache Flume (Wiki). https://cwiki.apache.org/confluence/display/FLUME/Home

48. Ravi Kalakota. 2015. The NoSQL and Spark Ecosystem: A C-Level Guide. Practical Analytics. Jun 2. https://practicalanalytics.co/2015/06/02/the-maturing-nosql-ecosystem-a-c-level-guide/

49. David Schatsky, Craig Muraskin, Ragu Gurumurthy. 2014. Demystifying Artificial Intelligence. Deloitte University Press. Nov 4. https://dupress.deloitte.com/dup-us-en/focus/cognitive-technologies/what-is-cognitive-technology.html

50. TechTarget (WhatIs.com). Turing Test. http://whatis.techtarget.com/definition/Turing-Test

51. IBM Newsroom. 2014. DBS Bank Engages IBM's Watson to Achieve Next Generation Client Experience. IBM. Jan 9. http://www-03.ibm.com/press/us/en/pressrelease/42868.wss

52. Jason Brownlee. 2016. Supervised and Unsupervised Machine Learning Algorithms. Machine Learning Mastery. Mar 16. http://machinelearning-mastery.com/supervised-and-unsupervised-machine-learning-algorithms

53. Saurabh Kumar. 2015. ICICI Bank Launches India's First Robotic Locker Facility. LiveMint. Aug 18. http://www.livemint.com/Industry/LarEXGeIghbiu3VeUMF2mL/ICICI-Bank-launches-Indias-first-robotic-locker-facility.html

54. Butler. 2017. 20+ Machine Learning As a Service Platforms. Butler Analytics. Apr 10. http://www.butleranalytics.com/20-machine-learning-service-platforms/

55. Dorian Pyle and Cristina San Jose. 2015. An Executive's Guide to Machine Learning. McKinsey (High Tech Insights). Jun. http://www.mckinsey.com/industries/high-tech/our-insights/an-executives-guide-to-machine-learning

56. Brainy Quote. Mahatma-Gandhi Quotes. https://www.brainyquote.com/quotes/quotes/m/mahatmagan103630.html

57. Clint Boulton. 2016. Why Banks Are Finally Cashing In on The Public Cloud. CIO. May 10. http://www.cio.com/article/3068517/cloud-computing/why-banks-are-finally-cashing-in-on-the-public-cloud.html

58. James Kaplan and Ishaan Seth. 2016. Banking on the Cloud. McKinsey (Digital Insights) (Interview). Apr. http://www.mckinsey.com/business-functions/digital-mckinsey/our-insights/banking-on-the-cloud

59. Stephen. J. Bigelow. Container vs. VM: What's the Difference? TechTarget (SearchServerVirtualization). http://searchservervirtualization.techtarget.com/answer/Containers-vs-VMs-Whats-the-difference

Additional Resources

1. Sunil Saxena. 2013. 7 Key Characteristics of Social Media. Easymedia. Aug 11. http://www.easymedia.in/7-key-characteristics-of-social-media/

2. Charlie Harper, Kimberley Thelwell, Patti Neumann. 2016. What Exactly Is Social Media Engagement? Why Do I Need It? Social Media Fuze. Jan 7. http://socialmediafuze.com/social-media-engagement/

3. Avinash Kaushik. Best Social Media Metrics: Conversation, Amplification, Applause, Economic Value. Kaushik. http://www.kaushik.net/avinash/best-social-media-metrics-conversation-amplification-applause-economic-value/

4. Jasmine Jaume. 2013. What IS Social Media Monitoring? Answers to Common Questions and Misconceptions. Brandwatch. Feb 20. https://www.brandwatch.com/2013/02/what-is-social-media-monitoring-answers-to-common-questions-and-misconceptions/

5. Jeffry Pilcher. 2012. Top 10 Best Banking Blogs – Readers' Choice 2012 Winners. The Financial Brand. Nov 8. http://thefinancialbrand. com/26152/best-banking-blogs-readers-choice-2012/
6. Jeffry Pilcher. 2014. Top 100 Hottest Bank & Credit Union YouTube Channels. The Financial Brand. Oct 3. http://thefinancialbrand. com/42904/power-100-2014-q3-youtube-banking/
7. See Kit Tang. 2015. How Social Media Is Reshaping Global Money Transfer. CNBC. Nov 12. http://www.cnbc.com/2015/11/12/start-up-fastacashs-xopo-app-lets-users-transfer-money-through-social-media.html
8. Mary Wisniewski. 2015. Pinterest Is Paying Off for These Big Banks — Here's Why. American Banker. Aug 5. http://www.american-banker.com/news/bank-technology/pinterest-is-paying-off-for-these-big-banks-heres-why-1075878-1.html
9. Sysomos. Different Types of Social Media Channels. SlideShare. http://www.slideshare.net/sysomos/ different-types-of-social-media-channels-sysomos
10. Curtis Foreman. 2017. 10 Types of Social Media and How Each Can Benefit Your Business. Hootsuite Blogs. June 20. http://blog.hootsuite. com/types-of-social-media/
11. Wikipedia. Social Currency. https://en.wikipedia.org/wiki/Social_currency
12. Incite Group Admin. 2013. What Is Your Social Currency? Jul 16. http://www.incite-group.com/customer-engagement/what-your-social-currency
13. HRzone. What Is Social Currency? http://www.hrzone.com/ hr-glossary/what-is-social-currency
14. Kurt Badenhausen. 2013. Subway, Google and Target Are Top Brands for Social Currency. *Forbes*. Mar 12. http:// www.forbes.com/sites/kurtbadenhausen/2013/03/12/ subway-google-and-target-are-top-brands-for-social-currency/
15. Cloud Foundry (Documentation). Cloud Foundry Overview. https:// docs.cloudfoundry.org/concepts/overview.html
16. *Fusionfarm* (This URL has been archived). http://blog.fusionfarm.com/ what-is-social-media-engagement-and-why-it-matters-for-your-business

3

DIGITAL INNOVATIONS FOR EMPLOYEES

Customers will never love a company until the employee loves it first.

Simon Sinek
author of Start with Why[1,2]

Based on the functional areas they work in, the banking and financial services personnel can be categorized as "front office" personnel, "middle office" personnel, and "back office" personnel. Front office personnel are those who interact more with customers and generate revenues. Sales agents, advisors, field agents, branch staff, brokers, relationship managers, and so on are examples of front office personnel. Back office personnel are those who manage transactional systems and processes. Support personnel, contact center personnel, IT, human resources, finance, procurement, and operations teams are all examples of back office personnel. Middle office personnel serve as the bridge between the front office and back office personnel. These are the employees who design the corporate strategy and manage risk. They also ensure that the financial enterprise complies with the regulatory needs of the regions and markets in which they operate.

The Degree of Relevancy of SMAC Technologies for Today's Financial Enterprise

SMAC technologies have transformed the way the front office, back office, and middle office operate. Mobile and cloud innovations have equipped the front office personnel of the financial enterprises with access to their back office systems from their pockets. Social media serves as a channel not only to engage the customer, but also to understand their needs and pain points. Analysis of social media feeds using big data analytics on the cloud helps middle office personnel strategize on the new products to be introduced. Big data analytics helps the middle office personnel identify fraud and risks early, take action, and comply with regulatory needs. Cloud is disrupting the back office systems. There is an increase in migration of customer relationship management, enterprise resource planning (ERP), and human resources (HR) systems to the cloud driven by the desire to help improve availability, reliability, and elasticity (ability to service increasing workloads and storage needs) of these systems while reducing the workload of IT personnel. The advances in business process management and case management technologies have automated large numbers of back-end processes enabling front-end personnel to easily perform tasks through their mobile apps. Processes that required days for their completion earlier now need only hours or minutes for their completion.

Table 3.1 provides the degree of relevancy of SMAC technologies to front office, middle office, and back office personnel.

The primary value of social technologies lies in areas where communication, collaboration, and messaging through non-traditional channels is required. Social technologies are also highly relevant in areas where wisdom of the "crowds" is desirable and where the "network effect" multiplies the value of the product or service. The front office personnel largely use "insights" from social media to understand the feedback about products or services they sell as well as to understand the potential customer's choices and preferences. The middle office personnel use social media for their analysis (be it product feedback analysis, identification of new features customers may want, or customer analysis). They use social media as a source for insights about the customer. In countries where privacy laws are relatively weak, they recommend approval or rejection of loans to lenders based on the credit worthiness of the social network of the

Table 3.1   Degree of Relevancy of SMAC Technologies for the Financial Industry Personnel

	SOCIAL	MOBILITY	ANALYTICS	CLOUD
Front Office Personnel	Medium	High	Medium	High
Middle Office Personnel	Medium	Low	High	High
Back Office Personnel	Medium	Low	Medium	High

lenders. The back office personnel, especially the contact center and customer support personnel, use social media to attend to customer complaints.

The degree of relevancy of mobile technology is low for the middle office and back office personnel as it is more valuable for those use cases (functionality) where either the functionality is dynamic (involves motion) or the end user of the functionality is on the move. For the middle office and back office, the value of mobile technology is limited to initiating workflows, approving requests of subordinates, and enabling them access enterprise information or undertaking compliance activities like travel expense filing, leave applications, and time recording outside official premises. However, for the front office personnel, mobile technology is a boon. It helps them be better prepared for their meetings with the customers and aids them in closing sales faster.

The degree of relevancy of analytics is the highest for the middle office personnel given that their primary job is to identify fraud, risk, and regulatory compliance issues. Mounds of content, both structured and unstructured, from both internal and external sources are analyzed using big data analytics (on cloud) by the middle office personnel, and any significant finding is reported to the relevant functions and business units. Front office and back office personnel leverage analytics more as a consumer. However, back office personnel may be involved in setting up the analytics infrastructure for the enterprise.

The value of the "cloud" lies in scenarios that need "anywhere anytime" access to enterprise information, a device-agnostic synchronized version of information is required or areas where scale (in computing or in storage) and elasticity of computing and storage resources are required. Given that front office personnel need to work in scenarios requiring anywhere anytime access to enterprise information, cloud technology is highly relevant to them. Typically, big data analytics is performed on the cloud. Hence, the cloud has been tagged as a highly relevant requirement for middle office personnel. Processes associated with back office personnel, especially the IT team, have been drastically altered by the gradual migration of enterprise systems to the cloud. Hence, the cloud has been tagged as a highly relevant requirement for back office personnel too.

Drivers behind the Use of SMAC Technologies
in Today's Financial Enterprise

By the end of this decade, half the workforce population will be from
"Generation Y," that is, those born after 1980 and before 2000.[3]

Those from Generation Y are digital natives, who are accustomed to
quick turnaround and do not like to work in a hierarchical structure.
They expect an "open culture" where they have enterprise information accessible anywhere, anytime, and on the device of their choice.
They are less loyal to the organization than the "Generation X" (those
born after the mid-1960s and before 1980) employees. They prefer
the organization to provide flexible working hours while also ensuring faster career growth. They expect their employers to equip them
with self-service tools that are as easy to work with and collaborative
as Facebook, Instagram, or other popular consumer tools. Employers
need to engage these Generation Y employees better in order to retain
this digital workforce.

Apart from a flatter organizational structure, flexible human
resource policies, startup culture, and work environment, the critical
elements for engaging the digital workforce are SMAC related. These
elements include anytime, anywhere access to enterprise information
and content on devices of their choice, tools to collaborate in real time
with other team members, ability to easily access experts agnostic of
location, faster decision making, and gamified interfaces to engage the
workforce.

Catering to the Demands of the Digital Workforce

Figure 3.1 provides a tag cloud of SMAC innovations increasingly
being used by various financial enterprises to address the needs of
their digital workforce.

The social technology innovations deployed by a few financial
enterprises are social CRM (customer relationship management), reputation management, social network analysis (for credit worthiness
assessment), and enterprise social. BNP Paribas is a good example of a
bank leveraging social media to manage their brand reputation when
they were fined by U.S. authorities for secretly conducting transactions with countries under sanctions.[4]

Figure 3.1 SMAC innovations for the employee.

The mobile technology innovations include mobile CRM, new employee engagement apps, wealth management apps, guided sales apps, customer 360 apps, financial advisors, employee productivity apps, manager approval apps, and mobile dashboards. Barclays, one of the leading banks in the United Kingdom, has rolled out apps for front office personnel on iPads, iPhones, and Android phones for aiding face-to-face interaction with customers at their branches.[5]

Big data innovations (usually executed on cloud) include fraud analytics and identifying high spending customers. HDFC Bank, a leading private bank in India, uses big data analytics to understand its customers' financial habits.

Table 3.2 provides a brief overview of the SMAC innovations being introduced by financial enterprises for enhancing the productivity of their employees.

Anytime, Anywhere, Any Device Access to Enterprise Information

Anytime, anywhere, any device access to enterprise data and content is a powerful productivity-enhancing booster to employees as well as employers. This capability by itself can help banks and financial institutions service more customers without the burden of having to open additional branches as well as to trim down branches. The evolution of banking from legacy transaction systems to centralized core banking systems to Internet banking has already established the foundational infrastructure for "anywhere" banking. The rapid evolution of wireless networks and mobile technology has enabled banks to go to where customers are instead of having customers go to the bank for their transactions.

Table 3.2   SMAC Innovations for the Employee

CATEGORY	INNOVATION	TARGET END USERS	PURPOSE
Social	Social CRM	Product managers	Identify product feedback and new features required from social media
	Reputation management	Marketing and corporate communications management team, customer support team	Monitor social media for any mischievous statements or negative news about the brand, its products or services, and respond appropriately
	Social network analysis for credit worthiness assessment	Lending managers of financial institutions	Leverage social network as a source of identifying risk. If the social network of the potential customer has creditworthy people, speed up lending process. Else slow down or reject loan applications
	Enterprise social	All employees within the enterprise	Enable employees to collaborate with others in their network, identify experts within the enterprise, and connect with them
Mobile	Mobile CRM	Sales staff and agents	CRM data available on mobile devices. Helps sales staff and agents plan their interactions with their customers better
	New employee engagement	Candidates who would like to become employees	Information about the company to engage potential recruits to the organization
	Wealth management, guided sales, customer 360, financial advisor	Investment/financial advisors, sales agents	These are usually iPad apps that help the front-end personnel understand the customer better and upsell and cross-sell the products of the company
	Employee productivity apps (leave application, travel expense request)	All employees	Enables employees to apply leave, file expenses on their mobile devices
	Manager approval apps	Managers and senior executives	Workflow-based apps that enable managers to approve requests of their reportees
	Mobile dashboards	Senior executives, unit heads	Provides a dashboard visualization for decision making
Big data analytics	Fraud analytics	Risk managers	Helps identify suspicious transactions, weed out false negatives, flag fraudulent scenarios
	Identifying high-spending customers	Marketing and sales	Identify customers for cross-selling or upselling products, provide offers to retain loyalty of customers

A good example is the "tablet banking" initiative, which is a common sight now in developing nations. The bank agents, equipped with iPads, go to their customers' residences for opening accounts. These agents can service customers at a time of their choice, even if it is outside branch working hours. Mobile applications (on tablets) enable these field agents to eliminate paper-based workflows and capture required information from customers through the iPad app. This immediately triggers the enterprise onboarding workflow (including any know your customer [KYC] processes) ICICI Bank, a leading bank in India, has been able to reduce the customer onboarding time from one-to-two weeks to one day through their tablet banking initiative. Through this initiative, they have also been able to reduce the number of customers coming over to branches for their account opening transactions.[6,7]

Sales and field agent modernization and advisory services are other areas that have been impacted by anytime, anywhere, any device capability. Before meeting (or selling to) a (potential) customer, the sales force need not be in an office to gather information about the customer. Mobile CRM apps can provide a 360-degree view of the customer on any device (typically a tablet device) anywhere, anytime for the sales representative or agent. Based on this, they can fine-tune their selling strategy during the course of their customer meeting and entice customers by providing them the best relevant offers. Guided sales mobile apps can also help these agents with next-best actions for selling their products and services (based on on-demand customer needs). The data source for these apps can be within the premises of the enterprise or on the cloud.

The anytime, anywhere, any device capability also helps in providing flexible working hours for the employees and enabling them to complete their tasks like leave applications and claiming expenses and approvals from their mobile device. This addresses one of the key demands of the digital native workforce, which is flexible work hours and conditions (i.e., work from any location).

Real-Time Collaboration and On-Demand Access to Experts

The Generation Y workforce is more attuned to a mode of communication that is closer to social networking platforms than emails. Ability to communicate instantly and ability to reach out to experts without any hierarchical constraints engage digital natives better. More and more banking and financial enterprises are moving toward enterprise social, a platform that enables employees across the enterprise to collaborate from computers or mobile devices. It has built-in social features to aid knowledge management and leverages social network analysis (SNA) to identify employee networks or expert teams around whom specific skills are centralized.[8]

RBS, a big U.K. bank, has piloted the rollout of "Facebook at Work" for 30% of their 100,000 employees to address their enterprise social platform needs. With a "Facebook-like" experience, this platform is quickly gaining the acceptance of their employees and is helping them collaborate better with each other. This platform is helping employees quickly reach out to experts (within the organization) for resolving complex customer queries and helping them respond to complex issues within seconds (rather than the hours it used to take them earlier).[9]

Faster Decision Making

In addition to changing employee demands, digital banking initiatives and changing customer demands make it imperative for large financial enterprises to decentralize authority. Whatever information and decision-making powers were earlier available only to senior executives today need to be made available to mid-level employees and in some cases, like reputation management, even to lower-level employees. Decisions associated with cyber security breaches, risk identification, reputation management, and fraud identification need to be data-driven, but rapid. More and more financial enterprises are leveraging advancements in technology associated with big data analytics and streaming analytics for automation of data extraction, transformation, and loading processes for many of these scenarios, and have enabled faster decision making. The source of data for these analytics can be within the enterprise or outside, structured or unstructured, and can be from any device (including point-of-sale [POS] devices) and any customer interaction channel.

One of the challenges the credit card companies have faced in the area of fraud detection traditionally has been the large amounts of false positives they run into. The false positives make them deny genuine credit card transactions of their customers. For example, denying a customer a genuine credit card transaction when (s)he is making a big purchase at a store is a case of a false positive. Gaining capability to analyze large amounts of real-time data and comparing them against existing data sets leveraging streaming analytics and big data analytics is helping fraud management software reduce false positives and thereby improve customer experience. In the above example, when the point-of-sale transaction is made at a store, various other data sets (customer's historical buying patterns, etc.) and fraud patterns are analyzed in real time to determine if this is a fraudulent transaction or not, and then a decision to approve or deny the transaction is made.[10]

Amex has seen a big improvement in their fraud detection and handling capability by leveraging big data analytics. Amex has one of the lowest fraud loss rates in the industry.[11]

Gamification

Digital natives need to be motivated to complete mundane tasks, and they do not like the enterprise to tell them what to complete and what to prioritize. They like more fun as part of their learning and work experience. More and more financial enterprises are adopting gamification to motivate their employees. Training as well internal systems are being gamified, leveraging the popular gamification platforms.

SMAC and Digital

So far, we have been discussing more about SMAC. Going forward, we will collectively use the word digital to refer to the set of technologies that enable businesses to provision new channels to interact with their customers, employees, and partners and improve their lives. SMAC technologies serve as the foundation for anything digital.

Digital Characteristics

Any interaction using digital technologies is intuitive to its end user and is simple to use. The end user can interact with the technology through any device, anytime, anywhere. The application or product using digital technologies already knows the end user and is personalized for their preferences. Digital technologies provide an omnichannel experience to the end user so that the user can begin a task through one channel and complete it through a different channel without having to redo the work. They are secure enough so that the end user trusts the product or application to store their preferences. It helps the end user collaborate easily with other users. It improves the productivity of the end user through the use of automation and enables "self-service" for the end user. Increasingly, digital also includes the use of artificial intelligence and the derivative cognitive technologies These are technologies that perform tasks associated with humans (like reasoning and learning), but can be done better now by these technologies through their machine learning ability.

Table 3.3 provides an overview of the how individual elements of SMAC technology come together to support the digital characteristics.

The combination of mobile and cloud technologies enable the end user to access information from the digital product or application anytime, with any device, anywhere. Cloud technologies and analytics (and social) help personalize the interactions while social (and mobile) technologies foster collaboration as well as support the digital products and applications in gathering the preferences of the end user. The combination of mobility and analytics helps in omnichannel experiences.

Prerequisites for Digital Enablement of Employees

Digital technologies have found a high adoption rate due to their simplicity, ease of use, intuitiveness, and resultant productivity gains. For the sustained success of employee digital transformation initiatives,

Table 3.3 Digital Characteristics and SMAC

DIGITAL CHARACTERISTIC	SOCIAL	MOBILITY	ANALYTICS	CLOUD
Anywhere, anytime, any device access		■		■
Personalization	■		■	■
Collaboration	■	■		
Omnichannel experience		■	■	

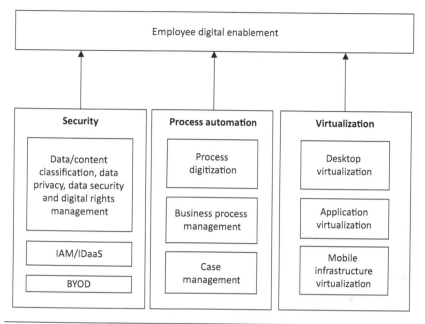

Figure 3.2 Foundational elements for employee digital enablement.

financial enterprises would need to establish the foundational pillars of security infrastructure, process automation infrastructure, and virtualization infrastructure for digital enablement of employees as shown in Figure 3.2.

Security Infrastructure

In the quest for simplicity and preference for lightweight technologies as part of digital transformation initiatives, there is a need to ensure that security and privacy are not overlooked. Much like the physical world, financial enterprises need to identify who should be provided what level of access for each of their digital assets, be it textual, graphical, or audiovisual. They still need to ensure that enterprise information is not misused. Thus, the security strategy for digitally enabling employees comprises of understanding what needs to be secured, who needs secure access to these enterprise software resources (applications, data, and content), and from what will they access these resources before delving into strategizing how they will need to be secured. The "how" of digital security for employees typically is addressed by identity and access management tools, single sign-on, and bring your own device (BYOD) implementation apart from information rights management (IRM).

> *Understanding what needs to be protected:* The biggest threat in enabling an internal application for anywhere, anytime access by the employee is the threat of leakage of sensitive data and content. Securing all the data and content managed by the enterprise (on-premise or on the cloud) is an expensive proposition. Any data and content protection initiative begins with identifying what needs to be protected by classifying the enterprise data and content into public, internal, sensitive, and secretive categories.

Any application dealing with secretive or sensitive data or content will have higher security restrictions than those handling internal or public data. Higher security restrictions may include encryption techniques for data at rest as well as data in motion, data anonymization (or making the data useless in case of leakage), restriction from downloading content onto the device, sharing it with others, and other data loss prevention (DLP) mechanisms. An assessment of where sensitive or secretive data (and content) reside, the inventory of applications handling sensitive data and enterprise guidelines for protection of this data go a long way toward standardizing the approach for protecting sensitive and secretive data (and content).

> *Understanding from whom enterprise software resources need to be secured:* In a world that is becoming more digital, the enterprise is becoming more and more dynamic from an organizational needs perspective. Newer employees join the organization as well as leave the organization more frequently. They change roles and belong to different groups. From an enterprise asset perspective, newer applications are being introduced more frequently. These may be on-premise or software as a service (SaaS)–based. It is necessary to ensure that the right people get access to the enterprise software resources at the right time and get the triangle of the user, the resource, and the permission reconfigured as frequently as needed. As much as possible, the process of onboarding of employees (and subcontractors), user provisioning, and asset (applications, content) allocation need to be automated. Identity and access management (IAM)

and identity and access management as a service (IDaaS) tools enable enterprises to centrally provision users and provide them different levels of access to enterprise software resources based on their roles and the groups to which they belong.

Understanding from what users will access enterprise software resources: The users accessing enterprise software resources may be using a laptop or a mobile device. From the beginning of this century, enterprises have permitted the use of (corporate-provided) laptops for accessing enterprise software resources due to the maturity of laptop hardening and virtual private network technologies along with established mechanisms for controlling laptops.

However, access from mobile devices is a relatively new requirement. Only the BlackBerry enterprise server was considered as being compliant to enterprise-grade security requirements, and hence only corporate-owned mobile devices, largely BlackBerry devices, were considered by large enterprises as a viable option for access to enterprise information. Even on BlackBerry devices, only emails and calendar functionality were made available. Only senior executives were considered to be privileged enough for this access, and they were provided with corporate-owned BlackBerry mobile devices.

With the entry of more digital natives into the workforce from the beginning of this decade, access to enterprise information on a mobile device is no more a privilege. Employees even at junior levels demand this. Providing corporate-owned devices for all employees for accessing enterprise information is no more economically feasible, especially for large enterprises, and there is a need to mobile-enable the employee on the device of their choice. With vast improvements in tools for enterprise mobility management (EMM), BYOD is easier to implement. Given the diversity in employee-owned mobile device specifications, most large enterprises limit "any device" access to only those whose security they have certified for compliance to corporate security policies, and these are largely Apple devices and a few specific makes/models of Android (and Microsoft Windows) devices.

Tools and techniques for securing digital enablement: A combination of tools are required for securing the digital enablement of employees. IAM tools help the enterprise IT in user provisioning and configuring access (including single sign-on) to enterprise software resources. IT teams can also delegate user administration to representatives from the business if required, and self-service is also supported for functions like password reset.

Identity as a service (IDaaS) tools help in securing access to SaaS applications using enterprise identity. They also help in identity federation and single sign-on across SaaS applications. (Figure 3.3)

IAM AND IDaaS

Employees (or partners or subcontractors) need access to applications, data, and content from multiple repositories (residing internally or externally to the organization) for performing their daily tasks. IAM is a framework (comprised of the people, processes, and tools) for providing access to enterprise software resources (applications and data). The IAM tools help the enterprise IT team in providing the "right level of access to the right people at the right time" through their authentication, authorization, and user management components. IAM tools typically have a centralized repository for storing the user (directory) attributes. These attributes may get synchronized with any virtual directory if required. The benefits of IAM tools are regulatory compliance and productivity gains, simplification of policy configuration, single sign-on, and self-service enablement for recurring tasks.[12]

Regulatory compliance and productivity benefits: User onboarding and offboarding is an involved process in large enterprises. User onboarding involves the manager of the resource raising a request to create the user identity credentials, specifying the enterprise software resources the user will need access to, providing the level of access required for each enterprise asset, and getting approvals before the IT team gets started. User offboarding too involves a similar process.

IAM tools typically have an associated workflow for supporting user and application onboarding, user and application offboarding, and providing and removing permissions to new applications while keeping track of the status of the request. Thus, IAM tools also support regulatory compliance needs and improve productivity.

Simplified policy configuration: Once the user identity is created, users are assigned to groups and roles instead of directly being assigned to each software resource. These users are assigned access policies or permissions based on the roles they take on and the groups they belong to. This ensures that once the user moves to a different department, or takes on a different role, their access permissions do not need to be reset individually. The IT department can provide the user with the right level of access to enterprise resources relevant for the role by just reassigning the user to a different group and role. IAM supports both role-based and rule-based permission assignment to users.

Single sign-on: One of the key experience requirements of digital natives include the ability to seamlessly move across different applications without having to login (enter their credentials) again and again for each application. Centralized session management capability of IAM tools help the already logged-in user to access other applications without having to enter their credentials again.

Self-service: Good security practices require the user's password to be changed at least once in two months. Instead of having the IT helpdesk support this process, IAM tools support self-service mechanisms for resetting or unlocking passwords. The centralized user credential management architecture also ensures that individual applications do not allow users to use their expired password credentials.

IAM has been implemented in one form or the other in most large financial enterprises.

IDaaS represents the evolution of IAM to the cloud. IDaaS is still in the evolutionary phase and may not have the full-blown identity and access management services and workflows as IAM, but nevertheless, when the sprawl of SaaS applications attains a significant threshold of the enterprise application portfolio, it is time to consider an IDaaS model. Small and medium financial enterprises are adopting IDaaS in a big way given that they have a negligible legacy application portfolio. IDaaS ensures that they do not need to make an expensive investment on an IAM solution implementation. Orrstown Bank, a bank operating around the Pennsylvania and Maryland regions, is adopting IDaaS.[13]

Given the sensitivity associated with moving identity management to cloud, most large financial enterprises use IAM for accessing on-premise applications and are exploring IDaaS for SaaS applications. IDaaS can be connected to an on-premise identity directory and is synchronized through standard protocols (like lightweight directory access protocol [LDAP] and active directory federation services [ADFS]), or through synchronization agents installed on the premises. The biggest benefit from IDaaS is the single sign-on capability possible across SaaS-based applications.

Microsoft Azure Active Directory, Ping Identity, Okta Identity Management, SailPoint IdentityNow, SalesForce, Oracle, and SAP are popular players in this market.

EMM tools (combined with mobile VPN tools) secure access to enterprise software resources from mobile devices. For a BYOD implementation, EMM tools enforce various levels of controls on personal devices through device management, app management, and mobile content management policies. Through containerization or app wrapping techniques, controls are enforced only on enterprise data on the device and not on the personal data. In case of loss of device or theft of personal device, only the enterprise content, data, and applications are wiped off and not the personal data.

A key threat for enterprises (that allow mobile access to enterprise content) is the loss of control of enterprise content once they allow the content (document) to be downloadable to the user's device. Most mobile content management software provide integrated rights management (InRM) capabilities that ensure preservation of information rights wherever they go. For example, if user A specifies that a document should be read only and uploads this protected document to a shared file repository (available as part of MCM), if user B downloads this document on his/her device and forwards this to user C, both

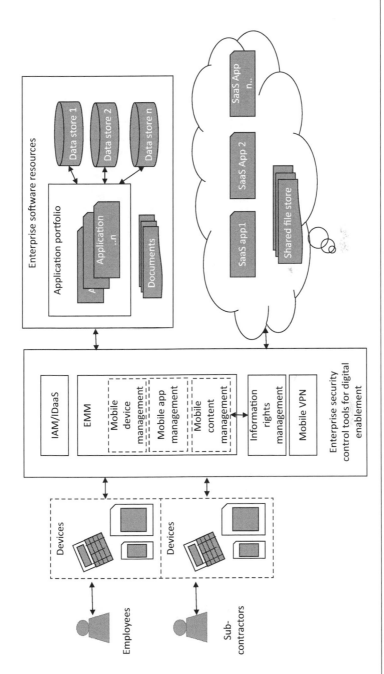

Figure 3.3 Security infrastructure for digital enablement of employees.

Table 3.4 Capability-Tool Map

CAPABILITY	TOOLS AND TECHNIQUES
Providing right people with right level of access to resources at the right time	IAM / IDaaS
Enabling anywhere-anytime-any device access	BYOD implementation using EMM tools (in combination with mobile VPN tools)
Ensuring protection of enterprise content on user devices	EMM (mobile content management feature integrated with information rights management (IRM))
Ensuring protection of sensitive data at rest (on device)	Encryption at app-level, EMM (mobile device management, mobile app management)
Ensuring protection from data loss in case of device theft or device loss	EMM (mobile device management, mobile app management)
Ensuring protection of sensitive data in motion	Secure sockets layer (SSL), mobile VPN, EMM
Single sign-on	IAM/ IDaaS
Ensuring continuous service to users and seamless switching across different public and private networks	Mobile VPN
Self-service capability (for password reset, unlocking)	IAM/IDaaS

user B and user C will not be able to edit the document, that is, rights are preserved. They will only be able to read the document.

EMM tools also come with a managed browser feature. This feature enables the user to access the intranet from the mobile device securely.

Table 3.4 provides a mapping of the tools and techniques against the capability they support.

Process Automation

Most banks and financial institutions focus on front-end channels when they start their digital journey. Back-end process automation is not the area they focus on, as back-end processes are complex, and these processes are based on legacy technologies as well as manual interventions. This results in below normal benefits from digital enablement. An iPad app for account opening is useless for front office personnel unless the back-end process to which it connects is a straight-through process.

A challenge for most financial enterprises is the high dependency on paper-based processes that also inhibits digital transformation projects from achieving their full potential. An average mortgage application (paper application) changes more than 30 different hands. On an average, half the account opening applications (paper-based) are rejected. Financial enterprises place a lot of demand on printing papers, and the dependency on paper-based processes has resulted in a need for more than 8,000-12,000 pages per year per person. This greatly increases chances of human error.[14]

Digitization can help in the transition toward a paperless office. This involves storing of documents on a document management system enabling faster search and retrieval of these documents. Usage of electronic signatures also improves productivity especially in cases where applications are rejected due to manual signature mismatch.

Business process management (BPM) tools enable modeling, monitoring, and optimization of business processes. Monitoring of processes leads to continuous improvement and optimization of business processes. BPM also requires the processes to be simplified if significant gains are to be achieved. One of the advantages of using a BPM tool is the reduced dependence on the IT department. Instead of depending on IT departments, the modeling, monitoring, and optimization of the business processes can be done by the business users themselves. BPM combined with service oriented architecture (SOA) enables faster creation of newer services and aid automation of processes. BPM is used for managing a process with an ordered set of activities. The order of activities is predictable, and the next step can be decided by the process itself.

Case management: Case management is used for managing a "problem" rather than a "process." A problem is an unordered set of activities. These activities occur in an unpredictable order and usually require a human to decide the next course of action or the next course of action based on preconditions.

Credit card dispute resolution is a good example for case management.

A case can be called the instantiation of a case type. A case type defines the activities and the optional document types that may be needed to support the activity. Case type also specifies the teams who must complete a set of activities to solve the business problem. A document type represents the classification of documents belonging to a case.

Alternately, a case can be defined as a collection of content/information and workflow for processing of the case (collaboration activities between knowledge workers). A case revolves around a subject (who may be a customer or an employee). While BPM revolves around automation of processes needing structured data, case management involves automation of processes or problems needing unstructured data and hence may involve interaction with content management systems. A case can have multiple participants (as part of the workflow), and each participant or case worker can add additional content (or perform an activity) that takes the case closer toward completion. Case management ultimately results in completion of a goal. The goal could be for example resolution of a customer complaint, a credit card dispute, loan origination, or account opening.

Case management software (tools) are commercially available as add-ons over BPM software. This software contains a case modeler for configuration of activities, participants, workflow, and preconditions as well as an interface that provides the status of where the case is in terms of resolution.

Process automation should also result in simplification wherever possible and reduction in the number of steps required for completing the process.

The implementation of digitization, BPM, and case management and exposing them as services (SOA approach) aids process automation. This can provide significant benefits to banks and financial institutions with a potential to achieve more than 20% cost savings. Though, on an average, banks may have more than 300 processes, focusing on automating fewer than 20 processes can give enormous benefits in terms of productivity enhancement, customer satisfaction, and faster time to market for new products and acts as a gateway for a "paperless office."

Account opening, loan origination, and mortgage application are all potential candidates for process automation.[15–17]

Virtualization

For today's employees, anywhere, anytime, and any device access to enterprise information doesn't stop at having specific apps on their mobile device targeted to perform a specific task and then accessing their applications on their laptops for other tasks. They expect to have access to all the data, applications, and content they need to complete their job without any location or device-specific constraint.

Implementing application and desktop virtualization addresses this need. Application virtualization enables the employee to use windows applications (executing remotely in the data center) on their mobile devices (or their personal desktops and even Mac machines) without having to install the operating system required to run the application. Full application virtualization enables the employee to use the application without even installing this application. Applications (to be virtualized) are prepared for virtualization at the data center by packaging them with the necessary files they need, and they are then delivered to the device on demand. These applications are centrally managed at the data center. All that the employee has to install on their local device is a client software that enables the application (on the device) to securely communicate with the data center (where the application actually gets executed). A virtualized application can have different instances for different operating systems. This enables the employee to access the virtualized application on one device and use another device to continue working on the same application from where they left.

Desktop virtualization enables the employee to gain access to their entire desktop (available at a data center) from anywhere on any device anytime securely. All the files existing on the desktop (virtual) are accessible on the device (as per the user's access permissions).

From an enterprise IT perspective, virtualized applications and desktops provide a centralized mechanism to manage applications and keep the operating system (on which the applications run) up-to-date with the latest software patches and security upgrades. This translates into less time supporting the users during installation of patch updates and operating system migrations. It also ensures that risk of any security breach due to an employee not updating the latest security patch on their desktop despite several reminders is mitigated.

Application and desktop virtualization capability enhances the BYOD experience and makes it wholesome for the employee.

Both application and desktop virtualization provide a "near-native" experience to the employee; that is, when using the desktop application on an iPad, the application will be touch-enabled, and when the same virtualized application is used on an Apple Mac machine, it is mouse-enabled. The user experience of virtualized applications on mobile devices is not as rich as a native mobile application, and hence application virtualization is largely used only if the enterprise has a large portfolio of legacy applications (that cannot be retired in the immediate future).[18]

Independent Bank, an Iona, Michigan-based bank, has implemented application virtualization and is realizing the benefits of cost reduction, better employee experience, and productivity.[19]

There are many vendors in the application and desktop virtualization space with VMware, Citrix, and Microsoft being the popular ones.

Better employee engagement of the digital workforce cannot just be realized with only technology and process initiatives. The culture also need to change. There is an increasing shift toward an open, non-hierarchical culture. Front offices as well as some of the IT departments are trying to adopt the "startup culture." They are bringing down boundaries between team members, and their offices have no cubicles. Team members are co-located to foster better collaboration among themselves and empathy. Flexible working hours are being explored. The future of work can move toward a sharing economy model where employees may work part-time and also work with competitors. In catering to part-time employees, it is necessary to have the right mix of control as well as the right mix of freedom. This is where application virtualization, desktop virtualization, and BYOD may be all the more relevant and help attract and retain talent, the best of which is in short supply.

Digital Workplace

Lately, the digital workplace is being touted as the answer to engage today's and tomorrow's digital workforce. In today's world, the digital workplace is treated more as an evolution of the intranet toward a social and collaborative mode.

However, from a roadmap perspective, the digital workplace will be a futuristic set of tools, technologies, and processes that are expected to be triggered as part of the onboarding process of the employee (Figure 3.4).

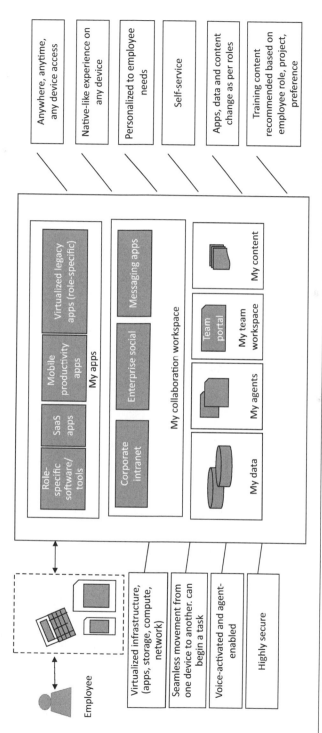

Figure 3.4 Digital workplace.

As part of the onboarding process, employees are expected to specify the choice of the devices from which they would want to work or access enterprise information. Once the onboarding process is complete, employees are expected to have a digital workspace, which is state-of-the-art, virtualized, and personalized to the role (and needs) of the employee. The applications, the tools, the data, and the content needed as part of the role of the employee are made available as part of the employee's digital workspace. The employee also has access to an enterprise social networking portal, a corporate intranet portal as well as messaging apps. The employee's team members are meanwhile sent automated notifications inviting them to connect with the new employee and add them to their social network. Digital workspace serves as the one-stop interface for the employee to access digital workplace capabilities. Any information needed by the employee is available through a search mechanism (supported by voice and digital personal assistants). Apps and content are personalized as per the role and behavior of the employee.

Nothing is installed on the employee's devices, and the applications, data, and content all reside in the data center or on the cloud. The digital workplace is self-service enabled and is supported by automated workflow. The employee can demand more apps, data, or content through self-service, and if authorized, they get these delivered onto their devices on demand. The infrastructure for the digital workplace is virtual. The employee can access the digital workplace from any device with a native-like experience. Digital workplace is voice enabled and supports personal digital assistants. The employee can start a task on one device and finish the task on another device. Digital workplace is highly secure.

Digital workplace is increasingly being explored as an employee engagement initiative. It is not just the IT department, but also the human resources department wanting to explore the concept of digital workplace. The digital workplace can be provisioned in an automated manner by IT.

Conclusion

Employees in banks and financial institutions are categorized into front office, middle office, and back office personnel based on whether their work profile involves direct customer interactions or revenue-generating activities, whether they are into defining strategy and identifying risk, or whether they are into operational activities. The entry of digital natives into the workforce is forcing the financial enterprises to focus on rolling out digital innovations to the employees to address the anywhere-anytime-any device access demands as well as faster decision-making demands. They are beginning to realize that the success of employee digital enablement initiatives depends on the security infrastructure readiness, the level of process automation, and their investment in virtualization initiatives. Digital workplace is increasingly being explored as a way to address the demands of the digital workforce while reducing the cost for the IT department and improving their productivity.

Points to ponder:

- Degree of relevancy of SMAC technologies for today's financial enterprise
- Entry of digital natives: the primary driver behind the use of SMAC technologies in today's financial enterprise
- Catering to the demands of the digital workforce
- SMAC and digital
- Prerequisites for digital enablement of employees
- Digital workplace

References

1. Facebook (Simon Sinek's Post). 2013. Jun 7. https://www.facebook.com/simonsinek/posts/10151694692851499
2. Cassie Paton. 2015. 37 Company Culture Quotes That Will Inspire Your Team. Enplug. Aug 25. https://enplug.com/blog/37-company-culture-quotes-that-will-inspire-your-team
3. PwC. Millenials at Work – Reshaping the Workplace. https://www.pwc.com/m1/en/services/consulting/documents/millennials-at-work.pdf
4. Ingrid. 2015. Online Reputation Management for Banks: The Lessons Learned from BNP Paribas. Talkwalker. Jul 8. https://www.talkwalker.com/case-studies/bnp-paribas-online-reputation-management
5. Pankaj Gupta. 2013. 7 Best Practices for Employee Mobile Device Rollout. Information Week – Bank Systems & Technology. Aug 20. http://www.banktech.com/channels/7-best-practices-for-employee-mobile-device-rollout/a/d-id/1296536

6. Raghunandan Kothamasu, Bhaskar Banerjee. The Paperless Branch. Leveraging a New Digital World. Capgemini Consulting. https://www. capgemini.com/resource-file-access/resource/pdf/paper_less_banking-leveraging_the_new_digital_world.pdf

7. Satrajit Sen. 2014. ICICI Bank: Banking on a Tab. Afaqs. Jan 13. http://www.afaqs.com/news/story/39659_ICICI-Bank-Banking-on-a-tab

8. Jeromy Anglim, Lea Waters. How to Conduct a Social Network Analysis: A Tool For Empowering Teams and Workgroups. SlideShare. http://www.slideshare.net/JeromyAnglim/how-to-conduct-a-social-network-analysis-a-tool-for-empowering-teams-and-work-groups

9. Matt Kapko. 2015. How a Big U.K. Bank Uses Facebook at Work for Collaboration. CIO. Nov 10. http://www.cio.com/article/3003867/collaboration/how-a-big-u-k-bank-uses-facebook-at-work-for-collaboration.html

10. Mary Shacklett. 2015. Improved Analytics Reduce False Positives in Credit Card Activity. TechRepublic. Jan 19. http://www.techrepublic.com/article/improved-analytics-reduce-false-positives-in-credit-card-activity/

11. Randy Bean. 2016. Inside American Express' Big Data Journey. Forbes. Apr 27. http://www.forbes.com/sites/ciocentral/2016/04/27/inside-american-express-big-data-journey/#4db5dbbb127f

12. KarinGroup (GammaTech). What Is Identity and Access Management? http://www.karingroup.com/eng/about/what_is_identity.pdf

13. SailPoint (Press Releases). 2015. SailPoint Sees Strong Market Traction for IDaaS Compliance Offering - Orrstown Bank Addresses Compliance Requirements, Improves Access Services. https://www.sailpoint.com/news/idaas-market-traction/

14. Capgemini Consulting. Backing Up the Digital Front – Digitizing the Banking Back Office. https://www.capgemini.com/resource-file-access/resource/pdf/backing_up_the_digital_front25_11_0.pdf

15. Prolifics. Case Management Offering in IBM BPM Advanced 8.5.5. http://www.prolifics.com/blog/case-management-offering-ibm-bpm-advanced-855

16. Advanced Case Management with IBM Case Manager http://www.redbooks.ibm.com

17. Tunde Olanrewaju. 2014. The Rise of the Digital Bank. McKinsey (Insights). July. http://www.mckinsey.com/business-functions/digital-mckinsey/our-insights/the-rise-of-the-digital-bank

18. Citrix. App Virtualization & VDI. https://www.citrix.com/virtualization/mobile-productivity.html

19. Sara Angeles. 2014. What Is Workspace Virtualization? And Does Your Business Need It? Business News Daily. Feb 20. http://www.business-newsdaily.com/5951-workspace-virtualization.html

4

NEW PARTNERSHIP MODELS

Digital Platforms and APIs

It doesn't matter much where your company sits in its industry
ecosystem, nor how vertically or horizontally integrated it
is—what matters is its relative "share of customer value" in the
final product or solution, and its cost of producing that value.[1,2]

Gary Hamel
management expert

Being a "digital business" is a constantly shifting goalpost. After the
dot-com boom (and bust), or what we call the "post-dot-com era,"
getting online (on the Internet) was considered enough to be a digital business. Thus for a bank, allowing online banking and Internet
banking was enough to be considered a digital leader. From the
beginning of this decade, with Apple, Google, and Facebook domi-
nating the mindshare of the consumers, partners, and employees, the
definition of digital business has converged around user experience,
consumer engagement through online and social marketing, social
presence, and mobile presence coupled with personalized experiences
leveraging big data analytics on the cloud. In this era, we have seen
digital technologies blurring the type of services provided by different
sectors. More and more technology and telecom companies are getting into payments space, while telcos and retail banks are considering
themselves more as retail businesses.

Digital business continues to evolve into an era where businesses
are exploring cognitive computing and artificial intelligence to take
their "digital journey" forward. Banks and financial institutions are
moving toward robo-advisors and digital-only banks.

Thus digital business is becoming synonymous with businesses leveraging automation, analytics, smart processes, and systems to solve problems for their customers, partners, and employees.

Rise of the New Market Segments

The benefits of going digital include new channels of customer engagement, higher automation, and the resultant higher productivity as well as reduced cost of business transactions. Thus digital technologies have been instrumental in making it feasible for businesses to serve new market segments. The new market segments introduced to economic literature by digital businesses include long tail economy, digital consumer economy, and on-demand or sharing economy.

Long Tail Economy

Historically, businesses have been able to make money by either serving a small number of customers making high-value purchases (also called the premium market segment) or a large number of customers making smaller-value purchases (also called the volume or mass market segment). For the mass market to be viable, the products sold at lower price points in bulk would also have to be of a homogeneous nature. The post-dot-com era showed that serving a large number of customers with diverse needs (who make low-value purchases) can still result in generating enough money for businesses. Amazon and Netflix are pioneers of this model.

Digital Consumer Economy

This market segment, powered by millennials, has been enabled by the social mobile analytics cloud (SMAC) technologies. This market segment is characterized by its focus on "virtual existence" and the use of compact devices for consuming products and services. Physical presence of the business is not a must for the digital consumer to transact, and similarly for businesses, physical presence of their customers is not a must to transact. A digital bank serves as a prime example of the digital consumer economy. Customers don't need to go physically to banks for their transactions. Banks don't need physical branches to serve their customers.

Sharing Economy

Uber and Airbnb are the primary examples of the sharing economy. The businesses operating in this segment are asset-light and data-driven. They cater to the real-time needs of their customers. The employees can be part-time or full-time employees. Customers need not be dedicated customers and can share the same product or service with other customers (remember UberPOOL). Uber, the world's largest taxi operator, is present in 77 countries, but owns no taxis; and Airbnb, the world's largest hotel chain, is present in 191 countries, and owns no hotels.

Long tail economy (serving customers with diverse needs), digital consumer economy (serving millennial customers), and the sharing economy (bringing luxury to the "not-so-rich") all reflect how digital technologies have transformed businesses into digital businesses and enabled them to service the underserved segments, thereby creating a new market for their products and services.

Serving the New Market Segments

Rather than the established banks and financial institutions, it has been the fintechs (financial technology startups that use technology for financial services) who have captured the new market segments. Payments, lending, and money transfer (and wealth management, to a smaller extent) have been the areas where the fintechs are increasingly disrupting the financial services sector. To take an example, more people are turning toward Lending Club, a fintech that is making news in the lending sector, traditionally a forte of the banks. Lending Club provides loans to customers at far cheaper prices than banks while fetching a higher return to lenders who may be individual investors or banks themselves. The loans are in the range of tens of thousands of dollars but still Lending Club is able to provide loans within a short time due to their use of analytics. Typically, the borrowers do not know who the lenders for their loans are. Their loans may have been fully provided by one individual or an institution, or may have been shared between multiple individuals or institutions.

Similarly, TransferWise, a fintech, has reduced the cost of transferring money across borders dramatically.

Established financial enterprises are finding that their dependency on legacy systems, their size as well as the need to comply with regulations constrain them from being nimble and agile to address the needs of the changing market, and this is resulting in the fintechs successfully taking away their existing or potential customers. They are strategizing on how new partnership models can help them gain footholds into the new market segments that have come into the world due to the advancement of digital technologies.

Partnering with the Ecosystem

Catering to the new market segments requires deploying new business models for engaging with customers directly or through partners. Traditionally, established financial enterprises have been focused on their core competency areas of business rather than any collaboration activities with their ecosystem. The success of the technology players like Apple, Facebook, and Amazon have shown how partnership with ecosystems can help grow business exponentially and how important is the wellbeing of the ecosystem to the wellbeing of the business of the enterprise itself. The mechanism for partnering can be through a business platform model or through the business API model.

Partnership Models

In this chapter, we will look at the new partnership models introduced by digital technologies or those required to address the needs of the new market segments introduced by digital technologies. We will not look at the traditional partnership models that financial enterprises already have with third-party vendors for back office functions or with brokerage houses and clearing houses.

Business Platform Model

A "platform" serves as a meeting ground for multiple stakeholders to collaboratively create something of greater value. These stakeholders can be producers/product sellers/service providers, intermediaries, and consumers of the product/service. The ecosystem players can also build products or services on top of the platform, co-creating value. Going forward in this book, "business platform," "digital platform," "digital business platform," and "platform" are all intended to mean the same.

Traditionally, business value has been generated through a "piped" business model. In this model, the supply chain is linear. A producer or service provider adds value to the input resources (raw materials) of the supply chain directly or potentially. An intermediary adds further value to the product or service before the product is consumed by the consumer for a fee. From a financial service perspective, we can look at banks taking deposits from investors and lending this to businesses at a higher interest rate as an example of a pipe. Other examples of the piped model can include the investment products of financial institutions being sold by a brokerage to end customers for a fee. Pipes can only generate linear business value, and sufficient effort needs to be spent targeting the right market segment, thereby increasing the cost of the product sold or the service provided. Consumers too need to make an effort to find the right producer or service provider for their needs.[3-5]

Digital business platforms automate the "match-making" tasks between the producer and the consumer. Network efforts widen the number of customers the producer can reach. Similarly, the consumers have a wider choice of producers. This reduces the cost of the product or service for the consumer. Automation due to digital technologies and a wider consumer base helps reduce the cost for the producers or service providers and makes digital platforms a viable business model. Thus, we have a Lending Club providing loans to customers at interest rates lower than established banks.

Thus digital business platforms have been instrumental in reducing the cost of premium products or services and making them affordable to a wider segment of people, thus making the market size bigger for those at the top of the supply chain. At the same time, the reduced cost of building scalable digital platforms, and the record speed at which they can be built, have reduced the entry barriers for new entrants. Products and services are being disintermediated or aggregated through new digital platforms, and established financial enterprises are feeling the heat with more and more disintermediaries being in closer touch with their customers. The combination of cloud, machine learning, big data analytics, and real-time analytics is also enabling platforms to address sharing economy needs of the customers. Just as Uber services the mobility needs of a customer by providing them an available cab (not owned by them) nearest to their location, we will see financial platforms providing loans to customers within a few seconds of them needing money.

Platforms address the long tail economy needs as well as sharing economy needs. Established financial enterprises can opt to participate (as producers or consumers) in existing platforms or build their own platform based on their strategic needs. Building a platform and owning it is beneficial if the platform usage data can be monetized.

For example, a platform like Lending Club is increasingly working with banks for lending through their platforms. For banks, lending through this platform helps them be more inclusive and helps serve customers they would not have been able to serve through the normal banking channels. On the other hand, Fidelity has invested in a fully-owned next-generation advisor technology platform to help their registered investment advisors and broker-dealers.[6]

Return on investment from business platforms: Platforms can be aggregation platforms (aggregating content from multiple internal and external sources), social platforms (helping people to connect), marketplace platforms (helping connect ecosystem sellers and buyers), or a combination of these. Platforms generate revenue for the owner through either a subscription model, a fee-per-transaction model, or a freemium model (free access for basic usage, but fee-based access for premium access or usage). Many times, enterprises invest in platforms not to directly generate revenues but for purposes like engagement, feedback collection, or just to gather data that may be helpful for future needs. This is true especially of social community platforms.

SOCIAL COMMUNITY PLATFORMS

In order to service their partners as well as customers, banks, and financial institutions have also created their own social community platforms. Partners and customers will be part of separate social communities. These communities, which are enabled by social technologies, are dedicated to gather suggestions and feedback provided by the partners and customers, as well as to help partners and customers mutually resolve issues. These communities are also gamified to provide virtual rewards to contributors who provide valuable suggestions, resolve issues, or generate content to keep the communities engaged and active. The social communities may be created on public social networking platforms like Facebook or through enterprise social platforms.

Characteristics of a digital business platform: While platforms have been in existence for a while, digital technologies have democratized the creation of business platforms and have enabled them to be scalable to cater to millions of users across the globe. Figure 4.1 depicts the elements of a business platform ecosystem.

At the edge of the business platform are the users of the platform (or the ecosystem players) whose *network effects* generate disruptive value that would not have been possible in a piped model. The *plug-and-play technical infrastructure* of the platform helps the providers integrate their own tools, products, or services. This infrastructure also includes security management tools and metering infrastructure for measuring and monitoring usage of the platform by providers and consumers. Profile data of the ecosystem users, metadata of product or service units traded through the platform, platform usage, and transaction data are all captured in real time and analyzed for helping the producers find the consumers for their products or services, and vice versa. This serves as the *data, analytics, and rules engine* element.

A perfect example of a successful digital platform is the iTunes App Store. Apple owns the platform. App developers can upload

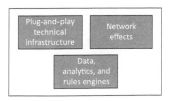

Figure 4.1   Elements of a business platform ecosystem.

(plug into the platform infrastructure) their mobile apps to the app store. iPhone and iPad users can download apps they need from the same app store. Any payment for app usage is channelized through the app store to the ecosystem app developers. For the buyers of Apple's mobile devices, the app store provides apps and tools of their choice, while for the ecosystem app developers, the app store provides a readily available medium for selling their products. The buyers have a range of sellers whose products they can choose from, and vice versa.

The app developers are allowed to specify what the app is about and how it works, while the users who download the apps are allowed to rate them and comment on them, thus helping other future users of the apps socially. This iTunes platform (App Store) helps Apple grow along with their ecosystem (benefiting from the network effects).

The app store stores the metadata of the mobile apps as well as the user profiles and preferences. Every device buyer has an individual iTunes account. Every device sold has a unique identifier and a device profile. Every app developer has a unique developer account. Every app is also associated with a unique identifier called the app ID. Thus, every app store transaction of the mobile device buyer as well as the app developer is recorded. To make the life of the app developer easy, Apple also provides development and testing tools that are readily integrated with its iTunes platform. Based on the preferences and transactions of the user, different apps are recommended for download for each user. The data, metadata, analytics, and rules behind the app store help in personalizing the interface for each user so that they are attracted more and more to visit the app store platform.

The technology enabling digital platforms: The success of digital platforms is dependent on how the platforms generate value for the ecosystem and are able to attract, engage, and retain more and more sellers (or providers) and buyers (or consumers). This in turn is based on how well the platforms can scale and how well the needs of the sellers are matched with the needs of the buyers. The platforms must be secure.

The network-effect gains of platforms are enabled by social technologies. Mobile technologies facilitate "ease-of-access" to end users of the platforms. They enable anywhere, anytime, any device access. Big data analytics and machine learning algorithms help platforms be data-driven. They support personalization to end users of the platform, matching the needs of millions of buyers or consumers with millions of sellers or providers. Cloud technologies address the computing and storage elasticity needs of the platform. They address the technical infrastructure scalability needs of the platform for supporting millions of users and millions of transactions across the globe. Thus digital technologies have reduced the entry barriers like time to market and cost to setup and maintain platforms.

Business API Model

Application programming interface (API) has largely been used in software development parlance to describe an interface to access some of the software program functionalities. Software programs expose their functionalities to external software programs through the API. The API defines the access boundaries and describes the input parameters it needs and the format of the output it would provide the caller.

The road to apps lies through APIs: A business API extends the concept of software API further into the business domain. Business API exposes business assets to the inside and outside world through the World Wide Web and makes business functions accessible over the network by means of standard protocols. It is managed, that is, discoverable by third parties, is secure to use, and is monitored for quality of service (QoS) attributes like performance, reliability, and availability. While the business API provider is bound by a service-level agreement (SLA), the consumers of business APIs have boundaries specified for usage and consumption. Business APIs can be monetized. In short, the business API is a product in itself.

Increasing adoption of business APIs has resulted in the growth of the "API economy" and has been driven by the huge success of technology players like Facebook (Facebook API) and Google (Google Maps API). Third-party developers can partner businesses by leveraging the APIs and creating new apps for usage by customers in ways that the enterprise might not have thought through. Online (and mobile) personal finance management (PFM) tools are perfect examples of the innovations possible through business API in the financial industry. Technology companies like Yodlee (now Envestnet) and Mint provide users access to an aggregated view of their multiple bank accounts within a single user interface, add value to this data, and help end users in tasks like spend analysis and budgeting. These PFM tools are able to access the end user's bank accounts (of course after taking the user's permission) through an API exposed by the banks where these users have their accounts.

Business APIs can be private (for internal use across the enterprise), restricted to partners, or open to the public. Private business APIs drive efficiency, foster reuse, shorten time to market for internal projects, and generate better productivity for the enterprise. Partner business APIs enable innovation co-creation and the creation of new markets for the enterprise. They facilitate third-party mobile apps to leverage the business assets and make available the enterprise assets to a wider audience. They attract more indirect consumers, serve as a valuable marketing channel, drive engagement with their users, and can generate usage of the exposed business assets in ways (and additional revenues) that the enterprise may not have imagined. Public business APIs serve as a new distribution channel to the enterprise, can generate additional business to the enterprise, and can serve as a product by themselves for the companies. The line between partner APIs and public APIs is very thin, though the purpose may be different as direct consumers of business APIs are largely third-party developer partners. The primary distinction between partner APIs and public APIs lies in the fact that partner APIs are aimed at creating targeted ecosystems for competitive benefits for the enterprise through the partners while public APIs are more open, can be used by anybody as long as they conform to the usage requirements and aid in the creation of a long tail market. The level of automation and self-service required for public APIs is higher than what is needed for partner APIs.

Regulations and standards spearheading business API adoption in financial enterprises: Established financial institutions, having been operational for the last few decades (many of them for centuries), have gathered enormous amounts of transactional and behavioral data about their customers. This serves as a competitive edge for these established enterprises and serves as an entry barrier for new players, especially the fintechs. Governments, especially in Europe, have been nudging the established financial players to be more open with sharing this customer data securely with third parties to provide better customer experience and to increase competition.

The Open Banking Standard and PSD2 are forcing established banks, especially in Europe, to take the API route for partnering. The Open Bank Project has already been in existence in Germany from the beginning of this decade, facilitating co-creation of innovative third-party applications for customers (using the data available with German banks) like the Social Finance application, KashFlow, the Singing Bank, SpendChart, Kinder Bank, Money Journey, Moneygarden, Speaking Bank, and so on.[7]

The United Kingdom has established the Open Banking Working Group to make banking in the United Kingdom conformant with the modern era by increasing competition and lowering banking costs. This group has come out with the Open Banking Standard, which recommends giving customers greater control over their financial data (available with the banks). The Open Banking Standard acknowledges that banking data, when made available in a standardized manner to third-party developers, can rapidly increase the number of innovative tools and applications available for the end customers to effectively manage their wealth. It recommends banks share data securely to customers and third parties (with the approval of customers) through open APIs. This would not only help retail customers but also business customers. Retail customers can leverage third-party tools integrating with open APIs to compare data from multiple banks and take the cheapest or the most suitable option for their needs like loans. The business customers use third-party software for their accounting purposes, which often requires the business customers to perform manual entries of financial data. With the availability of open APIs, third-party financial accounting software can integrate easily with the APIs and reduce manual entry efforts, thereby dramatically increasing the productivity of business consumers. The Open Banking Standard is expected to be fully implemented and operational before the end of this decade.[8]

Payment services directive 2 (PSD2), seeks to regulate financial innovations in Europe. This was introduced in January 2016 and mandates that banking consumers must be given the right to view consolidated information from their payment accounts through online services. This makes it imperative for banks to open their APIs to the outside world securely and enable their customers to use third-party apps for accessing their banking information and transferring money into or out of these accounts. Banks will need to ensure that customers provide their consent for third-party access to their accounts and have to protect customers against fraud as well as ensure the security of these accounts.[8]

While open banking regulations do result in more innovations for the customer and empower them with more options, established banks and financial institutions do face the threat of loss of customer stickiness and disintermediation by the third-party providers who are allowed to access their customers' accounts through their own APIs. We thus see a few large banks in the United States reluctant to share more data with PFM players (in the absence of regulations). However, these regulations can be seen as an opportunity that open up new channels and business segments for the established banks and financial institutions.

The perfect example for this is Citigroup's global API developer hub (developer.Citi.com), which helps Citi to connect with third-party developers to enable open innovation. This developer hub allows developers to register, get access to a sandbox environment, use Citi APIs and developer tools, and test their ideas. The developer hub is also meant to foster better collaboration with fintechs as well as commercial brands, thereby creating a valuable ecosystem for Citi to push their products and services directly or indirectly. Citi has allowed access to their APIs to commercial brands like Virgin Money and Mastercard, as well as 1-800-Flowers and honestbee, a concierge and services firm, thereby gaining access to newer customer segments.[9]

It is thus clear that opening up core assets to third-party developers requires a mature tool for creating, managing, securing, and publishing APIs to third-party developers. This is where API management tools come into the picture.

API Management

The success of business APIs depends on how well the APIs are externalized and realized. APIs needs to be easily discoverable and usable by third-party developers. From a realization perspective, the provisioning and management of APIs across their lifecycle should be seamless for the internal stakeholders and the technical infrastructure needs as well as enterprise security needs to be proactively addressed. Figure 4.2 depicts the varying concerns of third-party developers and enterprises when adopting business APIs.

The world of business APIs has multiple stakeholders like third-party app developers, enterprise product managers (API managers), enterprise IT, and enterprise API developers. For third-party app developers, the key concerns are about discovering APIs, knowing how to leverage the APIs and having tools to simulate or test the working of the APIs as well as analytics tools to review the operational metrics and usage aspects of apps using the APIs. For the product manager, the key concerns revolve around the time to market to create, update, publish, version, and publicize the API. For the API developer, the key concern is about how to securely configure and assemble an API from multiple services within a quick time instead of having to code APIs. For the operations manager, the key concerns are about how to scale technical infrastructure for the growing usage of the APIs, how to provision technical infrastructure on demand and how to secure the enterprise resources from external users who can play mischief.

As APIs grow in complexity and begin to cater to more users, security and scalability become very important, and the need for an API management tool is felt. There are advanced API management tools like IBM API management, MuleSoft, Apigee, Computer Associates' Layer 7, and WSO2 available in the market, which address the needs of both internal and external stakeholders. The main components of API management include the API gateway (which can be hosted on-premise or on cloud), the developer portal, and the management console for the IT managers. The API gateway separates the internal network from the external network and secures the enterprise when exposing enterprise assets as business APIs. The gateway also has connectors to back-end systems and databases. An API manager user interface helps product managers and API developers to create, assemble, secure, plan (monetize), version, and publish APIs, as well as cache and throttle API requests. Deprecation and retirement of APIs are also supported. There are screens that provide analytical views on API usage as well as

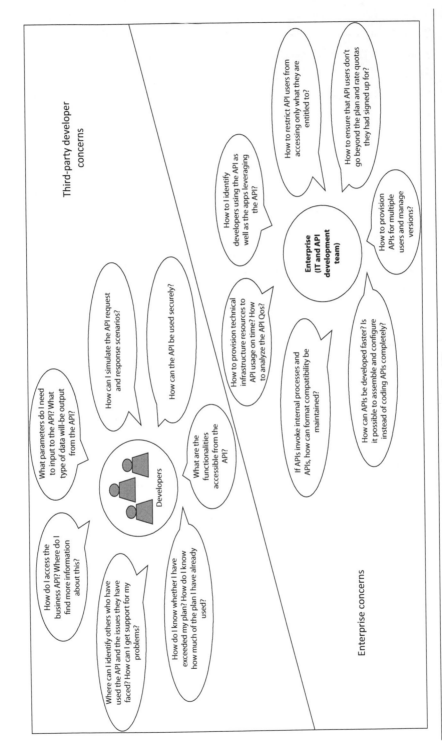

Figure 4.2   Operational concerns of third-party developers and enterprises adopting APIs.

depict the users and the apps registered for using the APIs. A management console helps the enterprise IT team scale technical infrastructure as per the needs of the API. It also helps in monitoring performance. A developer portal helps external third-party developers to sign up through a self-service mechanism, discover APIs, explore the APIs, and view documentation about the APIs. They also provide access to security keys that the developers would have to use along with their API requests to invoke the published API. Some of the developer portals also have social communities and forums to support development of APIs and discussion of issues regarding the usage of the API. API usage is metered, and the logs are analyzed through an analytical system. This system also alerts (or recommends) changes in plans for the third-party developer in case of a breach (or excess) in API plan usage.

For API management to succeed, API development must be treated as a business implementation rather than a technical implementation. Security and analytics must be embedded as part of the API development project and should not be an afterthought. API development must be flexible and agile. APIs should be creatable and publishable independent of the core assets (that they expose). Coding should be minimal, and instead APIs should be configurable.[10]

ARCHITECTURAL ASPECTS OF API MANAGEMENT

Figure 4.3 provides a perspective of how an API management layer fits into the enterprise deployment architecture.

External, third-party, or internal apps invoke the API published on the API gateway. The API gateway generates and validates a token through an identity management system, transforms the request into the format required by the enterprise integration layer component (ESB/BPM), and generates a response for the app to consume. Enterprise services are exposed through the enterprise integration layer components.

As per necessity, the API gateway takes care of caching the request as well as throttling the requests. Every API request is logged and analyzed for any policy or rate limit violation, and notifications are generated in case of any violation.

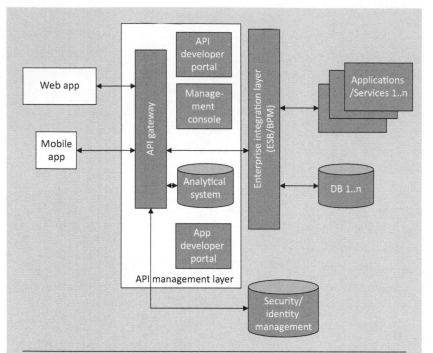

Figure 4.3   Retrofitting API management into the enterprise deployment architecture.

The API management layer provides an agility advantage for an enterprise saddled with legacy systems. As and when an existing functionality (owned by a legacy system) needs to be exposed, only that specific functionality can be carved out as a new service exposed by the enterprise integration layer, This can further be exposed by publishing an API endpoint from the API management layer for consumption by dependent apps. API versioning ensures that clients using existing API versions are not broken.

The API gateway can be load-balanced or distributed to accommodate for any redundancy requirements. Separate instances of API gateways may be used for internal requirements and external requirements.

API management helps in the availability of enterprise resources for a wide variety of devices. It can help in making available device-optimized APIs, that is, separate services (APIs) optimized for laptop and desktop as well as other devices. Architectural patterns like back-end for front-ends (BFF) can be supported. This pattern (especially useful for mobile app development) enables creation of separate services to be consumed for separate devices so that user experience is optimal. For optimizing performance, different services provide only as much data as the device can consume.[11]

ROI from APIs: Different types of APIs (internal, external, and partner API) bring in different types of return on investment (ROI). The primary ROI from internal APIs is faster time to market for internal application development (for those leveraging the API) and better productivity of developers. The primary ROI from partner APIs as well as public APIs is access to newer market segments and indirect customers. Different models can be used to monetize APIs.

It can be a "developer pays" model where the developer can pay based on usage basis, a per-transaction basis, or a periodic subscription basis. Developer pays models can also take the shape of freemium models where the basic features are accessible or a limited number of requests are permitted without any cost, but exceeding this limit will result in a fee. This fee may be further segmented into a tiered structure.

There is also a "developer gets paid" model, where the revenue is shared between the app developer and the API owner. In this model, the developer builds an app leveraging the API. Customers can download (and use) this app for a fee, which will be distributed between the app developer and the API provider. Public app stores (iTunes, Google Play Store) work on a developer gets paid model.

API can also be monetized in an indirect manner. Third-party apps can be allowed to access the API without any charge, but the API usage can be logged and analyzed to create newer services or products (which generate revenues) or provide intangible benefits.

In order to publicize APIs for third-party developers, many banks and financial institutions conduct "hackathons," time-bound events where third-party developers are invited to participate. In this event, developers are encouraged to develop a working prototype or even functional apps using the APIs exposed by the financial enterprises. The best prototypes and apps are suitably rewarded. The Royal Bank of Scotland and Citibank frequently conduct hackathons across different cities to foster open innovation.

Business Platforms versus Business APIs

Business APIs and business platforms are not mutually exclusive. Platforms can also be exposed to the outside worlds as APIs. Typically the business API model is employed as a strategy for partnering when businesses know that the assets they own are more valuable (for themselves as well as for customers) than the applications and services they are capable of providing by themselves (using these assets). Allowing third-party developers (and organizations) to build derivative services (and apps) over the APIs in innovative ways can help them cater to new market segments and unlock more value.

John Watton, the director of Expedia Affiliate Network (EAN), says that the rise of mobile apps has resulted in more than 80% of EAN's revenues being generated through their APIs.[12]

Twitter has seen its API bring 10 times more traffic than their websites.[13]

On the other hand, business platforms are used as a strategy when a new ecosystem can be created for long-term benefits or the ecosystem can provide substantial revenues (in the business segment) which the enterprises cannot ignore. Apple's dominance in the mobile device market is due to the robust ecosystem supported by their iTunes App Store platform. Uber and Airbnb drive the sharing economy needs (of taxi users and travelers needing accommodation) through their data-driven digital business platforms.

Addressing Needs of the Digital Consumer Economy

Though banks and financial institutions are making available their own mobile apps and experience management portals for engaging digital consumers, they are increasingly facing serious challenges from digital-only "challenger banks" like Moven, Atom, and BankMobile. Many banks have a fear of losing their existing customers to these challenger banks and take the route of ownership rather than collaboration with partners, especially in the developed economies like the United States and the United Kingdom.

Wherever providing vital digital services over their existing technology infrastructure is suboptimal, these banks are opting to setup their own digital-only banks as wholly owned subsidiaries or as a separate entity within the enterprise group and partner with fintechs only for specific needs.[14]

The digital-only banks focus on customer experience, agility, and ease of use and are not saddled by the legacy-centric technical infrastructure and processes of traditional banking systems. They instead use open-architecture systems and leverage the legacy systems only wherever necessary. The cost of servicing customers through digital channels is also low, and hence we see examples like the established Republic Bank & Trust Company setting up a digital-only MemoryBank.[15]

However, in non-U.S. and non-European markets, we do see examples of established banks partnering with fintechs in specific areas like payments and lending. In India, Yes Bank and RBL Bank are leveraging the payment and lending platforms of fintechs like Oxigen Services and ToneTag. Through these partnerships, the banks are benefited by gaining access to new customers while the fintechs benefit from access to funds.[16]

Navigating the Digital Ecosystem

Engaging with the ecosystem is imperative for success in the digital world. Table 4.1 provides a view of the new market segments introduced by digital technologies and the business models that need to be adopted to address the needs of these market segments. This table also provides the degree to which the ecosystem needs to be partnered.

Table 4.1 Approach to Cater to New Market Segments

NEW MARKET SEGMENT	BUSINESS MODEL	DEGREE OF PARTNERSHIP WITH ECOSYSTEMS
Long tail economy	Open innovation (API model)/platform model	High
Digital consumer economy	Fully owned subsidiary model (digital banks)	Low
Sharing economy	Platform model	High

Conclusion

Typically established financial enterprises have only partnered for non-core competencies like back-end systems development, maintenance, support and operations, or with brokerages.

The adoption of digital technologies has introduced new market segments and has changed business models. Fintechs and digital-only challenger banks are capturing the new market segments due to the advancement of digital technologies as well as their commoditization and democratization.

While on one hand, fintechs are squeezing the margins and profits of established financial enterprises, more and more standards like Open Banking Standard and regulations like PSD2 are also forcing banks to be more open.

Banks being saddled with legacy systems and processes are being forced to coopt rivals (as well as fintechs) as partners even on core competency areas.

Business models are evolving from "pipes to platform model."[4] They are adopting either the business platform model, the business API model, or a wholly owned digital bank subsidiary model to target the new market segments like the sharing economy segment, the digital consumer segment, and the long tail economy segment. Technology like API management tools, the cloud, big data analytics, social, and mobility are aiding the established banks in opening up APIs or setting up platforms securely and partnering with newer partner segments like third-party developers apart from traditional partners.

Points to ponder:

- Rise of the new market segments
- Serving the new market segments
- Partnering with the ecosystem

References

1. BrainyQuote. Ecosystem Quotes. http://www.brainyquote.com/quotes/keywords/ecosystem.html
2. Gary Hamel. 2009. Who Needs Employees Anyway? http://engaged-employees.blogspot.in/2009/

3. Mark Bonchek and Sangeet Paul Chaudhary. 2013. Three Elements of a Successful Platform Strategy. *Harvard Business Review*. Jan 31. https://hbr.org/2013/01/three-elements-of-a-successful-platform

4. Haydn Shaughnessy and Nick Vitalari. The Elastic Enterprise: The New Manifesto for Business Revolution. https://theelasticenterprise.com/

5. Pipes to Platforms. http://platformthinkinglabs.com/start-here/

6. Fidelity. Fidelity® Goes to Market with Next-Generation Advisor Technology Platform. https://www.fidelity.com/about-fidelity/individual-investing/next-generation-advisor-technology-platform?sf39189820=1

7. OpenBankProject. Apps-Applications That Use the Open Bank Project API. https://openbankproject.com/apps/

8. Sergio Chelbaud. 2016. What Is Open Banking and Why Does It Matter? The Financial Brand. May 16. https://thefinancialbrand.com/58913/open-banking-standard-api-regulation-fintech/

9. The Green Sheet. 2016. Citi Launches Global API Developer Hub to Enable Open Banking. http://www.greensheet.com/newswire.php?flag=display_story&id=43273

10. Isabelle Mauny. Best Practices for API Management. SlideShare. http://www.slideshare.net/wso2.org/best-practices-for-api-management

11. Sam Newman. 2015. Pattern: Building Backends for Frontends. http://samnewman.io/patterns/architectural/bff/#comment-2923121019

12. Travolution (This URL has been archived). http://www.travolution.com/articles/5576/open-apis-let-them-eat-cake-says-expedia-affiliate-network

13. Laura (Olson) Heritage. 2013. Introduction to IBM API Management and What's New. SlideShare. http://www.slideshare.net/patrickbouillaud/introduction-to-ibm-api-management

14. Jim Marous. 2014. Is It Time for Digital-Only Banking? The Financial Brand. Nov 12. https://thefinancialbrand.com/45095/comes-new-wave-digital-banks/

15. BI Intelligence. 2016. This Digital-Only Bank Promises High Returns. *Business Insider*. Oct 27. http://www.businessinsider.com/digital-only-bank-memorybank-promises-high-returns-2016-10?IR=T

16. Mugdha Variar and Pratik Bhakta. 2016. Banks, Fintech Startups Opt for Partnerships Post Demonetisation Drive. *Economic Times*. Nov 29. http://economictimes.indiatimes.com/small-biz/money/banks-fintech-startups-opt-for-partnerships-post-demonetisation-drive/articleshow/55677432.cms

5

DIGITAL INNOVATIONS
FOR THE CONSUMER

People will forget what you said. They will forget what you did.
But people will never forget how you made them feel.

Maya Angelou

American poet, memoirist, and civil rights activist[1,2]

From the beginning of this decade, branch transactions have seen a
fall (sometimes as high as 30%), while transactions from online and
mobile banking have been increasing rapidly (by around 10% every
year) across the developed economies spanning Western Europe and
North America. Less than 10% of customers visit a bank branch once
or more a week, while more than 80% of the customers use online or
mobile banking every week.[3,4]

The decline in the usage of traditional channels of banking and
increase in usage of digital channels have coincided with the rise of
digital consumers as a new market segment. Financial technology
companies (fintechs) have been successful in understanding the needs
of digital consumers and are gradually taking away digital consumers from traditional financial enterprises. This has led to customer
experience initiatives getting a larger (and sometimes dispropor-
tionate) share of the digital investments of an enterprise. Customer
experience transformation is seen as the most visible impact of digital
investments of an enterprise.

Customer experience can be defined as the outcome of a series of
direct or indirect interactions (moments of truth) between the enterprise (or brand) and the customer. It is how the customer feels during the series of interactions with the enterprise. A good experience
with the interaction when needing a product or a service results in the
prospect turning into a lead. A continuing good experience converts

the lead to a customer. Positive interactions with the enterprise after buying the product or consuming the service cement the relationship, improve loyalty, and turn the customer into an advocate for the enterprise, thereby multiplying the revenues for the enterprise. A bad experience for the customer during any stage of the relationship cycle can convert him/her into a detractor, thereby driving away potential new customers.

In the digital era, network effects can result in the rapid rise or fall of the enterprise. Good customer experience is seen as the gateway for influencing network effects positively. Identifying the "moments of truth," influencing the "moments of truth," and designing the "customer journey" right ensures good customer experience. How well a customer journey capitalizes on the moments of truth and influences them through contextual capabilities supported by digital technologies differentiates the experience.

In this chapter, brand and enterprise are used synonymously.

Identifying "Moments of Truth"

A "moment of truth" (MOT) is a concept pioneered by Jan Carlzon, the acclaimed former President and CEO of SAS Airlines and author of the book with the same name, *Moments of Truth*. MOT can be considered as the instances or the moments when the customer (or a prospect) has an interaction with the enterprise or brand. They provide an opportunity for the enterprise to influence the customer. As seen in Figure 5.1, a stimulus drives the traversal through a series of MOTs, starting with the "zero moment of truth" (ZMOT), followed by the "first moment of truth" (FMOT), further followed by the "second moment of truth" (SMOT), and the "third moment of truth" (TMOT). Many marketing gurus do not differentiate between SMOT and TMOT, but in this chapter, we treat them differently. Based on the extent to which enterprises attract potential customers to traverse through each subsequent MOT, the status of the customer changes from a prospect to a lead to a customer to an advocate, and the relationship between the enterprise and the customer strengthens.[5]

Figure 5.1 depicts the different actions taken by the customer (or prospect) at each moment of truth.

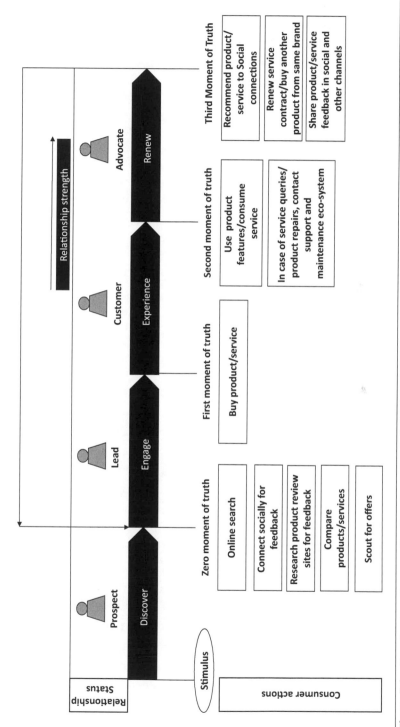

Figure 5.1 Map of customer (or prospect) actions at each "moment of truth."

Prior to Google introducing Google Search to the world, the traditional business-to-consumer (B2C) marketing model only had the stimulus directly leading to FMOT and SMOT. In this model, the customer (or prospective customer) was driven to buy a product or a service (FMOT) through the influence of stimulus like print or TV ads, communications from trade shows, or word of mouth.

Google has introduced ZMOT to the world largely through their popular search engine. ZMOT has resulted in consumers researching the products and services they are interested in from websites, product review sites, and other online and social sources before buying. Most of the time, the consumers have already decided what to buy before visiting a branch or financial agency to buy a product or service. ZMOT helps in this decision-making process to buy while Google searches filter the products or services that would be relevant for the consumer and drive the consumers toward ZMOT.[6]

The buying behaviors of online consumers are largely triggered from search-based mechanisms. Hence the stimulus (which was largely focused on driving consumers toward FMOT as part of traditional B2C strategy) has now changed toward encouraging people toward ZMOT. The stimulus for ZMOT could be email marketing or social media marketing in addition to the traditional stimulus.

ZMOT is the interaction (or set of interactions) that occurs when the customer (who is still a prospect) intends to discover a service or a product that fulfills their need or craving. In the online world, this is when the prospect "searches" for the service or product by stating their need. Results from search engines, social recommendations (recommendations from friends on social networks), pay-per-click ads, and targeted ads or personalized ads on websites or mobile apps can also be the place (virtual real estate) where ZMOT interaction occurs. How easily the product or service can be discovered in the appropriate channel (Web, mobile, social) plays a key role in influencing the prospect to get converted to a lead. With ZMOT becoming highly influential in the buying process, more analytics are being deployed for gaining insights about the prospective customers and personalizing ads toward the needs of the (prospective) consumers. Personalization has entered a complex phase where there is a need to provide the right level of information and content at the right time, right location, and right device to the right user.

FMOT is the interaction (set of interactions) when the lead needs to be encouraged or engaged to buy the product or service and turned into a customer. With digital consumers being "well-informed" consumers, the level of influence that the enterprise has at FMOT has diminished and has moved toward ZMOT. In the retail banking world, we are thus seeing a lot of sales activities (at bank branches) move toward digital marketing activities focused on influencing ZMOT and stimulus for ZMOT.

SMOT is the interaction (or series of interactions) that occurs after the customer has bought the product or signed up to consume the service and is experiencing the product or service. This is the time when the customer forms a perception about the product or service. Quality of service, ease of use of the product, and how well the product/service fulfills the promises made by the brand during the engagement process influence the experience of the customer and determine whether they would want to recommend this product or service to their social connections as well as stay loyal to the brand.

TMOT is when the customer, having experienced the product or service, recommends this to others. If the product or the service is at the end of its lifecycle, the customer stays loyal and goes in for another similar or related product from the same brand or renews the service. TMOT can thus become the ZMOT for the existing customers when going for a new product (from the same enterprise or brand) or renewing their service. TMOT can also be the ZMOT for other new prospects who plan to buy the product of the enterprise based on the recommendation of the existing customers.

It needs to be noted that one MOT may correspond to multiple interactions and need not be limited to just one direct or indirect interaction between the (prospective) customer and the enterprise. For example, the prospect may connect with existing buyers of product through social networking platforms, visit product review sites, compare product charges through third-party comparison sites as well as look at best offers before deciding to buy a product from the enterprise. In such a case, all the above interactions would be considered as being part of ZMOT.

From a banking and financial services perspective, any moment when a prospect thinks of either investing, lending, or borrowing money and goes online for discovering the products or services suitable for his/her need can be considered as the "stimulus." Appearing on top of the list (as part of search results or through social recommendations or positive word of mouth) and attracting the prospect to either visit the online portal, download a mobile app, visit the branch, or contact the call center for information is the ZMOT. Attracting the prospect to open an account or buy a financial product at a branch or online is the FMOT. Retention of the customer through frequent connects (one-to-one interactions) is SMOT. TMOT occurs when the customer is willing to be upsold or cross-sold more financial products from the same enterprise.[5,6]

Influencing "Moments of Truth"

The enterprise needs to treat each MOT separately and deploy a different set of tactics for influencing customers at each MOT. How well the enterprise influences the prospects or customers during each MOT decides the probability of the prospect entering into the next relationship stage. Table 5.1 describes the type of tactic used to influence the customers (or prospects) at different MOTs. At ZMOT, most of the tactics are focused on marketing and engagement of the prospect. At FMOT, the focus shifts to sales while continuing to keep the customer engaged. During SMOT, the focus shifts to servicing the customer and providing a good experience to the customer while keeping the customer engaged to lead them toward TMOT. The extent of influence the enterprise or the brand wields based on the experience of the customer from ZMOT until SMOT leads to the customer engaging with the enterprise on TMOT. It is to be noted that irrespective of the MOT, the enterprise needs to influence the customer (or prospect) with engagement tactics in order to encourage him or her to move into the next MOT.

Table 5.1   Tactic Types across MOTs

TACTIC TYPE	ZMOT	FMOT	SMOT	TMOT
Marketing	High	Medium	Low	Medium
Engagement	High	Medium	Medium	Medium
Sales	None	High	Low	Medium
Service	None	None	High	Medium

Figure 5.2 provides the different tactics used by the enterprise to influence the prospect (or customer) to move toward the next MOT. In this chapter, we deal only with the tactics relevant to the digital customer experience world. Print, TV advertising, and other forms of marketing, sales, and service tactics will not be covered.

Influencing ZMOT

Traditionally, the process of conversion of a prospect to a customer is through a marketing funnel that begins with tactics for catching eyeballs (through stimuli like print ads, TV ads, and trade shows). Prospects go through a series of steps right from awareness about the products or services to considering the product or service they would want to buy. Largely the sale occurs at the store or a bank branch (considering the banking industry). Sales effort for an enterprise is much higher than the marketing effort, and thus there is a need for more sales personnel.

However, ZMOT has changed the buying paradigm. The well-informed digital consumer goes through multiple sources of information like search results, product review sites, blogs about the product or service, YouTube videos, price comparison sites, and recommendations from social networks before deciding the product or service to buy. There is a high probability that the prospect may not even go through the website of the enterprise if it is not optimized for search engines, that is, the website link does not appear at the top of a search result. Understanding the keywords that the user may use when searching for a product or service is also very important the customer. The prospect most often makes up his or her mind on which financial product or service they would want to buy by the time they visit a branch. Bombarding a prospect with irrelevant information or content will not work with the well-informed digital consumer. Only content relevant (personalized) for the consumer at a channel they prefer may gather eyeballs. Ad-blockers may also block online ads. Thus the enterprise has to spend more effort in planning to attract each prospect differently based on their need, their demographic profile as well as preferences through the use of analytics. For the financial enterprise, data-driven (analytical) marketing of their products becomes as important as (or more important than) branch

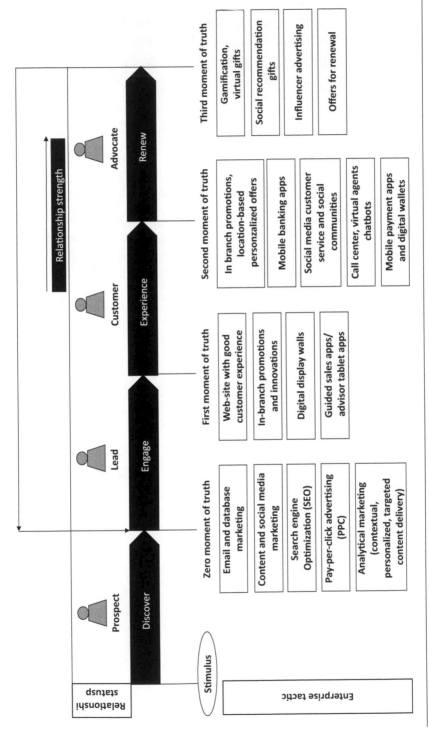

Figure 5.2 Tactics used by enterprises for influencing each MOT.

sales of these products. Given the disparate sources of stimulus, the enterprise needs to ensure that all relevant channels are covered for influencing the prospect. Thus digital marketing tactics need to be supplemented by marketing automation for influencing ZMOTs with each tactic being sufficiently tracked for analysis. Automation should enable the enterprise to provide the "right content" (online brochures, audio, podcasts, videos, photos) about the product or service at the "right place" (blogs, social networking sites), "right time," and "right channel" for influencing the prospect. While marketing tools do play a significant role in influencing ZMOTs, the success of the influencing tactics is highly dependent on analytics and customer insights.

The tactics used for ZMOTs include search engine optimization, email marketing, database marketing, affinity marketing, pay-per-click advertising, social and influencer marketing, answering queries in product review sites, as well as funding product review sites and content optimization. Digital marketing must ensure that these tactics are contextual, personalized, and targeted in order to engage the prospective customer. Contextual information, delivered especially with information in channels that the prospective customers would naturally consume, is a powerful tactic.[7]

The power of digital marketing lies in the test-and-learn approach it facilitates for marketers. Digital marketing leverages online tools and is supplemented by analytics. Thus, digital marketing, when done right, enables tracking and understanding the online behavior of the prospect and measuring the impact of marketing campaigns through analytics, and thereby helps in personalizing the tactics for different categories of users and increasing the chances of converting the prospect to a lead.

DIGITAL MARKETING TACTICS NEEDED FOR INFLUENCING ZMOT[8]

The importance of ZMOT in the digital buying process has resulted in digital marketing being critical to influence MOTs. Digital marketing is all about attracting and building a relationship with the prospects, leads, and customers who are online. Search engine optimization (SEO), pay-per-click (PPC), email marketing, website design, content marketing, social marketing, and influencer marketing can all be considered a part of digital marketing.

Search engine optimization (SEO): With search engines being the driver for most online transactions, coming out on top of the search results is very important to get noticed. Search engines throw up results based on algorithms, and the number of instances of specific keywords is an important decision factor for the rankings. Researching the key words typed in by users as part of their search, adding appropriate keywords and title tags to the website, and building links are all part of SEO activities that can push up rankings of the website. It is to be noted that search engines often change the algorithms for their ranking, and this can result in SEO strategy also having to be revisited.

Pay-per-click (PPC): PPC is generally used in consonance with SEO. These are "paid links" or "sponsored links" that appear as results when searching for specific key words through search engines. In order to distinguish paid links from normal links, these appear in a different color as part of search results. The enterprise needs to pay the search engine based on the number of users who have clicked the "paid links." Paid links typically lead to a landing page in the website of the enterprise. The landing page allows the user to find the required information and transact with the enterprise easily.

Email marketing: This is one of the oldest tactics used to generate online traffic for an enterprise. It is all about sending emails with advertisements to targeted users. Quite often, email addresses of prospective customers are sourced from third-party providers. Emails from unknown domains can often end up in spam folders. Many corporations as well as countries end up blacklisting bulk email senders, and this can reduce the efficacy of email marketing campaigns.

Database marketing: Many enterprises gather valuable profile and behavioral data of customers (and prospects) in their data warehouses through sweepstake campaigns as well as through their online transaction systems. This data is repurposed for targeted promotions of new products and services either through banner ads or email marketing. Both email and database marketing are direct marketing techniques.

Social Media Marketing: As the digital consumer looks to social networks and platforms for information and recommendation, enterprises actively advertise their products on social media. This advertising can be through dedicated pages on Facebook (Facebook walls), contests on Facebook for engaging users, blogs about products and services through blogging platforms or LinkedIn, or paying social influencers or celebrities to blog about their products and services. With user-generated content being equally important as corporate-generated content in the digital world, the comments from users on social networking platforms and product review sites are analyzed for feedback about their products and services and fine-tuning them.

Content marketing and optimization: In the digital world, prospects may not turn into leads and customers immediately. They need to be engaged frequently. Content marketing is used as a tactic for engaging prospects. High-quality informational content in the form of blogs or videos is often posted to social networking sites or to a preferred channel of the prospect with the hope that the informational content will help the prospect decide in favor of the product or service of the enterprise. The content needs to be highly engaging for the user to take a favorable action. The engagement level of the content can vary based on the type of content (text, audio, and video), the category of content (emotional, patriotic), the frequency of updates and freshness of content as well as the channel and device it is delivered to. Content needs to be optimized for the devices in which the prospect views it. Content can be optimized by understanding how the prospect came to the website using tracking uniform resource locators (URLs). To understand the customer pathway and the online behavior of the customer, the links that the customer clicks after entering the site are analyzed by Web analytics software, and content is personalized accordingly. Content can be personalized based on the profile, segment, and behavioral analytics of the prospect.

Analytical marketing: Leveraging Web and social analytics, content, promotions, and advertisements are contextualized and personalized to the needs of the user. This results in a higher possibility of conversion. Mobile devices can provide the locational context, and based on this, location-based offers can be pushed to the mobile apps. In-app marketing (mobile marketing) is also used for influencing ZMOT.

Banks and credit card providers also use affinity marketing to get introduced to a new set of target users or affinity groups. To take an example, JPMorgan Chase Bank partnered with Amazon for the Amazon.com Rewards Visa Signature card, which the customers of Amazon can sign up and use for their online purchases on Amazon. This is a win-win mechanism for both the business (JPMorgan Chase) and the affiliate (Amazon, in this case), and brings in e-commerce customers, a new market segment, as the customers of JPMorgan Chase Bank.[9]

Influencing FMOT

The intent of influencing FMOT is to turn the lead into a customer. From a financial enterprise perspective, the tactics to influence FMOT can be classified into online tactics and in-branch tactics.

Online Tactics   These are tactics that involve a website with an intuitive customer experience. Website visitors who have been attracted by clicking on the URLs, which appear as paid links or links from search engine results, are directly led to a landing page. This page enables the prospect to get onboarded intuitively as a customer. Easily findable offers and discounts for immediate onboarding accelerate the conversion of prospects and leads to customers. Other online tactics include product discounts for buying within a specific date and opt-in email promotions. An enterprise needs experience management tools and Web analytics for deploying online tactics.

In-Branch Tactics   These tactics include a mix of digital display advertising apart from human support. As part of display advertising, digital display walls or digital signage (which includes kiosks, touchscreens, high-end display screens, and curved screens) within branches provide relevant information about products and services. Retail banks, which are beginning to look more like high-end retail stores, are adopting digital signage for engaging customers and improving branch experience. Information displayed in digital signage tends to reduce the queries that the prospects or customers may tend to ask bank tellers or customer advisors. Videos displayed on digital signage enable a perception of reduced wait times for the customer. Credit unions like Michigan First Credit Union are leveraging digital signage to transform their in-branch customer experience. Many retail banks are also experimenting with contextual advertising leveraging digital signage. Once a customer walks into the branch, financial products based on the profile, spending, and investment patterns of the customer are displayed to encourage the customer to buy the product.[10]

In-branch tactics involving human support include branch staff enabled with mobile apps on their iPads for providing guidance to prospects and helping prospects get onboarded as customers quickly. These mobile devices can scan know your customer (KYC) documents and upload the documents to their secure content repositories, initiate the workflow for onboarding the customer, reduce wait time, and improve customer experience. These guided sales apps on iPads also equip branch advisors with queries to ask the customer (and fill the response into the app). The branch advisors are provided with the next question and next step automatically by the app based on the response provided to the previous question.

In order to attract the digital consumer segment, banks are making their branches look like high-end retail stores. State Bank of India, the leading public sector bank in India, is opening "digital stores" called sbiINTOUCH in prominent locations where Gen Y frequent. These branches help in improving the experience of their customer by providing a debit card (chip card) within ten minutes of opening their account. These branches have digital display walls that provide information about various products.

As part of in-branch tactics, financial enterprises are also exploring proximity marketing tactics. These tactics involve the use of beacons (which are sensors leveraging Bluetooth Low Energy protocol), which can communicate with the customers through their mobile apps and guide them (and provide them offers and promotions) based on their proximity to the beacons.

Influencing SMOT

At this stage, the customer has already been onboarded and is experiencing the product or consuming the service provided by the enterprise. The objective of influencing SMOT is to ensure that the customer has a good experience with the enterprise. The quality of the product or service sold and the support provided by the enterprise play an important factor in how the customer rates the experience.

During this MOT, enterprises need to stay connected with the customer, supporting them across channels and resolving any issues they may face when using the product or consuming the service. Quality products and services, personalized offers, customer delight initiatives, and inexpensive pricing help keep the customers engaged and loyal. How the enterprise services the customer is key to the customer staying through to the TMOT. The tactics used for SMOT can be divided into operational engagement tactics, service and support tactics, and after-sales marketing tactics.

Operational Engagement Tactics Traditionally, customers have been leveraging bank branches for their transactions. While local bank branches improve the relationship and connect with the customer, they increase the cost of operations for the bank and also reduce the productivity for the customers. With the advent of online channels and mobile, banks have been pushing their customers to use non-branch channels like Internet banking and mobile banking, and come over to the bank only for absolutely essential needs.

Internet and Mobile Banking Web-based Internet banking portals allow customers to view statements, transfer money, pay bills, track investments and spending, as well as invest in other financial products. Mobile banking apps that became functional with basic features like view transactions now support advanced features like transferring funds, paying bills as well as remote mobile deposit capture. The remote mobile deposit feature enables the customer to leverage the camera and scan features of mobile devices to capture a photo of a check, upload the image of the check, and deposit the check into their account through their mobile app without having to enter bank branches. A few banks in the United Kingdom, like Nationwide Building Society, have also extended some of the mobile banking features to wearables like Apple Watch and Android Wear through wearable apps. Features like Quick Balance are being made available on the wearables (which need to be paired with smartphones).

As part of their customer experience initiatives to enable customers to use the device of their choice, most banks have also come up with mobile wallets (to enable quick transfer of money and pay bills). Pockets, a mobile wallet from ICICI Bank, and PayZapp, a mobile wallet from HDFC Bank, are good examples.

Banks like American National Bank and First Green Bank have also teamed up with mobile payment vendors (Apple Pay, Android Pay) to facilitate payment (in retail stores) through their mobiles.

Given that Internet banking and mobile banking are the most frequently used tools by the customers, and the frequency of usage of these channels is higher than bank branch visits by the customer, the design of the Internet banking sites and mobile banking apps plays a crucial role in how the customer perceives the bank. The workflow and user experience of Internet bank sites and mobile banking apps of established banks often mirrors the way a bank teller would use the internal systems of the bank rather than how a customer would like to transact with the bank. This is leading to a lot of digital consumers beginning to look at "digital-only" challenger banks like Atom, Tandem, and Moven. These banks do not have any physical branches, but they still attract digital consumers through their ease of use and intuitive user experience.

Hashtag Banking As part of customer experience initiatives, banks are also leveraging social networking platforms for basic banking features likes statements, balance notification, and money transfer (up to a limited value). Leading private banks in India like Kotak Mahindra Bank and ICICI Bank allow banking using Twitter's hashtag and direct messaging features. Customers are required to specify the service they want (whether they want money transfer or bank balance) along with details like the money recipient's Twitter handle and the money to be transferred using hashtags (which help categorize tweets in Twitter). The customer is required to follow the bank (and the bank also follows the customer) to enable direct messaging. Once the customer sends the command to the bank's Twitter handle using a hashtag, they receive a unique code through a direct message (which ensures that others do not access this code). If the command is to transfer money, this code should be shared with the recipient. The bank tweets a link to the recipient's timeline to authenticate the recipient's Twitter account. Once the recipient authenticates his or her Twitter account using the link tweeted by the bank and the unique code shared by the sender, the money is transferred through a standard electronic funds transfer mechanism. Using Hashtag Banking, only small amounts (< US$200) are currently permitted for transfer. Figure 5.3 depicts a view of how Twitter Hashtag Banking works for money transfer.[11]

Service and Support Tactics   While call center (interactive voice response [IVR]), LiveChat, and phone banking have traditionally been used as standard mechanisms for resolving service issues and disputes, the cost of servicing customers through these channels is high. Social media and artificial intelligence (AI)-based virtual agents are being increasingly seen as cheaper and better options for servicing customers.

Tactics Leveraging Social Media   Online social communities and Twitter are largely used as customer service channels by banks and financial service enterprises.

INFLUENCING SMOT BY LEVERAGING ONLINE SOCIAL COMMUNITIES

Online social communities can be hosted on public social networking platforms or can be hosted on enterprise social platforms. These customer-to-customer (C2C) communities enable likeminded customers to collaborate with each other, post queries, and get answers from other customers who might have

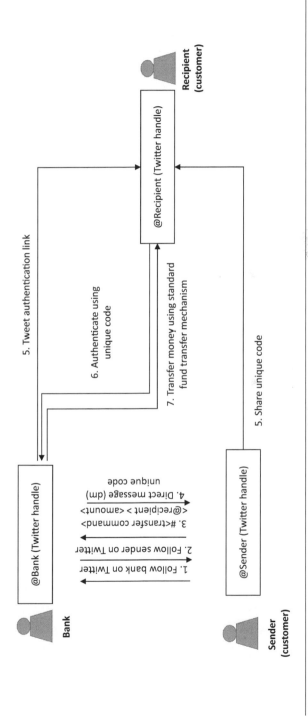

Figure 5.3   How Twitter Hashtag Banking works.

faced a similar issue (and got it addressed). These queries may also be answered by representatives from the financial enterprise (C2C communities also have representatives from the enterprise for either moderation or for answering queries that customers may not be able to). These C2C social communities are an inexpensive mechanism for enterprises to improve their customer experience. Customers themselves helping other customers by answering their queries also increases trust and helps in reducing calls to the more expensive call centers. In order to keep these communities active, enterprises also gamify C2C communities and reward customers who resolve more queries (beyond a threshold number).

LEVERAGING TWITTER TO INFLUENCE SMOT

Social media as a channel is a double-edged sword for enterprises. While it provides a more "personal" way to engage the customer and resolve a query or a simple problem faster, any unsatisfactory response gets amplified and spreads virally, leading to the brand name getting sullied. Savvy digital consumers, who know the power of social media, often complain about products and services using the Twitter platform. Twitter posts (tweets) spread virally across the world faster than other media channels. Hence, leading banks like HSBC, Barclays, NatWest, Lloyds TSB, and so on are leveraging Twitter as a channel for customer service.[12]

When any customer has an issue or query, these banks try to identify if the tweets are from their customers. For any queries that can potentially damage the reputation of the brand, the banks also tweet their replies to clarify their positions. For any genuine customer issues, they use the direct messaging feature of Twitter for one-to-one interaction with the customer. The direct messaging feature of Twitter ensures that conversations are not seen by anybody other than the customer, and this helps preserve the privacy of any confidential information required. Using direct messaging, however, requires the customers and the bank to follow each other (on Twitter). Quite often if the customer issue is resolved to their satisfaction, the customers express their gratitude publicly on Twitter, which helps the reputation of the brand.

Social media platforms like Facebook, Twitter as well as blogs provide an inexpensive way for banks and financial service enterprises to engage, support, and service their customers and play an important role in influencing ZMOT and SMOT in a big way, and TMOT and FMOT to a lesser extent. We thus see that more and more financial enterprises also capture the social networking identifiers (Twitter handle, Facebook login) as part of customer profile information in addition to their contact phone numbers and email IDs.

The way the enterprises treat social media distinguishes the leaders from the laggards. The leaders among financial enterprises have an integrated strategy toward social media. They have a dedicated team monitoring social media posts in real time (and responding to the comments when necessary) through their social media command centers. They have advanced tools for analyzing social media posts as well as mechanisms to respond immediately to customer queries and issues, handle reputation management issues, engage with prospective and active customers, as well as use social media for communicating with customers during emergencies and corporate events like mergers and acquisitions. User-generated comments are given importance, and mechanisms exist to integrate user-generated comments (as well as social media posts) with internal systems. These posts are leveraged for co-creating new products and services as well as serve as a springboard for generating leads and new consumers. Compared to the leaders, the laggards among financial enterprises treat social media channels (and initiatives) in a siloed manner, despite leveraging tools for handling social media.

Tactics Using Artificial Intelligence   Leading banks like Bank of America and Capital One are increasingly piloting chatbots for servicing customers. These chatbots leverage artificial intelligence (machine learning) to answer common queries of customers. Customers can either SMS these queries or converse with these virtual agents by talking to them (voice-activated chatbots). These chatbots can currently answer only basic queries, but over a period of time, machine learning will enable them to become better and more accurate as they answer more and more queries from the customer.

After-Sales Advertising Tactics   Upselling and cross-selling to an existing customer are always easier than selling to a new customer. The more products and services the same customer buys, the more profitable they are for the enterprise. Hence, even after a prospect or a lead becomes a customer, enterprises continue to persist with advertising and sales tactics to influence further sales. Digital channels leveraging mobile devices and social media help the enterprises to engage their customers better and make them increase their usage of a product or consumption of their service and retain their loyalty. Location-based offers and personalized offers are the typical after-sales advertising tactics used to influence SMOT.

Location-Based Offers   The biggest advantage of a mobile device like a smartphone or tablet is the contextual capabilities it can provide for enriching any interaction. Smartphones can provide the location of the device and thereby the location of a customer through mobile apps. Credit card providers can leverage the location of the customer to a branch or to an affiliate business (where a customer can buy an item using the credit card) and provide promotions and discounts based on their proximity to the affiliate. Thus, credit card providers can increase usage of the card.

As shown in Figure 5.4, any location-based offer typically leverages a mobile app (made available by the credit card provider) on the customer device and a software accessible to the credit card users for geofencing. The affiliate uploads the offers at specific locations to the credit card provider through an interface. Once the customer permits the mobile app on the device to access the location, offers, and promotions are pushed to the mobile app when they are within the boundaries of the geofence. The offers are contextualized based on rules and analytics.

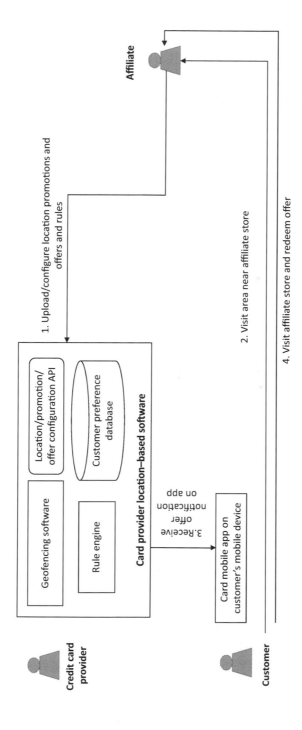

Figure 5.4 Generating location-based offers.

Credit card providers also tie up with location-based service provider partners and offer promotions to their customers and encourage them to spend using their credit cards. A perfect example is the tie-up Amex has with Foursquare. Foursquare is a popular mobile app for users to find local restaurants and other places of interest based on their location. The users also can view ratings of these places and make a decision to visit these locations or not. This app allows users to check in to a location (typically a tourist location or a retail business establishment) and announce this to their local phone contacts as well as contacts from their social networks. Users checking in more frequently to these locations gain badges and can get them converted to offers and discounts. This app has gained popularity as it provides offers and coupons for users to visit their places of interest (nearest to them), allows users to announce to their social connections where they are, and helps them meet up with their social community. Amex has tied up with Foursquare to provide offers to their Foursquare users at specific locations (if they use Amex cards for their purchases) thereby increasing customers to spend more (and save more) using Amex cards.

Personalized Offers Credit card companies have a rich database of customer profile information and their credit card transaction history. They mine this data to identify spend patterns of the customer. These patterns are married with contextual parameters like location, and personalized upsell and cross-sell offers are generated to targeted customers. These offers have a higher success rate in terms of influencing customers given the data-driven approach followed. During the first decade of this century, personalized offers were generated through rule-based mechanisms.

However, advancement in machine learning and analytics is helping automate the discovery of patterns and dynamic generation of offers and promotions. With more and more data, the accuracy of these patterns has also improved. Figure 5.5 depicts the process of generation of personalized offers. Product data, customer data, and customer transaction data are mined using advanced analytical algorithms, and the pattern is mined into a data store. A personalization engine or recommendation engine further gathers the context, marries the mined data, and generates personalized offers and recommendations to the customers (often on a real-time basis).

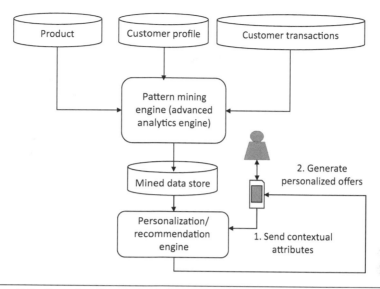

Figure 5.5   Generation of personalized offers.

Most leading credit card companies and retail banks now have a dedicated team of data scientists and analysts working on fine-tuning data mining algorithms for real-time personalization. These analytics teams are largely part of the middle office.

Influencing TMOT

Influencing SMOT encourages customers to stay loyal to the brand, encourages repeat customers for the products, and increases the share of wallet from each customer through a good customer experience. Apart from delivering high-quality products and services, the levers for great customer experience include attractive promotions, offers, attractive pricing, fostering engagement, and better relationships through contests and games. How the customer experiences SMOT leads them toward the TMOT, where they play the role of an advocate for the brand, product, or service and influence their social network to buy the product or consume the service of the enterprise. This brings in new customers to the enterprise for their products or services. Good experience during SMOT can also lead to the customer buying more products of the same category, or other products and services from the same enterprise. Service renewal and buying another new product (from the same brand) at the end of the lifecycle of the previous product is considered TMOT.

Tactics for influencing TMOT involve gamification techniques and social recommendation. Offers to customers for recommendations through social apps is an example. As part of this, a discount or an attractive offer for new customers is notified (as a feed) to the customer on the social platform, and the customer is encouraged to share this offer with a few of their friends in their social network. As each of these friends accept the offer, the customer is provided a real or a virtual gift or an offer. As part of their innovation programs, banks are exploring ways to mine the conversations of the users with their network using the social app (after taking the user's permission) and personalize offers contextually, taking into consideration privacy safeguards.

Other tactics for influencing TMOT include rewarding existing customers or influencers for turning advocates of their product or service, and encouraging them to share their good experiences with the public through social channels.

To influence customers to renew their service subscriptions or buy new products at the end of the older product's lifecycle, customers are also provided special offers, promotions, and discounts. The more the offers are contextual and target the needs of the user, the higher the chances of the customer renewing the subscription or buying a new product

Designing the Customer Journey Right

Many banks and credit card companies do well in terms of identifying MOTs and influencing them. This takes care of addressing individual touch points (or moments) of interaction with the customer. However, in today's world, more than a third of the customer interactions with the enterprise within a customer lifecycle (after they signup as a customer) span across multiple touch points and channels, and multiple departments of the organization (sales, billing, service, etc.). For a good customer experience, the customer journey has to be designed well. Despite taking measures to influence MOTs (or individual touch points), many banks and credit card companies fall short in customer satisfaction surveys because of their focus only on MOTs rather than customer journeys.

The customer journey can be defined as the sum of the experiences (of the customer) across the entire customer lifecycle across multiple channels, multiple touch points (i.e., MOTs), and multiple functions of the enterprise. It is the journey when interacting with the enterprise or brand through the eyes of the customer. Some of the examples of a journey include onboarding of the customer, account opening, payments, funds transfer, new card issual, new loan grant, reporting of loss of card or stolen card, and so on. When it comes to customer satisfaction (CSAT) ratings, there is a much stronger correlation between the overall experiences of the customer journey across a lifecycle than the experience of the customer at each touch point.

Not all customer journeys matter, and only the top few customer journeys impact customer satisfaction. Knowing the journeys that impact the CSAT ratings heavily is key to transforming the customer experience. Enterprises that are rated highly for their customer experience know the priority journeys to focus on. They keep refining this journey and introducing innovations to differentiate themselves from their competitors.

Customer journey mapping is the technique used for visually representing the customer journey. A customer journey map represents what a customer does between various touch points and helps in understanding the way the customers interact with the enterprise or brand. It takes into account all the channels used by the customer for interaction and spans across all the departments the customer interacts with (as part of their interaction with the enterprise). The success of digital transformation implementations (which typically span over a couple of years) is dependent on how well the customer journey is mapped. The customer journey maps (CJMs) help in identifying troublesome spots in their current online journey (the troublesome spots can be the reasons why customers may not use specific pages or screens, or do not go beyond a specific page or screen to complete their online transaction). It can also help in discovering the needs and motivations of the customer for their specific online behavior as well as the emotions associated with it. CJMs also capture the emotions of a customer at various stages of their journey. Large U.K. banks like HSBC Bank have leveraged CJMs to transform their customer experience.[13]

BUILDING A CUSTOMER JOURNEY MAP

The typical process of building a CJM involves workshops with business stakeholders to identify objectives of specific customer processes, conducting user research, and gathering inputs on the path taken for specific customer journeys through a mix of ethnography studies, in-branch observation and analytics, visualizing (and depicting) the current way the customers interact with each touch point through the journey, identifying the needs of customers as well as the issues the customer has when interacting with these touch points, and depicting the future state desirable customer journey along with a plan for implementing this.

Figure 5.6 depicts the (sample) customer journey of how the customer can transfer funds to a new payee on a mobile device through a mobile banking app. It outlines the different stages of the customer journey, the tasks performed by the user, their expectations (and the gap in expectations), and the ideas for improvement. In this example, the gaps are that the user is asked to enter a lot of information about the bank details of the sender, has no option for real-time transfer, and does not know the balance available in the account after the funds transfer to the payee. The improvement ideas include enabling the user to select from a list of bank branch codes, providing options for real-time transfer mechanisms, and sending SMS notification of bank balance after the completion of funds transfer. If multiple channels are involved for the scenario, the channel mapping for each user task is also specified.

Measuring Customer Experience

For an enterprise, customer experience is measured across different stages, that is, how well they are able to attract leads, how well they are able to convert leads to customers, and how well they are able to retain and service customers. How well they are able to attract leads is measured through metrics like number of visits (traffic to website),

User persona: Digital native mobile customer using mobile app   **Scenario:** Transfer funds to new customer

	Add payee	Validate receiver	Initiate fund transfer	Confirm
Steps				
User tasks	• Specify payee (account holder) name • Specify account number • Specify branch details • Submit details	• Receive OTP (one-time password) for validation • Confirm payee addition	• Select payee • Specify amount for transfer • Specify schedule for transfer	• Confirm funds transfer
Issues	• Too many details to be typed in for adding payee		• No immediate fund transfer option available	• No notifications received about balance in account after actual transfer of funds
Bank tasks	• Authenticate payee account	• Confirm payee addition has been requested by genuine customer	• Validate availability of funds	• Transfer funds to receiver • Acknowledge transfer to sender • Debit transferred amount from sender's account
Improve-ment ideas	• Provide list of bank and branch codes as readily available dropdown selection list		• Provide real-time transfer options (RTGS and IMPS)	• Send SMS notification to user after funds transfer specifying balance in account

Figure 5.6 Sample customer journey for funds transfer through mobile apps.

number of brand mentions, number of pages per visit, campaign effectiveness, and so on. How well enterprises are able to convert leads to customers is measured through metrics like conversion rate, number of completed transactions, and so on. How well the enterprises are able to retain customers, service them, and convert them to advocates are measured using metrics like frequency of visits, average revenue per user, upsell and cross-sell rate, share of wallet, net promoter score (difference between the percentage of advocates and the percentage of detractors), average handling time (AHT), first contact resolution, customer satisfaction (CSAT), customer effort score (CES), and so on. These metrics are usually captured through surveys as well as Web analytic tools, social, and text analytic tools, as well as advanced audience measurement tools. A few of the above metrics are derived metrics. When measuring customer experience, all possible channels of customer interaction must be considered to generate a holistic view.[14]

Customer Experience Transformation Strategy

Customer experience transformation can have different goals. It can be to engage or attract customers, to retain loyalty of existing customers, or to improve the lives of customers through productivity improvement and self-service.

Enterprises launch digital customer experience (DCX) transformation initiatives in order to help them succeed in converting the series of interactions with each of their existing and prospective customers into a trusted relationship. In order to succeed in their DCX transformation initiatives, enterprises must consider DCX transformation not as a single step, but as a series of steps.

The "Engagement" Step

For a prospective customer, "engagement" is the beginning of initial interaction with the enterprise. From the perspective of existing customers, engagement is about motivating them to interact further with the enterprise. Engagement capabilities are relatively easier to acquire for an enterprise, given that it largely requires omnichannel delivery systems with minimal or no dependency on internal IT systems.

Campaigns and contests on social platforms like Facebook are good examples of engagement initiatives.

The "Enable Customer Productivity" Step

This step involves providing tools to the customer, which dramatically reduces the time required for addressing their current needs (from the enterprise). Successfully implementing productivity initiatives for the customer brings them closer to the enterprise. Acquiring this capability requires investment in omnichannel delivery systems in addition to business process management (and automation) systems. Mobile banking and wallet apps are excellent examples of productivity initiatives for the customer.

The "Enable Self-Service" Step

Bringing in the self-service element, especially for supporting and servicing the customer, makes the customer realize that the enterprise is keen to ensure that they are able to use their products and services for betterment of their lives, resulting in a healthy relationship status between customers and enterprises. Acquiring self-service capability is a much more complex exercise. This may require case management systems in addition to business process management (and automation) and omnichannel delivery systems. The relationship with the customer gets better as the enterprise is trying to make it easier for the customer to interact with them. Online payment dispute resolution mechanisms for credit cards can be considered a good example of implementing the self-service step (leveraging case management solutions).

The "Enable Personalization" Step

Implementing personalization signals to the customer that the enterprise has understood the customer's needs well enough. At this stage, the customer has a trusted relationship with the enterprise, and their future needs from the enterprise are well anticipated by the personalized recommendations based on their current and past needs. Successful implementation of personalization leads to customers willing to invest in newer relationships or enhance their relationship (by buying other products and services) with the same enterprise. Providing more accurate personalized recommendations requires time, given that acquiring this capability is dependent on the analysis of the history of the customer's interactions with the enterprise. Analytics and machine learning systems are required to blend with the omnichannel, business process management (and automation), and case management systems for providing this capability. Customer experience (management) platforms are often leveraged when the enterprise reaches the enable personalization step. Recommendations on investment products as per the account balance and risk profile can be considered an example of personalization.

Climbing the Digital Customer Experience (DCX) Success Ladder

Figure 5.7 depicts the series of steps in the DCX success ladder. It shows the dependency between the enterprise efforts to influence the customer and the strength of the relationship with the customer. This ladder depicts how the enterprise efforts have to increase if they need to convert a prospect to a lead, a lead to a customer, and a customer to an advocate. In other words, the relationship strength of the customer (with the enterprise) is directly proportional to the efforts put in by the enterprise to influence the customer. As and when the enterprise climbs up each CX step in the DCX ladder, the more knowledge

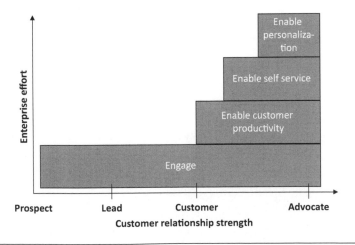

Figure 5.7 The DCX success ladder.

it gains about the customer, the better the relationship with the customer.

In order to convert a prospect to a lead and a lead to a customer, the enterprise needs to engage with the customer. If the customer is to be retained and turned into an advocate, the enterprise needs to start making an impact on the life of the customer by increasing their productivity by providing them tools, enabling self-service. Once they understand the customer better and start providing them what they want (personalization), the customer will start becoming an advocate. It needs to be noted that engagement does not stop with the prospect becoming a lead and the lead getting converted to a customer. A customer will still have to be engaged if they need to become an advocate.

Climbing the DCX ladder successfully enables the enterprise to acquire capability to attract future customers, retain and delight existing customers, build on their trusted relationships with their existing customers, and enable the customers as well as the enterprise to mutually benefit from each other.

Enabling Transformation of Digital Customer Experience

For DCX transformation initiatives to succeed in attracting new customers, retaining existing customers, and converting them to advocates of the brand, the enterprise must have capabilities to engage and support the customers across any device and any channel. Enterprises need to support omnichannel or any-channel capabilities; deliver the right content to the right user at the right time; track, monitor, and measure the impact of each tactic on each MOT for every prospect or customer; and provide a seamless experience for the customer from marketing to sales to service. The omnichannel capabilities must enable the customer to start a transaction from one channel, move seamlessly to another channel without losing the work they have already completed as part of the transaction in the earlier channel, and complete their unfinished work.

Customer relationship management (CRM), marketing automation platform, analytics, customer experience platform, content management systems, portals and websites, social platforms, mobile apps, and location-based services serve as the enablers for equipping the enterprises with the above capabilities.

Customer Relationship Management (CRM)

Retail-focused banking and financial service enterprises have been using CRM for a long time now for managing customers from a sales and service perspective. CRM helps in capturing information about the customer, tracking conversations with the customer throughout their lifecycle and targeting the right customers. CRM is largely used by the sales and customer service personnel to get an all-around view of the customers. Traditionally, implementing CRM has been a complex affair and has been expensive to maintain on-premise as well. Different businesses within the same enterprise sell different products in different ways. Sales process is not standardized and it is still not uncommon to find that different businesses within the same enterprise have different CRM.

Figure 5.8 depicts the high-level functionality supported by a CRM.

The role of the CRM has been steadily increasing over the last decade. In order to address the challenges of managing their digitally native customers as well as to make life easier for their sales personnel, financial enterprises are investing more on integrating social data (social media feeds from customers) with their CRM (social CRM) and equipping their sales personnel and agents with anytime, anywhere, any device access to CRM (mobile CRM). Financial enterprises are also investing in standardizing and simplifying their sales and service processes, while enhancing their capability to be more agile in handling their customer needs. They are investing in migrating their CRM from on-premise to cloud-based versions (software-as-a-service model)

Thus CRM plays a vital role in enabling financial enterprises to influence FMOT and SMOT for their customers. Oracle's Siebel CRM, Salesforce SFDC's CRM, SAP CRM, and Microsoft Dynamics CRM are preferred by large financial enterprises. Open source CRM like SugarCRM is also seeing an increased adoption by small and medium-sized financial enterprises.

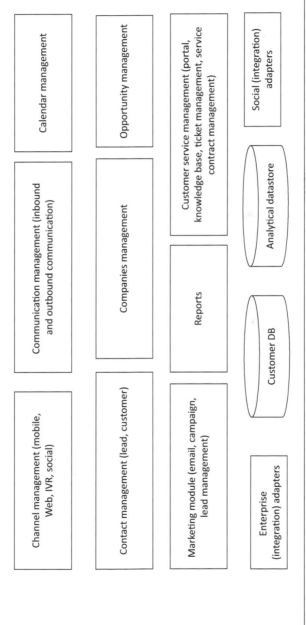

Figure 5.8 CRM overview.

Marketing Automation Platform

CRM serves as a handy tool for the sales and service personnel to manage already onboarded customers and influence them during their FMOT and SMOT. However, attracting leads and nurturing every lead with the aim of converting them to customers over a period of time goes beyond what a standard CRM can provide.

Hitherto marketing teams have been using multiple tools for the tasks related to lead management and tactics for influencing ZMOT. Diverse tools are used for email marketing, lead management, and nurturing and campaign management. There is minimal or no handshake (and collaboration) between the marketing and the sales team, and a manual or at best semiautomated process is associated with converting leads to customers. This keeps the lead conversion ratio low, and there is no easy way to track the return on investment (ROI) on marketing activities.[15]

In the last few years, marketing automation platforms (MAPs) that enable tracking the activity of leads, fostering a two-way communication between the enterprise and the leads, automating the process of capturing and nurturing leads, lead scoring and calculation, building the lead or contact list and segmenting them, email marketing, and campaign management have gained popularity. MAPs integrate well with content management systems and CRM and thus facilitate the publishing of the right content to the right lead at the right time through the right channel and aid seamless integration between marketing and sales teams. MAPs can serve as the underlying technology for enabling marketing processes and workflows. They have modules to ensure that only authorized users (from the marketing department) have access to confidential client (or lead) information and seamlessly pass on the filtered leads to the sales team so that they can convert the lead to a customer and don't miss out on any leads. MAPs support effective tracking of leads, campaigns, and related activity of leads across channels (mobile, Web, social). Analytical modules (of MAPs) help segment leads. These modules also integrate well with Web analytics tools and social analytics tools. Lead activity is well analyzed, and the right content can be better targeted to the right leads based on their preferences and online behavior on websites and social platforms, thus increasing the chances of the lead becoming a customer.

The benefits of MAPs include higher conversion of leads to customers, improved productivity of marketing teams, measuring the effectiveness of campaigns, reduction in marketing costs, and better collaboration between marketing and sales teams. There are at least two dozen MAP vendors, and this is growing. Popular among them include Adobe, Oracle Eloqua, IBM Unica, SAS Marketing Automation, Marketo, Hubspot, and so on. Marketing automation has seen higher adoption in business-to-business (B2B) marketing (where the target customers are limited when compared to B2C markets). MAPs play a vital role when influencing prospective customers or leads during their ZMOT. Some of the MAPs go beyond ZMOT and help personalize offers to existing customers to retain their loyalty. MAPs are largely installed on the cloud. Banks like First National Bank (South Africa), Czech National Bank, and Home Credit & Finance Bank are examples of banks using MAPs. Figure 5.9 provides a high-level overview of MAP components.

Of late, MAPs are evolving into digital marketing hubs. In addition to marketing automation capabilities, digital marketing hub products leverage big data to personalize content for the leads as well as target offers (and create effective marketing campaigns) for existing customers. The digital marketing hub enables better targeting by analyzing customer transaction data across the different channels.

Many CRM services have an add-on marketing automation module that supports some of the basic MAP features like campaign management, email management, and lead management, but MAPs can have more features for engagement of leads. The level of engagement analytics available in MAPs have more depth.

Customer Experience Management Platforms

Portals, which enable customers to search for the products, view product information, and sign up and transact with the enterprise, have been built with the assumption that customers will interact with the enterprise online only through a computer browser. They were not optimized for customers accessing portals through smartphones or tablets. Enabling personalization of the portal user interface based on multiple parameters like customer preferences (stored in external data stores) and online behavior across different channels was not easy to

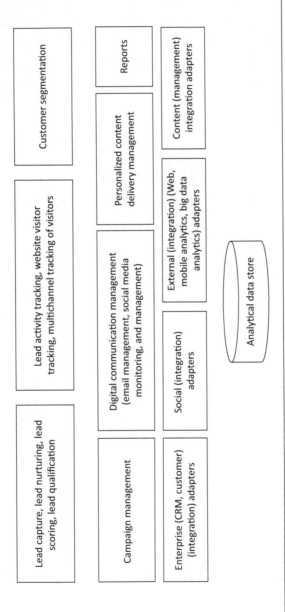

Figure 5.9 MAP overview.

achieve for the business. It was not easy to configure the portals for such changes by the business users themselves, and these required the involvement of the IT team and developers.

Customer experience platforms (CXPs) represent an evolution of the portal infrastructure for the digital consumers. CXPs separate out content management and content delivery. CXPs inherently realize that the needs of businesses, content creators, and developers (IT departments) are different. They enable business users to manage content as well as configure delivery of content across different device types (computers, tablets, smartphones) through a template-based approach. CXPs also have connectors to CRM services and may also have their own customer profile databases. They provide an interface to enable personalization of content to the users across different devices. CXPs help the business users model the customer journey and also help simulate the experience of the customer on different devices. Once the business user is satisfied, the webpages can be pushed into the production environment (which is accessible to the customer). Permissions for customers can be configured. Online behavior of customers is logged for analytics.

As shown in Figure 5.10, the components of a standard CXP include a content management system (templates, what you see is what you get (WYSIWYG) editor, workflows, content (and webpage) publisher), portal infrastructure (for hosting Web pages and device-agnostic widgets), content rendering engine (for device-agnostic access), customer data repository, data connectors to CRM services, commerce engines and enterprise services, social connectors, analytics engine, reports, and admin portal.

CXPs play a big role in FMOT and SMOT. Adobe, Sitecore, and Backbase are the popular CXP vendors. Leading banks like ABN AMRO, Barclays, Westpac, and ING Group are examples of financial enterprises adopting CXPs.

Analytics and Customer Insights

Enterprises understand what is working and what is not working with regards to engaging customers as well as what the customers want and do not want by investing in analytics. The insights from analytics help them fine-tune their tactics. In the digital world, the complexity comes from the fact that the customer can choose to interact with the enterprise on any channel through any device at a time of their

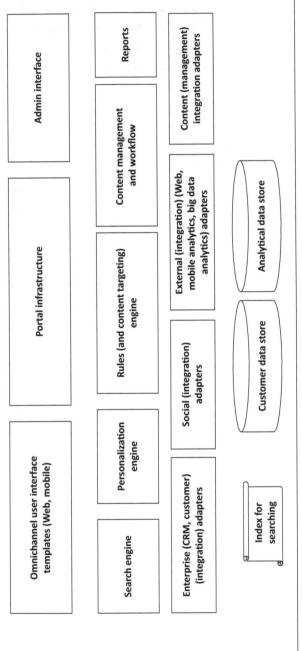

Figure 5.10 CXP components.

choosing. Thus, analytics for customer experience can involve Web analytics, social analytics, and mobile app analytics. Most often the data for analytics can be of both a structured and unstructured nature. The data can be voluminous and get created at breakneck velocity, and thus involve big data analytics as well as real-time analytics. Insights are derived when data from the Web, social, mobile, and traditional channels (like branches and call centers) are correlated with sales data, marketing data, and customer data.

Figure 5.11 depicts the process of leveraging analytics from customer interactions across channels and applying the intelligence gained from this to improve the customer experience. As with any analytical processing, customer experience analytics involves data capture, data processing and analysis, and applying this for business purposes like personalization, recommendations, targeted engagement, as well as data visualizations. The process of preparation for data capture involves the enterprise deploying hooks or logs in their engagement tactics (websites, mobile, and social apps). Logs are generated at various stages of customer activity and this logged data is usually transmitted to cloud-based analytical tools. Cloud-based analytical tools (Google Analytics, Adobe, Webtrends, IBM Coremetrics, etc.) perform the first level data processing and analysis.

Feeds from Web analytics, social analytics, and mobile analytics providers are further analyzed and correlated with enterprise data (customer transaction data, customer profile data, sales data, marketing data) to generate insights on what is working and what is not, what is the experience of the customers, where they are spending more time and where they are exiting, and so on.

Analytics serve as a vital input for the enterprise to adjust their tactics for influencing MOTs. The value of analytics spans across ZMOT, FMOT, SMOT, and TMOT.

Other Enablers

Content management systems, customer data store (cleaned up data of customers that serves as a single source of truth across the enterprise), mobile apps, social pages and apps, social media monitoring,

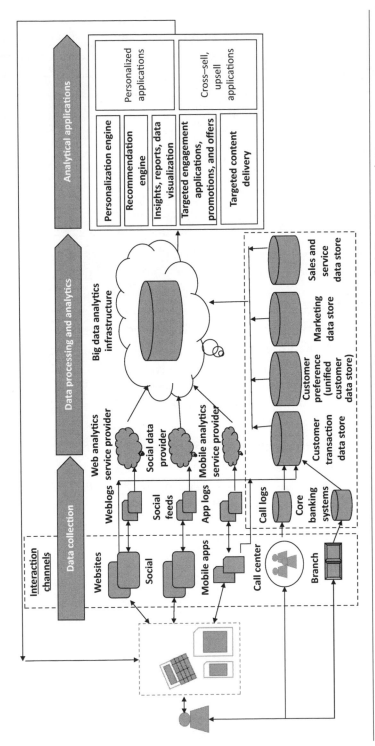

Figure 5.11 Generating intelligence from omnichannel customer interactions and applying the intelligence for better customer experience.

proximity marketing enablers like beacons, and sensors also serve as enablers for customer experience initiatives.

Content management systems include Web content management systems as well as digital asset management systems for storing rich media.

Targeted marketing tactics will fail if the customer data is not clean. Hence the customer data store should contain only cleaned up data about the customer, and this should serve as the single source of truth. Cleaning up customer data and having a 360-degree view of the customer may require the use of master data management technology.

Content management systems and customer data stores are not being covered in detail in this chapter, as these are systems that the enterprise has already been using before the SMAC era. Beacons and sensors are still being explored in branches. Mobile apps, social media monitoring, social pages and apps have already been covered in an earlier chapter (SMAC Primer).

Security and Privacy

Supporting single sign-on and social logins is imperative for a good customer experience. "No password" mechanisms like biometric identification and facial recognition techniques are being explored by banks for their mobile apps.

We are entering an interesting world where analyzing customer behavior is entering into grey areas, raising concerns with regards to individual privacy and raising the hackles of government regulators. Tracking customer behavior is increasingly being challenged by various governments and is seen to be violating data privacy regulations. Customers are demanding that they be informed of how their digital footprints are being used. Privacy preserving data mining (PPDM) techniques are being explored for customer analytics so that privacy regulations can be complied with.

The Coming of Age of Marketing Technology

Over the last decade, the Marketing organization under the Chief Marketing Officer (CMO), also referred to as the CMO organization going forward, has involved multiple creative agencies and external vendors for their digital marketing activities. This has led to a marketing technology sprawl with diverse "point" tools (which are used for specific purposes). The evolution of digital marketing has also contributed to this sprawl. To take an example, there are more than 40 tools available in the market only for email marketing, and it is not uncommon to find the CMO organization use more than one tool for email marketing. If all the tasks done by today's CMO organization are considered (like influencer marketing, content optimization, loyalty management, personalization management, ad management, etc.), the CMO organization has more than 1800 tools to choose from.[16]

MAPs and CXPs are reducing the marketing technology sprawl. MAPs are bringing together the functionality required for the marketers for creating, managing, and tracking leads along with analytics for assessing the ROI of marketing tactics. CXPs are bringing together the tools necessary for engaging the customer. Both MAPs and CXPs have also reduced the dependency on the IT organization and can be operated by the CMO organization itself. Gradually, the need for the IT organization is getting limited to platform customization and software integration tasks rather than building whole systems from scratch.

Reconfiguration of Marketing, Sales, and IT
Organization within the Financial Enterprise

The rise of digital consumers has disrupted the marketing and sales organizations within financial enterprises in a big way. With buying patterns of the customers changing and "decision to buy" being made in the online world, more and more activities that were earlier considered to be part of the sales organization have moved to the marketing organization. When it comes to digital technology investments, the CMO organization has an equal or higher budget than the chief information officer/IT (CIO) of the organization. With the advent of CRM, enterprises have already embarked on sales process simplification and optimization. Over the last three years, the CMO organization has embarked on marketing process automation. After the stabilization of marketing automation initiatives, more software investments from the CMO organization are getting into integrating the marketing organization with the sales organization (integration with CRM services and e-commerce platforms).

Figure 5.12 depicts the technology sprawl of the CMO organization spreading across (interaction channel) properties, applications, and data (and content) stores needed by the CMO organization for managing the customer experience. We can thus see why the technology budgets of the CMO organization have increased.

DOES THE CMO ORGANIZATION HAVE TO INVEST IN THE ENTIRE MARKETING TECHNOLOGY STACK TO MANAGE DIGITAL CUSTOMER EXPERIENCE?

The boundaries between CRM services, MAPs, and CXPs have been thinning. As most of the vendors take a platform approach to project themselves as the solution provider to reduce the diverse toolsets the CMO (and sales organization) have to deal with, there is an overlap between the functionality provided by each of them. Most financial enterprises already have the tools (custom-built or packaged) required for influencing MOTs in one way or the other, and it is not necessary to have all the above enablers to improve the experience of their customers.

A marketing automation strategy that involves assessment of the capabilities already within the enterprise and the gaps will provide a clear picture of the platforms that make sense for the enterprise to procure.

Desirable Habits for a Financial Enterprise for Enhancing Customer Experience

For succeeding in gaining digital consumers as their customers, enterprises need to undergo a big change in the way they engage with a prospective customer and the way they transact with a customer. Here are the desirable habits for the enterprise when dealing with digitally native customers.

It's All about Listening to the Customer

Gone are the days of information push. The digitally native customer is fickle-minded. Any good service is amplified and made known

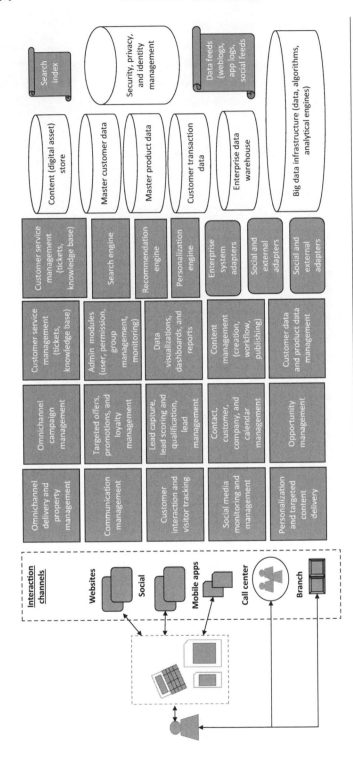

Figure 5.12 Technology capabilities required by the CMO organization.[17]

to the world through social media and product review sites. And so is bad service. Customers cannot be expected to consume whatever information is pushed by the enterprise. They need to be listened to. User comments are as important to the enterprise as what the enterprise communicates. Enterprises need to have mechanisms to monitor and analyze what is being said about them (and their products and services) in the product review sites and social media and to use this feedback to improve the way they engage or transact with their customers. Quick response to customer issues is an important part of customer experience.

It's Not Just Customers, but Even Leads (and Prospective Customers) Who Need to Be Understood

Gone are the days of trigger-happy email marketing. Emails that are not personalized to the needs of the prospective customers will be treated as spam and can potentially cause annoyance. An annoyed prospect will not become a customer. And it may not stop at that. They can express their annoyance in social media and bring disrepute to the brand image. It is necessary for the enterprise to capture the preferences of the leads, build trust, and personalize communications. Leveraging influencers for blogging about the product or service can help improve trust.

It's All about Customer Centricity

Gone are the days when banks and financial institutions were considered to be important for all financial transactions. Fintechs have leapfrogged ahead in popularity over banks and financial institutions because of their focus on customer centricity and customer experience. Banks and financial institutions have been thinking about only scenarios where a customer or prospect will need a bank or financial service and have tried to digitally enrich only these scenarios. They have rarely looked at scenarios where a prospect or a customer may need money (and not necessarily a bank). This is where fintechs are gaining popularity. The need of the hour is for the banks and financial institutions to think in terms of user personas instead of just the users. The context of usage is as important as the usage itself.

It's All about MOTs

Not engaging the prospective customer in their ZMOT results in the prospect not getting converted to a customer. If the enterprise makes all the effort to attract the prospect during ZMOT but makes the FMOT unattractive, the probability of the prospect turning into a customer is low. If ZMOT and FMOT are taken care of, but the customer has a bad experience with the product or service (their SMOT interactions with the enterprise), the customer will not stay loyal and may drive away potential customers. To remain in business in the digital world, the enterprise must stay engaged with the customer across all MOTs through marketing automation and personalized content delivery, leveraging a mix of data (insights), (experience) design, and technology capabilities.

It's All about Seamless Collaboration within the Enterprise

In the digital world, more sales functions have moved to marketing. Before coming to FMOT, a customer has already decided the product they are going to buy. The transition from marketing to sales to service must be seamless. No handshake between marketing and sales leads to missed customer conversions. Customer engagement doesn't end with a sale and needs to be continued even after the prospect has become a lead and the lead has become a customer, and further, an advocate.

Conclusion

Customer experience is a journey. Or, in other words, it is an aggregate of the experiences that the customer has at different interaction moments with the enterprise. Each stage of interaction on the customer journey is a moment of truth for the enterprise. Digital technology has transformed the way the customer interacts (or buys a product or service) from the enterprise. They research well before they buy a product or service. This is the zero moment of truth. By the time a customer has come to a branch, the customer has already decided on the product they want to buy. Thus it is imperative for the enterprise to engage the prospective customer well during the ZMOT if they wish to convert them to a customer. The engagement has to continue throughout the customer lifecycle (from a lead to prospect to customer to advocate) for the success of an enterprise. Banks and financial services are investing in digital marketing to engage the customer during the different moments of truth. For the customer to stay loyal, it is necessary for the handover from marketing to sales to service to be seamless. We thus see a lot of technology investment for automating sales, marketing, and service being made by the CMO organization.

Different tactics leveraging technology need to be adopted to influence the customer during different moments of truth and encourage them to stay loyal to the brand or enterprise.

As quoted by Steve Jobs, "You have got to start with customer experience and work back toward the technology." For enterprises to succeed in transforming the experience of their digital customers, they would need to identify the moments of truth, influence these moments of truth by adopting different tactics, and design the entire customer journey well. The enablers for this include customer relationship management software, marketing automation platforms, customer experience platforms, analytics, content management systems, unified master customer data repositories, channel properties (websites, mobile apps), and miscellaneous other tactics like proximity marketing, location-based services, and so on. It is key that any strategy for customer experience takes into account the need for omnichannel access for the customer, ability to perform different steps of the customer journey through different devices, and personalization of the user interface, data, and content as per customer needs.

Abbreviations Expanded

MOTs   moments of truth.
ZMOT   zero moment of truth.
FMOT   first moment of truth.
SMOT   second moment of truth.
TMOT   third moment of truth.
CJM   customer journey map.
B2C   business-to-consumer.

NEFT National Electronic Funds Transfer (an electronic fund transfer system maintained by the Reserve Bank of India, the Indian equivalent of the U.S. Federal Reserve).

RTGS real-time gross settlement (a real-time funds transfer and settlement system maintained by the Reserve Bank of India, the Indian equivalent of the U.S. Federal Reserve).

IMPS Immediate Payment Service, an instant interbank electronic funds transfer service through mobile phones. This service is provided by the National Payments Corporation of India (NPCI) and supported by the Reserve Bank of India and Indian Banks Association.

Points to ponder:

- What is a moment of truth?
- How can the enterprise influence the moments of truth?
- How should the customer journey be designed?
- How can the enterprise climb the digital customer experience success ladder?
- What are the enablers for digital customer experience?
- What is marketing technology?
- What is the impact of digital technologies on the sales, marketing, and IT organization of financial enterprises?

References

1. Good Reads. Maya Angelou Quotes https://www.goodreads.com/author/quotes/3503.Maya_Angelou
2. Wikipedia. Maya Angelou. https://en.wikipedia.org/wiki/Maya_Angelou
3. Lance Boge, Tom Bittner, Virginia Sertich. 2010. Do Physical Bank Branches Still Hold Value? Gensler Research & Insight. http://www.gensler.com/research-insight/research/retail-banking-trends
4. Sky News. Digital Banking Growth Poses Risk to Branches. 2014. http://news.sky.com/story/digital-banking-growth-po9.ses-risk-to-branches-10397599
5. Douglas Karr. 2012. Zero Moment of Truth. SlideShare. Nov 10. http://www.slideshare.net/douglaskarr/zmot-zero-moment-of-truth?next_slideshow=1
6. Dale Denham. 2016. Selling in ZMOT. SlideShare. Sep 28. http://www.slideshare.net/therealdaledenham/selling-in-zmot-zero-moment-of-truth

7. Nick Garner. 2013. ZMOT & Influence-Growing Importance of ZMOT. SlideShare. Oct 7. http://www.slideshare.net/90DigitalAgency/zmot-influence-growing-importance-of-zmot
8. Marketing Schools. Types of Marketing Strategies. http://www.marketing-schools.org/types-of-marketing.html
9. Marketing Schools. Affinity Marketing. http://www.marketing-schools.org/types-of-marketing/affinity-marketing.html
10. Christopher Hall. 2015. Banks are Banking on Digital Signage. DigitalSignageToday. Aug 28. http://www.digitalsignagetoday.com/articles/banks-are-banking-on-digital-signage/
11. Vivina Vishwanathan. 2015. One Minute Guide: Hashtag Banking. LiveMint. Jul 5. http://www.livemint.com/Money/PaklJWALLp7ttemZp9oleL/One-minute-guide-hashtag-banking.html
12. Adrian Swinscoe. 2012. Customer Service: Which Retail Banks Are Most Responsive on Twitter? BrandWatch (Blog). May 16. https://www.brandwatch.com/blog/customer-service-which-retail-banks-are-most-responsive-on-twitter/
13. Researchomatic. Customer Experience Journey Mapping in HSBCs Bank UK. http://www.researchomatic.com/Customer-Experience-Journey-Mapping-In-Hsbc-Bank-Uk-72237.html#buytopicstep
14. Oracle (White Paper). 2015. Customer Experience (CX) Metrics and Key Performance Indicators. http://www.oracle.com/us/products/applications/cx-metrics-kpi-dictionary-1966465.pdf
15. Maryka Burger. 2016. What is the Difference Between Marketing Automation & CRM? SharpSpring. Feb 23. https://sharpspring.com/marketing-automation-vs-crm/
16. Marketing Technology Landscape. 2015. Chief Martec. Jan. http://cdn.chiefmartec.com/wp-content/uploads/2015/01/marketing_technology_jan2015.png
17. Disruptive Digital. CMO View of Digital Architecture (image). https://disruptivedigital.files.wordpress.com/2015/05/cmo-view-of-digital-architecture.png

Additional Resources

1. CXOToday News Desk. 2016. Marketing Automation- 4 Mistakes to Avoid. CXO Today. Dec 26. http://www.cxotoday.com/story/4-mistakes-to-avoid-while-driving-marketing-automation/
2. CXOToday News Desk. 2016. Marketing Automation- 4 Mistakes to Avoid. CXO Today. Dec 26. http://www.cxotoday.com/story/4-mistakes-to-avoid-while-driving-marketing-automation/
3. Robert SIciliano CSP. 2014. Why Proximity Marketing Is the Next Big Thing for Retail. American Express (OPEN Forum). Dec 2. https://www.americanexpress.com/us/small-business/openforum/articles/tracking-beacons-business-vs-consumer/

4. Wes Prichard. 2014. Big Data for Location-Based Offers in Banking. Oracle (Big Data Blog). Jul 11. https://blogs.oracle.com/bigdata/big-data-for-location-based-offers-in-banking

5. Ajay Gupta and Vik Sohoni. 2016. Digital Marketing Really Matters for US Banks Even As Branches Show Significant Staying Power. McKinsey (Digital Insights). Dec 1. http://www.mckinsey.com/business-functions/digital-mckinsey/our-insights/digital-blog/digital-marketing-really-matters-for-us-banks-even-as-branches-show-significant-staying-power?cid=other-alt-mip-mck-oth-1612

6. Luis Cortes. 2015. Moments of Truth, Systems of Record and Systems ff Engagement: It All Fits Together with Red Hat Jboss Fuse. Jun 10. Redhat. https://www.redhat.com/en/about/blog/moments-truth-systems-record-and-systems-engagement-it-all-fits-together-red-hat-jboss-fuse

7. KPMG Nunwood. 2015. A Look at Customer Journey Mapping in the Financial Services Sector. KPMG Nunwood. Jul 7. http://www.nunwood.com/a-look-at-customer-journey-mapping-in-the-financial-services-sector/

8. Edwin van Bommel, David Edelman, and Kelly Ungerman. Digitizing the Consumer Decision Journey. McKinsey (Marketing & Sales Insights). http://www.mckinsey.com/business-functions/marketing-and-sales/our-insights/digitizing-the-consumer-decision-journey

9. David Baker. 2015. Mapping the Customer Journey. LinkedIn (Pulse). Feb 17. https://www.linkedin.com/pulse/mapping-customer-journey-david-a-baker

10. Simon Herd. 2015. How to create effective customer journey maps. LinkedIn (Pulse). Nov 6. https://www.linkedin.com/pulse/how-create-effective-customer-journey-maps-simon-herd?articleId=7966921122566037782#comments-7966921122566037782&trk=sushi_topic_posts

11. Investopedia. Back Office. http://www.investopedia.com/terms/b/backoffice.asp

12. The Customer Journey Consultancy. What is Customer Journey? http://customerjourney.uk.com/customer-journey/what-is-customer-journey/

13. ICICI Bank. ICICIBankPay (Information). http://www.icicibank.com/Personal-Banking/insta-banking/internet-banking/twitter-banking/transactions.page

14. News Room. 2015. ICICI Bank Launches Banking Services on Twitter. ICICI Bank. Jan 19. http://www.icicibank.com/aboutus/article.page?identifier=news-icici-bank-launches-banking-services-on-twitter-20151901130220548

15. American Banker. http://www.americanbanker.com/

16. Ray. 2015. Banks That Have Implemented Social Media Payments through Facebook and Twitter. Let's Talk Payments (LTP). Apr 25. http://letstalkpayments.com/banks-that-have-implemented-social-media-payments-through-facebook-and-twitter-2/

17. Lon. S. Cohen. 2009. 5 Ways Banks Are Using Social Media. Mashable. Sep 11. http://mashable.com/2009/09/11/banks-social-media/#Q.kdlUO19Oqf

18. Geoff Livingston. 2011. The State of Influencer Theory on the Social Web. SmartBrief. Jul 15. http://smartblogs.com/social-media/2011/07/15/the-state-of-influencer-theory-on-the-social-web/

19. Jay Baer. Social Media Influencers versus Brand Advocates Infographic. Convince&Convert. http://www.convinceandconvert.com/content-marketing/social-media-influencers-versus-brand-advocates-infographic/

20. GroupHigh. Social Media Influencers. http://www.grouphigh.com/social-media-influencers/

21. Christina Newberry. 2017. Influencer Marketing on Social Media: Everything You Need to Know. Hootsuite. Apr 19. https://blog.hootsuite.com/how-to-find-social-media-influencers/

22. Marketing-Schools. Business to Business Marketing. http://www.marketing-schools.org/types-of-marketing/b2b-marketing.html

23. Marketing-Schools. Analytical Marketing. http://www.marketing-schools.org/types-of-marketing/analytical-marketing.html

24. Marketing-Schools. Article Marketing. http://www.marketing-schools.org/types-of-marketing/article-marketing.html

25. Marketing-Schools. Facebook Marketing. http://www.marketing-schools.org/types-of-marketing/facebook-marketing.html

26. Marketing-Schools. Long Tail Marketing. http://www.marketing-schools.org/types-of-marketing/long-tail-marketing.html

27. Marketing-Schools. Business to Business Marketing. http://www.marketing-schools.org/types-of-marketing/contextual-marketing.html

28. Marketing-Schools. Contextual Marketing. http://www.marketing-schools.org/types-of-marketing/e-commerce-marketing.html

29. Marketing-Schools. Integrated Marketing. http://www.marketing-schools.org/types-of-marketing/integrated-marketing.html

30. Marketing-Schools. Influencer Marketing. http://www.marketing-schools.org/types-of-marketing/influencer-marketing.html

31. Marketing-Schools. Mobile Marketing. http://www.marketing-schools.org/types-of-marketing/mobile-marketing.html

32. Marketing-Schools. Multichannel Marketing. http://www.marketing-schools.org/types-of-marketing/multichannel-marketing.html

33. Marketing-Schools. Cross-Media Marketing. http://www.marketing-schools.org/types-of-marketing/cross-media-marketing.html

34. Marketing-Schools. Neuromarketing. http://www.marketing-schools.org/types-of-marketing/neuromarketing.html

35. Marketing-Schools. Next-Best-Action Marketing. http://www.marketing-schools.org/types-of-marketing/next-best-action-marketing.html

36. Marketing-Schools. Consumer Generated Marketing. http://www.marketing-schools.org/types-of-marketing/consumer-generated-marketing.html

37. Marketing-Schools. Targeted Marketing. http://www.marketing-schools.org/types-of-marketing/targeted-marketing.html

38. Marketing-Schools. Closed Loop Marketing. http://www.marketing-schools.org/types-of-marketing/closed-loop-marketing.html

39. Marketing-Schools. Post-Click Marketing. http://www.marketing-schools.org/types-of-marketing/post-click-marketing.html
40. Marketing-Schools. Internet Marketing. http://www.marketing-schools.org/types-of-marketing/internet-marketing.html
41. Marketing-Schools. Cloud Marketing. http://www.marketing-schools.org/types-of-marketing/cloud-marketing.html
42. Wikipedia. Digital Native. https://en.wikipedia.org/wiki/Digital_native
43. Ofer Zur and Azzia Walker. 2016. On Digital Immigrants and Digital Natives: How the Digital Divide Affects Families, Educational Institutions, and the Workplace. Zur Institute. http://www.zurinstitute.com/digital_divide.html
44. Abbey Klaassen. 2009. Using Social Media to Listen to Consumers. *AdvertisingAge*. Mar 30. http://adage.com/article/digital/digital-marketing-social-media-listen-consumers/135605/
45. Vikki Zelkin. 2014. The Role of Rewards in Retaining the Vocal Minority and the Silent Majority. *Digital Marketing Magazine*. Aug 27. http://digitalmarketingmagazine.co.uk/customer-experience/the-role-of-rewards-in-retaining-the-vocal-minority-and-the-silent-majority/918
46. Consumer Futures. (This URL has been archived and currently redirects to Citizens Advice Scotland website.) http://www.consumerfutures.org.uk/files/2014/03/Realising-consumer-rights.pdf
47. Olivier Denecker, Sameer Gulati, and Marc Niederkorn. 2014. The Digital Battle That Banks Must Win. McKinsey (Financial Services Insights). Aug. http://www.mckinsey.com/insights/financial_services/the_digital_battle_that_banks_must_win)
48. Tunde Olanrewaju. 2014. The Rise of the Digital Bank. McKinsey (Digital Insights). July. http://www.mckinsey.com/insights/business_technology/the_rise_of_the_digital_bank
49. Edwin van Bommel and David Edelman. 2015. Adapting to Digital Consumer Decision Journeys in Banking. McKinsey (Financial Services Insights). Feb. http://www.mckinsey.com/insights/financial_services/adapting_to_digital_consumer_decision_journeys_in_banking
50. Nationwide. (This URL has been archived.) http://www.nationwide.co.uk/support/ways-to-bank/digital-wallet/features-and-benefits
51. Cadie Thompson. 2014. Can Apple Win the Mobile Wallet War? CNBC. Nov. 3. http://www.cnbc.com/id/102140953
52. Tom Jackson. 2014. Cape Town Goes Cashless as Mobile Payment Apps Take Off. BBC News. Dec 5. http://www.bbc.com/news/business-30184359
53. Heistmade. Designing the Smart Bank. http://www.heistmade.com/banks/
54. Luis Cortes. 2015. Moments of Truth, Systems Of Record And Systems Of Engagement: It All Fits Together with Red Hat Jboss Fuse. Red Hat. Jun 10. https://www.redhat.com/en/about/blog/moments-truth-systems-record-and-systems-engagement-it-all-fits-together-red-hat-jboss-fuse

6

DIGITAL TRANSFORMATION AND IMPACT OF SMAC TECHNOLOGIES ON CULTURE, THINKING, IT PRACTICES, ORGANIZATIONAL STRUCTURES, AND GOVERNANCE

In five years, the biggest banks in the world won't be banks, they'll be tech companies.

Brett King

CEO of Moven, a digital-only bank[1]

Digital transformation means different things for different stakeholders. For a customer, digital transformation enables self-service. It saves time. The customer no longer needs to go to a bank branch at a specific time to open accounts or to transfer money to their friends or relatives. They can do this by touching a button on their own device anywhere, anytime. The mobile bank app as well as the Internet bank site know their preferences and provide them information personalized to their needs. It is truly omnichannel, that is, customers can initiate a transaction through their mobile device and complete this on their desktop without having to redo their transaction from scratch.

For an employee, digital transformation implies that they can collaborate faster with their coworkers as well as agents and customers and get work done faster. They are equipped with real-time data that provides them with a 360-degree view of the customer, right when they begin conversations with their customers. It helps them address the needs of the customer better and faster.

For a financial enterprise, digital transformation helps them to be more data-driven. It helps them automate mundane tasks of the employees, improve productivity of the employees, target customers better and attract more digital native customers, increase revenues, and bank the unbanked.

Digital transformation is not something that can be achieved as a one-time activity with a planned end date. It is a continuously evolving exercise and the benefits will be realized incrementally. The gains from digital transformation can be sustained only when the financial enterprise is supported by an agile organization that is flexible to rapidly changing customer demographics and needs.

Critical Success Factors for Digital Transformation Initiatives

Across industries, large enterprises succeed or fail in their digital transformation initiatives based on how they leverage their design, data, and delivery capabilities to enrich context and bring value to their interactions with their customers. These capabilities need not be "fully owned" capabilities. They can be borrowed from the ecosystem. Success in the digital space depends on how these enterprises move away from their risk-averse approach, how quickly they deploy (and enhance) their products, and how open they are to collaborating with their partners as well as customers.

In this chapter, applications developed using SMAC technologies are grouped under the umbrella of digital applications and products. Both digital applications and products are spoken of in the same breath and intend to mean the same. Similarly, "established financial enterprises" and "established banks and financial institutions" are intended to mean the same.

Short Release Cycles, Continuous Evolution, and
a Minimum Value Product Approach

Due to the highly evolving nature of digital technologies and their applications, taking a big bang approach to digital transformation is not beneficial. It is necessary to take an experimental approach. A single process, which is of value to the customer, can be chosen initially for the experiment and the digital concept, prototype, and product with bare minimum features can be built (around this process) within a short period of three to four weeks and released to production for user feedback. If the product is well-received by the users, it can be further improved with more features and can start covering more processes over further iterations of short release cycles. The objective is for the product to get better (to continuously improve) in close collaboration with the user.

Fail Fast Approach

Digital transformation projects require a measured risk-taking attitude. All innovational experiments may not succeed. Some may disrupt the market and provide substantial gains for the business, some of them may just provide incremental gains for the business while some may fail. Innovations need to be monitored for success and failure indicators early in their evolution cycle. If the innovative product does not reach critical mass in terms of customer adoption within the initial few releases, the innovative experiment can be stopped and the team can be reallocated to another new experiment. The objective here is to fail fast without spending too much money. This is what systematic innovation is all about. It makes sufficient budgets available for innovation but ensures that too much money is not spent on non-value-adding innovations, while also ensuring that failure does not result in stopping experimentation altogether.

Partnering with the Ecosystem Players

Given their focus on very specific processes as well as absence of legacy systems, the user experience and customer centricity of products developed by technology startups are superior to those that can be provided by established financial enterprises. Partnerships with technology startups (and fintechs) enable better customer engagement for the established banks and financial institutions while providing an expanded customer reach for the fintech players for their products.

Opening up Hitherto Closed Systems to External Players through APIs

Historically, established banks and financial institutions have leveraged the data they possess for their own application usage and have hardly ever made it available for use by external organizations as part of their security and competitive strategy. However, the success of technology players like Google and Facebook (who are more open with sharing their expertise in technology with the world by open sourcing the technology frameworks they use) have made the established players realize that innovation is occurring more outside than inside their own enterprises. By allowing external access of their data (with appropriate monitoring and control systems in place), they can monetize their data better and also get closer to their customers. The maturity of API management software (like Apigee, Layer 7, WSO2) helps in exposing the internal business applications (and data) as secure APIs, and this has helped in the growth of the API economy.

Open Innovation

Innovative ideas, especially related to the needs of customers, come more often from outside the enterprise than within. Crowdsourcing ideas, evaluating feasibility of these ideas and prioritizing them, quickly turning these ideas into prototypes, beta-testing these working prototypes with end users, and taking a decision to either scale or shelve these prototypes based on the user feedback all require a change in mindset. Instead of pushing products to the customers based on the value perceived by the enterprise, an outside-in approach of co-creating innovative products with customers and partners has a greater chance of success. An idea-management or innovation-exchange platform that enables enterprises to gather and prioritize ideas from employees, partners, and customers works as a starting point for CIO organizations embarking on digital transformation initiatives.

Why Aren't Established Financial Enterprises as Nimble as the Fintechs?

The older and more established the enterprise, the higher the likelihood of the enterprise being saddled with legacy systems, processes, and infrastructure. Out of the close to US$400 billion spend on IT in 2015 and 2016, banks ended up allocating more than 60% of this spend towards servicing their legacy systems and only the remainder was routed towards new projects.[2]

Inheritance of Legacy Systems

Legacy systems prove to be a drag on the IT organization and affect their readiness for digital transformation initiatives. Any bank that has acquired or built application systems over the last 30-plus years is bound to have an application portfolio consisting of a heterogeneous mix of technologies, many of which would have no skill pool available in the market. Building new digital front-end applications, which requires integration with such applications (for which the resource pool is limited), brings down the flexibility of such banks to repurpose the data they own toward innovative digital use cases.

Layers of Handshakes from Development to Deployment

Given the regulatory compliance controls on the financial enterprises industry, most IT groups in banks and financial institutions would just want to ensure that they are on the right side of the law (an attitude of leaving the systems unchanged if they are not broken). The HR policies and the incentivizing structure tends to favor the status quo as against disruption. IT managers are keen to ensure that any new feature enhancement doesn't impact existing systems and hence try to mitigate risk by increasing the number of gatekeepers from the time new code is deployed on the development environment to the time it goes live for the customers.

THE COST AND EFFORT FOR ADDING A NEW DATE FIELD IN A REPORTING APPLICATION

One of the business divisions of an established global bank required an additional field to appear as part of the reports sent periodically to a regulator. The business asked IT to provide an estimate for adding an additional date field for their reports. As is the norm, the IT manager contacted the vendor maintaining the 35-year-old legacy application for the estimate. The developer (from the vendor organization) estimated the work to take 10 days. The vendor delivery manager added up contingency efforts and gave a 30-day estimate for the change to the bank's IT manager. The bank's IT manager added efforts for regression testing, system and integration testing, apart from the user acceptance testing and application deployment efforts, and provided a budgetary effort of 90 elapsed days and an estimated costing of US$45,000 for this effort. The business had no alternative other than approving this budget, as it was a mandatory regulatory compliance requirement. Thus, the cost of adding just one date field in a report built on a legacy system ended up with a US$45,000 bill for the business with a 90-day waiting period.

Stove-Pipe Architecture

Enterprises with legacy systems, built more for reliability than flexibility, end up with a large number of non-standardized point-to-point integration between applications. IT systems acquired due to mergers and acquisitions compound this problem further. New digital applications requiring interaction with any back-end system of record end up being dependent on long-duration complex integration activities (which by themselves get carved out into separate integration projects), impacting their time to market plans. Even if front-end digital applications adopt the required agile development infrastructure, the dependency on slow systems of record and systems of integration curbs the short-release development and deployment capabilities of the IT organization.

Partial Agile Adoption

Though many banks and financial institutions are adopting agile development methodologies, they are partial at best. While the new digital front-end applications are being developed in an agile manner, changes to the back-end systems (with which they need to be integrated) are made in a waterfall model (a sequential software development methodology) due to their inherent legacy nature. This hinders the established banks and financial institutions from reaping the business benefits of agile development, namely, faster speed to market, higher productivity, and better delivery quality.

Coming out of "Too-Big-to-Change" Syndrome

Application development for today's digital needs requires large enterprises to shift out of their traditional ways of working, which restrain creativity and innovation. They need to explore adoption of the "startup" way of working wherever possible. This shift impacts software development methodologies followed, architectural techniques deployed, the way the business and the software development team collaborate, as well as the way the software development teams work with the IT operations teams, and thereby the organizational structure.

Changes to Software Development Methodology

Software development involves collaboration and handshakes between multiple parties in a large enterprise. These stakeholders are the end users (customers), the business team who represent the customers and foot the bill for the application development (and deployment), and the IT team, which further involves the business analysts (the functional experts), software architects, application designers, the software developers, the testers, and then the IT operations team who deploy, manage, monitor, and support the application.

Traditionally, application development projects in established financial enterprises follow a waterfall methodology (as shown in Figure 6.1), a sequential set of activities ranging from requirements gathering, to application architecture and design, to application development, to application testing, to application deployment, maintenance, and support. Here the assumption is that the business team (who represents the end users) knows all the end-user requirements up front. An average application implementation begins with the requirements-gathering phase, which takes about two to three months of intensive requirements gathering and documentation by business analysts. If the application development is outsourced, the vendors also ensure that the next set of activities related to application architecture and design does not begin until the business

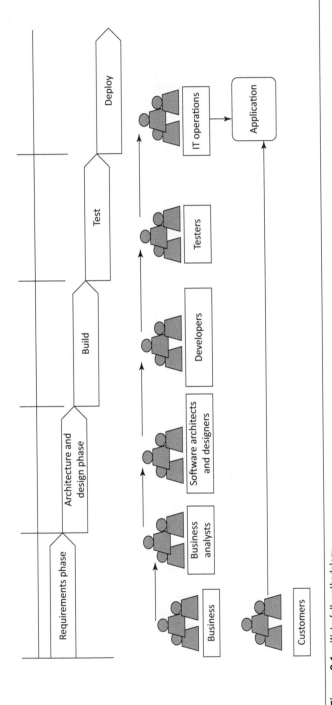

Figure 6.1   Waterfall methodology.

owner signs off that there is no change to the requirement. As part of the subsequent architecture and design phase, the software architects and application designers translate the functional requirements to technical requirements and evaluate and recommend the appropriate technology for the requirements based on an exhaustive criteria leading to a rulebook for the application developers. If a third-party software package is required, an additional software procurement process (driven by the vendor management organization) also kicks in. Depending on the complexity of the functional requirements, this architecture and design phase too may take anywhere from two to four months. Until this stage, which is almost six months after the beginning of the project, all that the business team may have is a set of documents and, if lucky, a basic low-level prototype of the application. The subsequent application development takes another six to eight months, followed by two to three months of system testing, integration testing, and end-user application test. Finally, by the time the application is deployed in production and made available for the end users, it is more than a year since the requirements would have been conceived (based on business need). The longer the gap between the requirements-gathering phase and application deployment, the higher the chances of end-user expectations changing, leading to suboptimal usage of the application and quite often failure of these application projects. If during this entire application development lifecycle, there is any change needed by the business team, a change request process triggers, resulting in rework, effort, and cost overruns.

The waterfall methodology works fairly well for developing back-end systems of record, which need to be stable, reliable, available, and secure. The business dynamics (and the assumptions) behind the existence of these systems do not change for a longer duration.

However, when this methodology is applied to development of digital applications or systems of engagement, this will lead to failure given that the business dynamics keep changing and customers also expect any digital application they use to provide them an experience comparable to a Google or a Facebook product. Inability to accommodate changing requirements during the course of the development of the applications is an additional constraint imposed by the waterfall model. This is where agile development methodology is gaining traction.

Agile development methodology (Figure 6.2) is all about better ways of developing high-quality software. It is based on a manifesto, supported

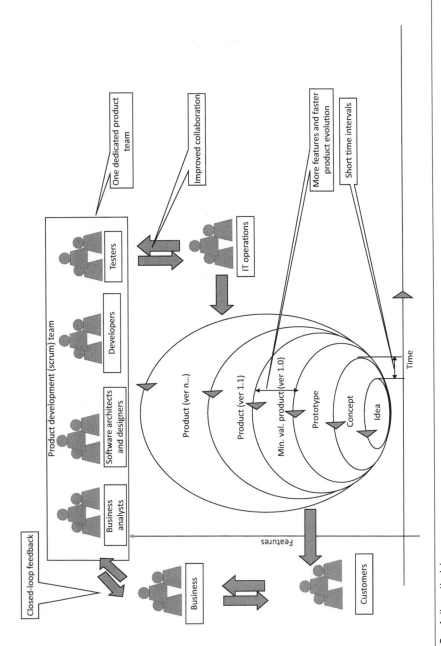

Figure 6.2 Agile methodology.

by 12 principles, that lays stress on being flexible to change, building continuously evolving better quality software, and fostering better collaboration between the different stakeholders, namely the business and the IT teams. The business team, which works closely with the end customer, is involved throughout the development cycle (across multiple releases) so that there is enough room for the customer feedback getting reflected in the software delivered. Each incremental release of the product gets developed as part of a sprint. The duration of each sprint ranges from two to four weeks and has something of value to the customers in terms of features. Instead of a big bang approach, a minimum viable product with prioritized features is delivered, so that the customers can use them early and provide their feedback for improvement. "Working software over comprehensive documentation" is the motto. The lower priority features as well as feedback from customers get accumulated into the product backlog (these are the features that are built into the product as part of the next few sprints). A product owner manages this backlog, and the backlog is distributed or prioritized through a series of sprints. Each sprint has a sprint backlog against which the team plans its sprint.

Contrary to teams leveraging the waterfall software development methodology, the agile teams are self-contained; that is, the business analysts, the architect, the designers, the application developers, and the testers are all part of the same team and are guided by a scrum master. A product owner plans the vision for the product and prioritizes the features that should go into each incremental release of the product.

Agile development can be implemented using various methods like scrum (the most popular method), Kanban, extreme programming (XP), pair programming, feature-driven development (FDD), test-driven development (TDD), Lean software development, and so on.

In order to transform the entire organization from waterfall methodology adherents to agile development adherents, there is a need for a mindset change (across the enterprise) as depicted in Figure 6.3.

The success of agile methodology adoption in a large enterprise is highly dependent on the support of the senior management. More and more banks are hiring *agile coaches* to guide them through the change management required (due to the adoption of agile methodology) across their lines of businesses. The *agile coaches* work across different teams and have executive backing. Both organizations that are new to agile development and those that have adopted agile (but have

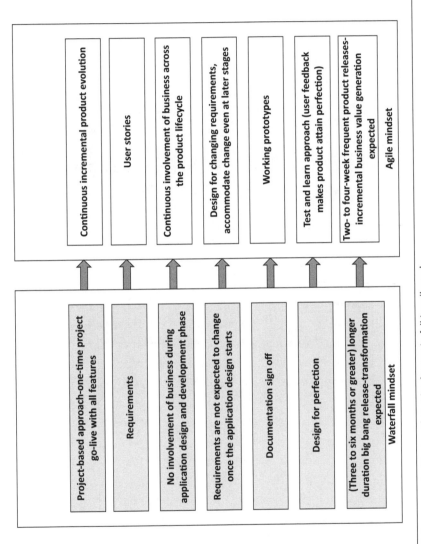

Figure 6.3 Mindset changes required for transformation from waterfall to agile mode.

not yet attained the optimal productivity gains in terms of software development) hire *agile coaches*.

SCRUM DEVELOPMENT TERMINOLOGIES[3,4]

Scrum is an iterative agile development framework that focuses on a highly motivated self-organizing team (preferably co-located) working toward a common goal: delivering continuously evolving high-quality software that meets the changing needs of the customer. The ideal team would be a team (not exceeding a dozen members) consisting of a product owner who defines the product vision and prioritizes features; a scrum master who motivates the entire team and removes hindrances the team faces in achieving their goal; and a set of business analysts, architects, designers, developers, and testers to build and enhance the product.

User story describes the requirements of the user and the reason for this requirement in simplistic terms. For example: "As a bank customer, I would need the mobile app to provide me a view of my weekly account transactions so that I know where I spend my money."

The user stories (as well as any improvements suggested by other stakeholders) go into the *Product backlog*, the running master list of features (of the product) sequenced as per descending priority.

Sprint is the definite period (preferably less than four weeks) during which one or more product backlog items are completed. An agile (scrum) product can be built over a series of sprints. *Sprint backlog* lists the set of tasks that should be completed within a sprint.

Sprint backlog need not be an item in product backlog. For example, the sprint backlog may involve setting up the automation test tool for usage by the scrum team, and this backlog is definitely not a product feature.

Velocity of a sprint is how much work an agile team can accomplish within a sprint in terms of *story points* (an arbitrary measure required to complete a user story), which serves as a guideline for estimation of future efforts

Sprint burndown charts and *release burnup charts* help the team in visualizing the progress. A sprint burndown chart shows the amount of work (number of tasks) remaining in the sprint backlog while the release burnup chart provides a visualization of what has been achieved so far (cumulative story points completed so far) in each sprint.

The five events associated with a scrum lifecycle are *sprint planning* (at the start of a sprint), *daily scrum meetings* or *stand-up meetings* (during the course of a sprint), *sprint review meetings* (to review the work completed as well as pending at the end of a sprint), *sprint retrospective meetings* (to identify what went well and what didn't work well), and an optional *backlog grooming meeting* (to facilitate reprioritization of product backlog).

Tools and Automation: Vital Ingredients for the Agile Development Recipe   For agile development to be successful, there is a need to leverage tools like JIRA, ChatOps tools like Slack, continuous integration tools like Jenkins, automated build tools like Ant and Grunt, code versioning tools like GitHub, code coverage tools, and code quality tools like SonarQube, apart from automated test coverage tools and frameworks like JUnit, NUnit, JsUnit, etc. Achieving build automation, continuous integration, and test automation is a vital ingredient for the success of agile development.

Scaling Agile   Ideally, an agile sprint team should not have more than a dozen people. However, when there is a need to reduce the product backlog faster, or in other words, build more features of a product within a timeframe (which is too short for one self-contained team of less than dozen people), we may need to scale to multiple agile development teams across different locations. When scaling agile teams, less dependency between teams (as little as possible), frequent communication, and more collaboration between different teams needs to be fostered so that the quality of the code and frequent product release cycles are maintained. This is where frameworks like Scaled Agile Framework (SAFe), Disciplined Agile Delivery (DAD), and Large-Scale Scrum (LeSS) are helpful.

Dean Leffingwell's SAFe, which facilitates implementing agile at scale, buckets large agile product development teams into portfolio, program, and teams and has seen increasing adoption across large banks. Nordea, Northern Europe's largest financial group, worked with a popular SAFe agile consultancy and adopted SAFe for their digital banking experience initiative. The initiative included more than six dozen members spread across multiple teams. Adopting SAFe (coupled with the senior management backing this adoption) has seen increased efficiency, more creativity, and better collaboration among team members leading to the success of the digital banking experience initiative. Other units in Nordea are beginning to explore adoption of SAFe for their initiatives.[5]

Agile methodology aids innovation and facilitates the rapid evolution of idea to concept to prototype to product. Agile methodology is designed to accommodate changes to requirements at later stages of product development. This potent combination of ability to accommodate changes at later stages of product evolution, short release cycles, better delivery quality, lower defects, and closer collaboration among stakeholders has made agile development adoption the key priority for IT organizations of both large, medium, and small financial institutions.

Integrating DevOps into Software Development Lifecycle   The long time to market in established financial enterprises is due to the barriers (communication layers) between business and IT teams as well as the barriers within the IT team; that is, the communication layers between software development, the testing team and the IT operations team. The misalignment between business and IT (comprising the software developers and testers) can be bridged by implementing agile development.

Despite implementing agile development practices, many enterprises face the last mile problem in their goal of delivering applications within a short span of time. While the software development is agile, the deployment and operations teams still take a long time to deploy the software to production. DevOps aims to bridge the gap between the development team, testing team, and operations team leveraging continuous integration, continuous deployment, and automation, reducing the time to deploy drastically.

The tools used for DevOps facilitate the specification of "infrastructure as code." Proactive monitoring, logging, and instrumentation foster direct communication of production issues to developers and reduce downtimes. Figure 6.4 provides a snapshot of the principles, practices, and tools used in DevOps.[6,7]

The impact of DevOps is felt not just on practices and tools, but also on organizational culture. DevOps requires development teams to work closely with operations teams. Operations team members are included as part of each sprint so that there is adequate version planning for releases. Requirements for each sprint include operational requirements like performance, scalability, and so on, under which the applications/products/services need to function. Code from each developer (or development team) is frequently integrated with a common source control repository. Building of code is automated and largely done from the central repository. Development and test environments are provisioned within a short time. Build also requires automated test scripts to be executed and passed before code is deployed onto production environments through containers like Docker. Due to containerization, there are not many differences between the production environment and the test environment. Deployment is automated and can be as frequent as every hour. Thus, better collaboration due to inclusion of operations team members as part of the project team, continuous integration, and continuous deployment, combined with automated scripting enables short product release cycles. Barclays Bank has embarked on a major 18-month initiative to increase the footprint of agile and DevOps across the banking enterprise. They currently have 500-plus teams leveraging these methodologies. Agile and DevOps adoption has helped the bank reduce the time to market for their applications to four weeks.[8]

Figure 6.5 depicts how the barriers between different teams starts falling as the enterprise starts moving from waterfall to agile to DevOps. With agile adoption, the barriers between the business and project teams (product development team consisting of software architect, designers, developers, and testers) come down, but the IT operations team remains separate. With agile plus DevOps adoption, the IT operation team also becomes part of the common team.

Agile development coupled with DevOps (continuous integration plus continuous deployment) and containerization infrastructures

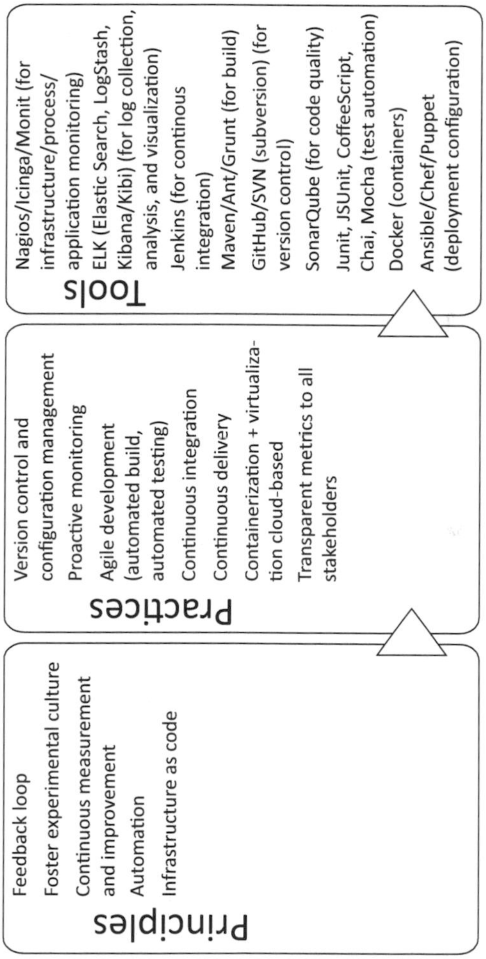

Principles

Feedback loop
Foster experimental culture
Continuous measurement and improvement
Automation
Infrastructure as code

Practices

Version control and configuration management
Proactive monitoring
Agile development (automated build, automated testing)
Continuous integration
Continuous delivery
Containerization + virtualization cloud-based
Transparent metrics to all stakeholders

Tools

Nagios/Icinga/Monit (for infrastructure/process/application monitoring)
ELK (Elastic Search, LogStash, Kibana/Kibi) (for log collection, analysis, and visualization)
Jenkins (for continous integration)
Maven/Ant/Grunt (for build)
GitHub/SVN (subversion) (for version control)
SonarQube (for code quality)
Junit, JSUnit, CoffeeScript, Chai, Mocha (test automation)
Docker (containers)
Ansible/Chef/Puppet (deployment configuration)

Figure 6.4 DevOps in a nutshell.

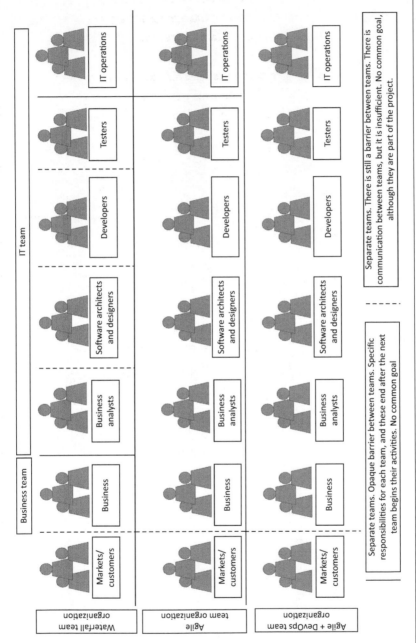

Figure 6.5 Transitioning from waterfall to agile, to agile plus devOps teams.

like Puppet, Chef, and Docker can amplify developer productivity exponentially and drastically reduce product release cycles. While DevOps is applicable to development (and enhancement) of digital and cloud-based engagement applications, it must be sparing for critical legacy application enhancements.

Integrating Human-Centric Design Process into Software Development Lifecycle   The left brain/right brain dominance theory propounds the belief that dominant left-brainers think differently from those who use their right brains dominantly. Left-brainers are largely logical and analytical in their approach to solving problems. They are good at tasks that involve language, numbers, and reasoning. In contrast, right-brainers are good at facial recognition, understanding, and displaying emotions as well as visual aspects like color and images. They are creative and intuitive.[9]

EMBEDDING EMOTION INTO DIGITAL INTERFACES

The popular digital products we know of today have gained people's acceptance because they are simple and easy to use. They have intuitive user interfaces. End users do not need to be taught how to use them. They understand the context of the end user well. Their interfaces empathize with the user. All the above qualities emphasize the need for a process to involve right-brain thinking into the software development cycle of digital products.

Creativity and user experience bring the human element to any digital product and thus become critical aspects of digital product development.

Good digital experience requires going beyond "who" the end user is by understanding and anticipating "when, where, and how" the end user will use the product. This calls for including both UX (user experience) designers (who are more creative) as well as user interface (UI) developers (who are more analytical) as part of the development team. Engaging with end users in design workshops aids UX designers in understanding the persona of the end user as well as the customer journey in using the product.

User experience is qualitative. It influences the emotions with which the user interacts with the product or service and finds value in the interaction.

USER EXPERIENCE HONEYCOMB

Peter Morville's User Experience Honeycomb framework captures the factors behind a meaningful and valuable experience (user experience as well as customer experience). According to this framework, the end-user experience is dependent on factors like usefulness (product needs to be original and fulfill a need), findability, accessibility (product must be accessible even by people with disabilities), and credibility of content, apart from usability (product must be easy to use) and desirability (product must be made desirable through the use of images and/or other design elements) of the interface. This framework can also help us compare the user experience provided by different websites.[10,11]

Traditionally, most enterprises have focused on only the user interface design for their applications. In a digital world, any application, product, or service development needs to go beyond user interface design and embrace user experience (UX) design, service design, and design thinking as part of their lifecycle.

UX Design The UX design process involves activities and tasks related to user research and analysis, concept design, prototyping, and testing (remote usability testing with the end user) for understanding the end-user experience. These activities are iteratively performed until a good working prototype meeting the end-user expectations is delivered. All these activities are completed within a short span of a few days or weeks. In addition to visual designs (low-fidelity and high-fidelity wireframes), information architecture, and design artifacts, user personas and customer journeys act as the most important tools for humanizing the digital interfaces. Other tools and artifacts, like mental models, concept maps, content inventory, and user and task flow charts are also generated as part of UX design process and help in providing a common understanding of the desired user experience for the product stakeholders.[12]

USER PERSONA

A user persona categorizes users into groups or hypothesizes end users into groups. The persona description captures "a day-in-the-life-of-the-persona" and outlines the attributes, challenges, and needs of the persona. It also gives a scenario map that correlates scenarios, needs, and the features that address the needs and behavior of the persona when the scenario occurs. User persona thus not only highlights the kind of users who use a feature, but the contextual and behavioral conditions pertaining to the feature usage. For a mobile banking app, student users could be an example of a persona. Persona descriptions are typically one or two-slide descriptions with a profile photo of a sample user.

UX design process reduces the risk of the product features not being used (developing features that nobody would use) while at the same time ensuring that vital features required by the end user are not left out of the product. This process also ensures that the product interface is simple, intuitive, and easy to use, thereby increasing the rate of adoption and thereby the success of the product.

Service Design   In the digital world, the boundary between products and services and thus user experience design and service design is very thin. The end user consuming a service (through an interface) is a customer, and thus design of the service affects the customer experience. In addition to the techniques used for UX design, the design of the interfaces of the service need to take into account the service touch points or the channels of engaging the customer. These channels for a banking service can be a phone banking interface, a call center, the bank teller or agent, an ATM, a kiosk, online, mobile, or social. The techniques used for service design include ethnography (understanding the relationship between the service context and the customers), user studies and personas, customer journey maps, service blueprinting, ideation, and storyboarding.

CUSTOMER JOURNEY MAPPING

Customer journey mapping is an important technique that outlines how the customer can use the service over a period of time (a series of important instances or "moments of truth" over a journey). It captures the needs of the customer at each "moment of truth" and how an interaction with the service at that moment of truth can fulfill the needs of the customer and delight the customer. From a banking perspective, a moment of truth can be any time the customer is in need of money.

The customer journey can thus be defined as the interaction that a customer has with different channels at each moment of truth, and customer experience can be defined as the cumulative experience the customer has from the service over a series of such interactions across channels.

SERVICE BLUEPRINTING

Interaction with a service typically triggers a sequence of actions and processes. Service blueprinting describes this sequence and distributes them into the front stage (actions and processes) and back stage (actions and processes).

Service design is critical to improving the customer satisfaction and delighting the customer.[11]

Design Thinking This is a popular process used to encourage out-of-box thinking for solving problems, fostering innovations. Design thinking is iterative in nature. The approach involves defining the problem, observing people's needs, identifying constraints and boundaries, ideating (co-creating solutions with the customers or end users), prioritizing the ideas, quickly prototyping the solutions and testing them with the users, and moving on to the next problem. The objective is to fail fast and not spend too much time on nonproductive prototypes. If the prototype is successful, it can move on to the next stages of business funding or implementation. If it fails, it is time to move on to next project.

It is a bottom-up approach involving end users in design workshops coming up with ideas (however silly they may be) and adopting experimental and iterative approaches to find solutions to problems. The objective is to imagine solutions that bring out not just explicit needs but also make implicit needs explicit. The solutions are imagined from the perspective of different stakeholders, resulting in an empathetic solution that addresses their needs. More than an analytical approach, design thinking relies on a creative approach to solve problems. Design thinking can be used for user experience design, service design, and product design as well as solving strategic needs of business and society. Design thinkers need "right-brained" skills. They need to be empathetic, optimistic, encourage collaborative and integrative thinking, and be willing to experiment. Leading financial enterprises like Fidelity Investments and Deutsche Bank have adopted design thinking. This process is increasingly being applied beyond customer experience innovations and is finding its way into areas like strategy. Exclusive design thinking sessions are being conducted for senior executives. [13]

Changes to Architecture

Figure 6.6 depicts the typical digital reference architecture (for repurposing the existing systems for digital initiatives).

Tables 6.1, 6.2, and 6.3 describe the layers of digital reference architecture.

It needs to be noted that Analytics is often not considered as a "System of Engagement." It is often considered as a "System of Intelligence" and mirrors the "Middle Office functionality." Digital transformation requires shifts in architectural thinking, namely adopting two-speed architecture, a shift toward lightweight decentralized microservice architecture, realizing that any systems built will need to be securely exposed as APIs to the external world, and

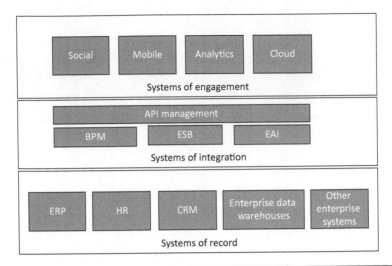

Figure 6.6   Typical digital reference architecture.

Table 6.1   Systems of Engagement (SOEs)

	DESCRIPTION
Definition	Systems that enable direct interaction with customers or that generate something of value for customers are categorized as system of engagement (SOE).
Instances	Customer-facing mobile apps, Web or mobile sites, and social networking platforms
Synonymous functionality	SOEs mirror front office processes.
Characteristics	SOEs need to be flexible to accommodate rapidly changing customer requirements and feedback. Short time to market, agility, flexibility, and rapid evolution are the implicit requirements for any SOE. SOEs are expected to be more innovative and lightweight applications. Building SOEs requires a "design-for-change" mindset.

Table 6.2   Systems of Integration

	DESCRIPTION
Definition	SORs are decoupled from the SOEs through integration systems. These enable SOEs to communicate with SOR. This communication is largely real time, but a few communication scenarios can also take place in batch mode.
Instances	Enterprise service bus (ESB), business process management (BPM) tools, microservices, application programming interface (API) management tools, and enterprise application integration (EAI) tools are considered to be integration systems. Microservices and API management that foster decentralization and reconfiguration of processes are the popular integration mechanisms that enable SOEs to integrate with SORs.
Characteristics	Evolution is slower than SOEs, but faster than SORs.

Table 6.3   Systems of Record (SOR)

	DESCRIPTION
Definition	Existing systems that acquire, process, store, and manage transactional data are grouped as systems of record (SOR).
Instances	Traditional ERP, human resource (HR) management) systems, customer relationship management (CRM), database and enterprise data warehouses, and even core banking systems can be grouped under SOR.
Synonymous functionality	SORs mirror and aid back office processes.
Characteristics	SORs evolve very gradually. SORs are expected to be highly available, accurate, stable, and reliable. SORs largely have requirements that do not change frequently, and if there are any changes required, associated change management procedures need to be triggered

allowing every interaction with the system to be instrumented for analytics and being cloud-ready.

Two-Speed Architecture   Established banking and financial enterprises, which have already been in business for decades, if not centuries, have a vital advantage over the new-age fintech disruptors. They have loads and loads of valuable data about their customers gathered from the period in which they have been in business. If any digital transformation initiative has to be beneficial for these financial institutions, the existing systems (which handle this data) have to be leveraged and repurposed. Implementing greenfield digital transformation initiatives without leveraging the existing systems will be way too expensive. Adopting two-speed architecture is one of the ways by which established banks and financial enterprises can aim to leverage their existing systems and data and address the needs of the digital world.

Customer-facing digital applications need to evolve rapidly and cater to changing customer needs. However, the existing systems on which they depend for data are not tailor-made for agility. Any change to the existing systems may have cascading impacts on other systems, and hence changes to these systems will need to be accompanied by a lengthy change management process, thereby slowing down the speed required for digital consumer-facing applications. In order to succeed in their digital transformation initiatives, the established financial enterprises need to architect their digital application portfolio, keeping in mind the different speeds at which their systems evolve.

Handling two-speed architecture begins with separating out those applications and systems that are customer-facing (and will need to adopt agility) from those systems that need stability, accuracy, and availability.[14] This is followed by setting up separate teams for handling SOEs and SORs, deploying a nimble integration infrastructure, and supporting real-time analytics.

SORs are decoupled from the SOEs through systems of integration. Microservices and API management, which foster decentralization and reconfiguration of processes, are popular integration mechanisms that enable SOEs to integrate with SORs. Two-Speed architecture is evolving into Multi-Speed architecture.

Shift toward Light weight, Decentralized Microservice Architecture   One of the key problems constraining the time to market of SOEs has been that any changes needed to the Web services (upon which they depend) may require a long duration of time. This is because of the prolonged nature of these services. Each service may provide more than one capability, and hence any changes may impact multiple functionalities. Microservices' architectural style can help address this problem, and use of this style introduces modularity into the architecture.

Microservices are cloud-friendly lightweight services enabling decentralization of development. Microservice patterns require fine-graining of these services. Each service must support only one independent business capability. They should be independently "developable" and "deployable." Each microservice can be developed using different programming languages and can use different databases. In fact, having a separate data store for each microservice and deploying each microservice in containers (like Docker) is encouraged. They aid automation and aid adoption of DevOps. Microservices are accessible through Hypertext Transfer Protocol (HTTP).

Netflix OSS components are often used for implementing microservices.

API Management   SOEs can be Web applications or mobile apps. The SORs, with which they need to integrate, may have been exposed to other systems by means of a more heavy data payload that may not be suitable for lightweight, faster SOE requirements. Getting the SORs to expose lesser payload may require a lengthy Web service development process. Web services with a heavier payload may need to coexist with Web services with a lesser payload. These are the problems that an API management problem addresses. They enable versioning of services, allow quick configuration of new Web services such as APIs, and support caching. API management tools also help in securing the Web services and APIs, publishing the APIs for any non-bank external applications to discover and use, isolating the internal SORs from external SOEs by means of an API gateway, metering the usage of APIs, and also providing analytics of API usage.

Various tools like WSO2, Apigee, CA Layer 7, Microsoft Azure API management, and MuleSoft API management have increased the adoption of API management.

Instrumentation   All customer interactions through SOEs are instrumented, captured, and analyzed. Analytics help in identifying performance and experience improvements needed to the product (these are included as features for further releases of the SOE). Real-time analysis of the instrumented data helps in personalizing user interfaces as well as making the customer experience better.

Being Cloud-Ready   Digital applications need to be built assuming that workloads can be distributed across public and private clouds, and will automatically scale (as and when the workloads increase). Digital applications must also be built keeping in mind the need for "zero downtime" during application upgrades.

Changes to Teams and Organizational Structure

The Rise of the CDiO   During the early stages of digital evolution of the enterprise, it makes sense to centralize all the digital initiatives under one centralized horizontal with a chief digital officer (CDiO) as the leader. Quite often, CDO is meant to be either a chief data officer or a chief development officer. Hence in this book, we use the term CDiO to refer to the chief digital officer.

The CDiO works closely with the Chief Information Officer (CIO), Chief Innovation Officer, the Chief Technology Officer (CTO), the Chief Marketing Officer (CMO) as well as the line of business (LOB) heads to chalk out the digital strategy (and roadmap) for the organization, build the digital capabilities necessary for the organization, and roll out digital initiatives. There are both internal and external goals for the CDiO. From an internal perspective, the CDiO has to set up an organizational unit to reduce the reliance on "shadow IT," especially by the marketing (CMO) unit, work with the IT organization (CIO), and enable adoption and reuse of any digital platforms or tools across LOBs. From an external perspective, the CDiO needs to act as the innovation champion for digital transformation initiatives of the organization and increase revenues for the organization by helping them get closer to the customers.

As digital technologies enrich customer interactions of the enterprise by enabling them to apply the three Ds, namely design, data, and delivery, to the contextual parameters, many digital organizations also reflect this structurally, as shown in Figure 6.7. A team focused on design (headed by the chief experience officer), a team focused on analytics (containing data scientists to design analytical algorithms, big data experts, statisticians, and business analysts) as well as the digital delivery team (user interface development experts skilled in building next-generation digital (Web and mobile) interfaces). The design team collaborates with the LOBs as well as the

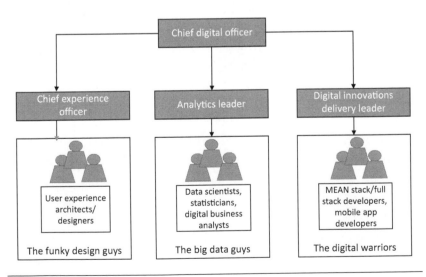

Figure 6.7   Digital Organization.

marketing organization (under the CMO) to test ideas and concepts. The analytics team also works with the LOBs as well as horizontal functions (marketing, sales, finance, etc.) as well as the IT team to identify the data for analysis. The digital delivery team is a Lean team meant to work only on digital innovations (taking the concepts provided by the digital design team and converting them to working technical prototypes). Once the prototypes are tested with the end users and found successful, the IT organization (under the CIO) takes up the subsequent work of scaling the prototype into the end product. This digital delivery team includes full stack developers (developers skilled in front-end, middleware, and back-end/database technologies), MEAN stack (MongoDB, Express.js, AngularJS, and Node.js) developers and specialist developers conversant with microservices architecture, DevOps, as well as containerization tools like Puppet, Chef, and Docker.

The digital organization quite often works with IT organization and leverages their capability to evaluate vendors and sign up contracts with any technology vendors.

Until the digital capabilities of the banks and financial institutions attain maturity, the digital organization under the CDiO largely functions as a center of excellence (CoE). Profit and loss responsibility will still lie with the individual LOBs.

Once the digital capabilities of the financial enterprise are mature, the centralized model may be disbanded, and each LOB may have their own digital team under a digital director. Alternately, a hybrid model, where there is still a small central digital team under a CDiO and digital directors from each LOB have a dotted line reporting to the CDiO, can also be adopted. In the hybrid model, the central digital unit is responsible for providing standards and recommending frameworks for digital transformation of LOBs. It is up to the digital directors of LOBs to tailor the standards and frameworks as per the needs of the LOB.

Addressing Organizational Needs for Supporting Two-Speed Architecture As part of two-speed architecture, SOEs and SORs are expected to have separate IT teams. The SOE development team follows an agile development methodology and adopts continuous integration. They may not be held accountable to the same standards of maturity as the SOR teams. The SOR team focuses on a more stable and lengthier iteration cycle and adheres to all enterprise processes. Typically, any SOR changes that may be required are planned for completion before the SOE iterations (dependent on them) begin.

Cultural and Mindset Changes Needed   With banking and financial institutions being highly regulated sectors across the world, established financial enterprises have been highly risk-averse. This culture restricts the tendency to innovate with multiple gates being present from business need conception to delivery. The culture of "do not disturb until something is broken" pervades the enterprise. With fintechs beginning to look disruptive (partially due to them not being subjected to the same regulations as the established financial institutions), the established financial enterprise needs to reward a risk-taking culture and adopt a startup culture at least in a few divisions that are customer-facing. IT organizations, especially software development organizations, need to reflect a product-based organization as against the current project-based organizations (projects have a start date and end date and there is no pressure to continuously improve, while products have the chance of becoming successful only if they continuously evolve as per the needs of the customer). If the entire organization needs to be agile, barriers between teams have to be brought down, and there should be more collaboration between the business and the IT (and the operations team).

Conclusion

Fintechs are eating into the business of established financial enterprises, especially in the world of digital banking and digital finance. In their digital transformation journey, established financial enterprises are facing the multipronged challenges of being "too large to

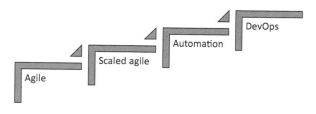

Figure 6.8   Transition roadmap to gain capability for short product release cycles.

move, too slow to change," and being saddled with legacy IT systems. Given the highly regulated nature of the banking and financial services industry and the high cost of IT failure, established financial enterprises try to keep risk as far away as possible by bringing in more processes and layers, thereby leading to application and product releases taking a long time to get delivered. On an average, deploying a single line of code requires filling up 20-plus forms and 40-plus days to complete the process of deployment.[7]

The road to agility lies in mindset, process, technology, and cultural changes. Adopting scaled agile software development, DevOps, and two-speed architecture, apart from adopting the nimble culture of a product-based organizational structure, can help the established financial enterprises in their digital transformation journey.

In order to reduce time to market, the entire value chain (of digital product lifecycle) needs to become agile and nimble. For this, the established financial enterprises need to move from waterfall to agile software development, and then move on to agile at scale (SAFe) adoption, followed by automation and DevOps as shown in Figure 6.8.

Figure 6.9 summarizes the changes to the software development practices and IT organization as well as architecture that large financial enterprises need to make for succeeding in their digital transformation journeys.

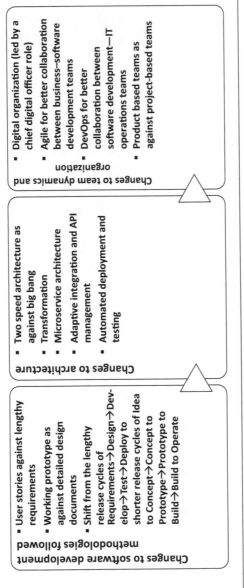

Figure 6.9 Changes that established financial enterprises need to make for success in the digital financial world.

Points to ponder:

- Critical success factors for digital transformation initiatives.
- Why aren't established financial enterprises as nimble as fintechs?
- Changes required to software development methodology, architecture, and organizational structure for success in the digital world.

References

1. Michael J. Casey. 2015. Bold Bet That Banking Industry Is Poised for Serious Disruption. *The Wall Street Journal* (Blogs). Jun 5. http://blogs.wsj.com/moneybeat/2015/06/05/bold-bet-that-banking-industry-is-poised-for-serious-disruption-horizons/
2. Celent. How Much Do Banks Spend on Technology? Infogram. https://infogram.com/how-much-do-banks-spend-on-IT
3. Wikipedia. Scrum (Software Development). https://en.wikipedia.org/wiki/Scrum_(software_development)
4. World of Agile. Fascinating World of Agile (Scrum). http://www.worldofagile.com/scrum/scrum-events/
5. Scaled Agile. Case Study: Nordea (Northern Europe's Largest Financial Group Increases Efficiency with SAFe). http://scaledagileframework.com/nordea/
6. Ernest Mueller. DevOps 101. SlideShare. http://www.slideshare.net/mxyzplk/devops-101
7. Tomer Levy. 9 Open Source DevOps Tools We Love. https://devops.com/2015/08/07/9-open-source-devops-tools-love/
8. Caroline Donnelly. 2016. Barclays Banks on Agile and DevOps to Tackle Competitive Threats in Fintech. Computer Weekly. Jul 1. http://www.computerweekly.com/news/450299551/Barclays-banks-on-agile-and-DevOps-to-tackle-competitive-threats-in-fintech
9. Kendra Cherry. 2017. Left Brain vs. Right Brain Dominance: The Surprising Truth. Verywell. Jun 1. https://www.verywell.com/left-brain-vs-right-brain-2795005
10. Usability.gov. User Experience Basics. https://www.usability.gov/what-and-why/user-experience.html
11. Sylvain Cottong. 2009. User Experience Design, Service Design & Design Thinking. SlideShare. Aug 18. http://www.slideshare.net/sylvain/ux-design-service-design-design-thinking?qid=a48b112a-93e8-4c6c-bd9c-74a5160dd0d6&v=&b=&from_search=4
12. Peter Morville. 2004. User Experience Design. *Semantic Studios*. 21 June. http://semanticstudios.com/user_experience_design/

13. Marcus Evans. Interview with Christpher Whitlock. 2015. Design Thinking for Banking & Financial Services Industry. Market Wired. Sep 16. http://www.marketwired.com/press-release/design-thinking-for-banking-financial-services-industry-2056127.htm

14. Oliver Bessert, Chris Ip, and Jürgen Laartz. 2014. A Two-Speed IT Architecture for the Digital Enterprise. McKinsey (Insights). Dec. http://www.mckinsey.com/business-functions/digital-mckinsey/our-insights/a-two-speed-it-architecture-for-the-digital-enterprise

7

2020 BANKING TRENDS

Nothing stops an organization faster than people who believe that the way you worked yesterday is the best way to work tomorrow.

Jon Madonna
eminent business leader[1]

Whenever we consider the topic of the "future of banking," questions narrow down to: How would a bank function in 2020? Would branches exist? Would it only be digital banks all over the world? Will a customer continue to converse with a human in a bank for his or her service needs? What are the other new technologies that could impact banking?

Based on how digital technologies have been rapidly evolving and are being deployed by the financial enterprises, Figure 7.1 depicts our view of how banks will evolve into 2020.

In the pre-digital banking era, (real) customers had to visit (real or physical) bank branches for their money transactions.

In the current "digital banking era," most of the transactions involving money can be performed virtually or digitally. There is no need for a customer to visit a real branch, and we thus see more and more "digital-only" banks coming into existence. The Internet banking website or the mobile apps, that is, the "digital" properties of the bank act as a "virtual" branch for a customer.

Over the next few years, the coming together of artificial intelligence and the Internet of Things (IOT) will enable even virtual customers to transact with physical as well as virtual bank branches. Virtual personal assistants (like Apple Siri, Google Now, Microsoft Cortana, Amazon Alexa, and potentially other virtual assistants) can act on behalf of customers and transact with banks for financial transactions. Though this may sound far-fetched, robots will soon walk into a branch and

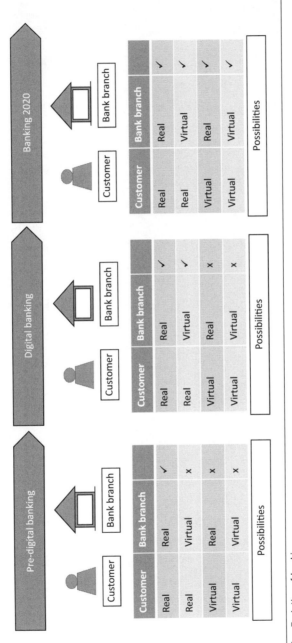

Figure 7.1 Evolution of banking.

perform basic financial transactions on behalf of authorized customers. Virtual personal assistants and robots act as a virtual customers. The possibilities enabled by advancement in the IOT technologies include "smart" refrigerators ordering milk from supermarkets on behalf of a customer. These smart refrigerators can proactively identify the need for stocking up on milk once all milk packets (or bottles) placed in the refrigerator are consumed and pay the supermarket for the order by initiating transactions for debiting money from the account of the customer and crediting this to the supermarket's account.

Technology has moved from assisting the banking enterprise to powering the banking enterprise, thereby causing disruptions in the way a bank functions. Thus, what we know as a bank in the near future will be starkly different from what it is today.

Financial Industry 2020 Digital Trends

Figure 7.2 depicts the financial industry 2020 digital trends. Based on the number of enterprises adopting these trends and the maturity of the technology shaping these trends, we categorize these trends into those attaining maturity, those gaining traction, and those which are at early stages.

From "Digital" to "Phygital" Banking

A recent McKinsey Global Survey points out that while the number of young customers trying to discover more information about financial products online has increased, more than 75% of the customers still express the need for a physical branch nearby to support them when they have any issues. Bank branches still seem to be an emotional need for customers, especially when they need support. In fact, the number of branches a bank has in and around their neighborhood serves as an important parameter for these customers to decide in favor of buying a product from the bank. Thus bank branches will continue to play an important role in the next few years.[2]

By 2020, we may not see the disappearance of the bank branch, but will see a fusion of physical and digital experiences into what is increasingly called a "phygital" or "digical" experience in the marketing world. A physical (bank) branch would not only employ people but also employ robots for servicing people. Branches would look

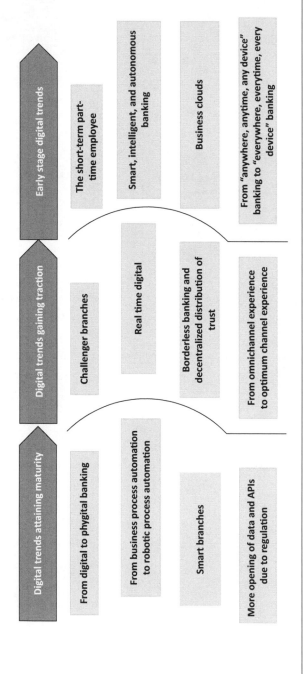

Figure 7.2   Financial industry digital trends 2020.

more like high-end retail stores. Banks may employ robots to welcome prospects and customers to the branch. They may also perform basic banking tasks for the customer.

With the help of augmented reality and virtual reality, the digital walls will provide an immersive visual experience for customers within the branch.

Banco Bradesco, a leading private bank in Brazil, is a pioneer in phygital experience banking. Their Bradesco Next branches leverage biometric sensors to identify customers, robots to welcome customers, interactive touch screens, remote financial advisors available through video conference, gesture-based touchless screens and interactive touch tables to provide personalized banking to customers for a highly engaging phygital experience without needing to employ human beings in the branch.

Smart Branches

When it comes to omnichannel experience, banks have been able to provide a seamless experience across digital channels (social, mobile, and Web) to the customer. But the seamlessness has largely excluded the in-branch experience for most transactions. The rapid deployment of artificial intelligence (AI) will enable the in-branch experience and digital channel experience to be seamless. Facial recognition and voice recognition technologies will enable the branch to recognize the customer as soon as they step in to the branch and provide personalized services to the customer. AI will also enable the branch staff to become smart enough to anticipate the needs of their (high net worth) customers based on their online behavior and proactively address their needs, taking customer experience to the next level. Customers will be able to initiate more and more transactions in the branch and complete any unfinished tasks online and vice versa.

The physical branch would have personalized digital walls enabled by facial recognition technology, voice recognition, gesture recognition, or a mix of two or more of these and recommend the financial product that would best suit the needs of the customer.

The Bank of Tokyo-Mitsubishi UFJ employs a humanoid robot for intelligent customer service in one of their high-end Tokyo branches. The customer robot, called Nao, leverages AI (gesture recognition, facial recognition) and answers questions from customers as per the context.[3]

Challenger Branches

We have seen pure e-commerce retail players open brick-and-mortar retail stores to get closer to their customers. These stores are more an experience center for the customers rather than a full-scale transactional store. Examples include Myntra (http://www.myntra.com), an online fashion retailer in India, and Lenskart (http://www.lenskart.com), an online eye-care optical store in India.

In order to gain scale, challenger banks will also feel the need to open physical or phygital branches. They will need to take this route not only to gain the confidence of those customers who feel safer dealing with only those banks having a physical presence, but also to provide an immersive experience to their customers. While we see the likes of big banks in the United Kingdom like HSBC, Lloyds, RBS, and Barclays closing more branches, in the recent past, we see challenger banks like Metro Bank opening more and more branches.[4] The absence of legacy systems for challenger banks would help them provide a higher level of experience to the customers.

From "Anywhere, Anytime, Any Device" Banking to
"Everywhere, Everytime, Every Device" Banking

Networks have evolved from 2G to 4G in a short span of time, even in the not-so-developed world of Asia, Africa, and Latin America. Parts of the developed world (like South Korea) are preparing for the rollout of 5G networks in 2017. In today's world, more people have access to mobile devices than toilets. Spotty networks are gradually becoming a thing of the past. Wireless networks (and Internet connectivity) are almost becoming so pervasive (especially in the developed world), that they are increasingly being considered the "sixth element of nature."

There is a growing concern that making customers download an app from an app store is not an efficient way to retain them, and installable mobile Web apps, which work on mobile browsers, can perform the same tasks efficiently and help retain customers if they are able to use the app immediately without having to download it. We are thus seeing Progressive Web apps gaining acceptance in place of native mobile apps. Technology approaches like Progressive Web apps (PWA) are leveraging the power of mobile browsers (like Google Chrome 50 and above) and trying to make network availability an irrelevant factor in the design of apps. PWAs are bringing push notifications, offline synchronization, and rich and native-like user experience to mobile Web applications.

We are thus seeing digital delivery move from the age of "anywhere, anytime, any device" banking to "everywhere, everytime, every device" banking.

From Business Process Automation to Robotic Process Automation

Business processes that are repeatable have been automated using business process management and enterprise application integration. Financial enterprises still have a number of repeatable processes that require human intervention. These are processes that could not be automated due to the involvement of multiple legacy systems or systems that may require a lot of code changes (and the cost of making changes to code does not justify the return on investment or ROI). Robotic process automation (RPA) leverages computer programs (called robots or bots) that learn the way the end user works on the system (leveraging the user interface) and reproduces this, thereby automating the task and providing immense productivity benefits, apart from higher accuracy and better predictability. The advantage of leveraging RPA lies in the fact that code in the existing systems need not be changed, and RPA can exist outside the system and be controlled by the operations team.

Banking industry processes are highly conducive to adoption of RPA. Examples of processes that can be automated are reconciliation (of data from multiple sources), reporting (from multiple data sources), and repeatable processes (involving two or more systems) that have highly frequent data entry needs. Implementing RPA depends on the complexity of the process. Clerical processes involving data entry of one or more systems based on inputs from two or more systems typically require about two months for implementation. RPA for clerical processes have the highest success rate and generate the maximum

ROI. Successful RPA implementations for such processes have generated productivity efficiency gains of more than 70%. End-to-end repeatable processes, which are rules-based, typically need double this time for implementation. RPA for such processes are known to have generated more than 40% productivity efficiency gains. Knowledge-based processes may involve the use of artificial intelligence, and automation of these processes would need three or more months based on the complexity. The candidate knowledge-based processes to be automated using robots would need to be carefully selected for generating a good ROI. For enterprises wanting to adopt RPA, the roadmap is to start with simple business processes, then gradually move toward implementing RPA for rules-based end-to-end processes, and finally take up implementing RPA for knowledge processes.

Scores of RPA vendors have sprung up in the last few years. The popular ones among them include Blue Prism, UiPath, and Automation Anywhere. Banks take the center of excellence (CoE) route toward implementing RPA. This involves the identification of processes for RPA, prioritizing these processes, evaluating RPA tools, piloting RPA for candidate processes, measuring the success, and refining the approach before bringing more processes into RPA.

Raiffeisen Bank International, a Central and Eastern European bank, is a good example.[5]

Borderless Banking and Decentralized Distribution of Trust

Immigrants wanting to send money to their near and dear ones residing in their country of origin form a significant portion of the remittance economy in the world. For too long, foreign remittances needed the immigrants to open bank accounts (opening a bank account was out of reach for many immigrants employed in blue collar jobs). Stringent anti-money laundering procedures resulted in prohibitive costs for banks transferring money across borders. As a result, those wanting to remit money across borders needed to cough up a significant portion of the money they transferred as transfer fees. The remittance economy also had a limited number of players, leaving no choice to the remitters.

Fintechs have tapped into the remittance economy opportunities by bringing down fees for money transfers across borders drastically through innovative approaches involving mobile apps and blockchain technology, the underlying cryptocurrency technology behind bitcoin.

TransferWise, a fintech focusing on cross-border money transfers, reported that by the end of 2015, they were transferring more than US$750 million per month across borders. Banks in Europe like LHV, the largest bank in Estonia, as well as a few U.K. banks are now integrating their mobile apps with the APIs provided by TransferWise for leveraging their cross-border money transfer capability.[6]

Many fintechs are also leveraging blockchain for cross-border money transfer. One of the approaches is to convert the amount to be transferred into bitcoins (as per the exchange rate) or cryptocurrency, transfer the bitcoins (or cryptocurrency), and convert the bitcoins (or cryptocurrency) to the currency.

Ripple is another private company leveraging their "distributed ledger technology" (a synonym for blockchain) to facilitate the cross-border transfer of money. Ripple is positioning itself as the competitor for SWIFT, the traditional interbank exchange pioneer, by facilitating real-time cross-border payments at fees that are a fraction of traditional cross-border payment fees. Ripple is signing up banks across many geographies as clients for using its protocol for cross-border money transfer. National Bank of Abu Dhabi, a Middle Eastern bank, is a prime example.[7]

Due to immense competition from blockchain-based startups, SWIFT is also exploring partnerships with fintechs as well as exploring the use of blockchain-based technology to make its cross-border money transfers more efficient and faster. It is also working with a consortium of banks on a global payment initiative for improving the speed, transparency, and experience of cross-border money transfer.

BLOCKCHAIN AND DISTRIBUTED TRUST COMPUTING

Despite bitcoin facing the heat from various government regulators in the last couple of years (due to the suspicion of bitcoin being used by money launderers), blockchain, which is the underlying technology behind bitcoin (and other virtual currencies) is gaining increasing support from various financial enterprises. Regulators have also evinced interest in this technology. They increasingly see blockchain as a highly secure technology for reducing operational costs for any transactions that involve an intermediary.

A blockchain is essentially a decentralized and distributed database that is secure and cannot be easily tampered with. Every transaction is recorded into a block along with a timestamp. This block is broadcast to different computing nodes (that store these blocks). Once the validity of transactions is established (by consensus across different nodes), each block has a link to the previous block, thus establishing a chain of blocks and sequence of events. These blocks are transparent and open for audit to everybody. Thus every computing node in the network validates the transaction and has a copy of the blockchain.

The need for an intermediary can be eliminated by the use of blockchains due to their inherent design of immutability. When it comes to digital money transfer, one of the challenge is to tackle "double spending," that is, ensuring that the same digital information is not retransmitted or exchanged for another subsequent transaction.

Or in other words, money that has been spent on an earlier transaction is not duplicated or used again for another transaction. Using a blockchain, every transaction can be recorded into a block and cannot be changed retrospectively, thus ensuring that "double spending" is prevented.

Blockchains are applicable wherever an intermediary is involved in storing, distributing, or transacting information. These are also applicable wherever an asset is stored, distributed, or transacted. We are thus seeing blockchain technology being applied not only in the financial industry but also in the music industry to prevent piracy. Blockchain also supports "smart contracts" (or dynamic contracts). These are auto-executing contracts (built on top of blockchain technology) that are triggered when an event occurs.

Blockchain technology is now available as public blockchain (where anybody can validate transactions) as well as private blockchains (that are accessible only to the participant entities). Given the sensitivity of the banking and financial service industry to anything public, we see more and more banks come together and take a consortium approach toward blockchain. They are more open to exploring private blockchains than public blockchains for their use cases. Private blockchain ensures the availability of the blockchain network only to a limited number of entities (banks) and is a closed network. Any third-party entities needing access to the blockchain can be "invited" to the network by the participants.

Given the hype around blockchain, numerous open source software as well as private vendors are venturing into the blockchain and distributed applications space. Ethereum is a public blockchain framework that also supports smart contracts natively. Linux foundation Hyperledger is a framework that supports private blockchain. Blockchain software from the R3 consortium and Ripple are also gaining support from various banks.

Executing blockchain transactions requires enormous computing power, and this can inhibit the adoption of this technology. We are increasingly seeing "blockchain as a service" coming into the picture with the entry of Microsoft and IBM. Both of them support different frameworks of blockchain on their cloud offerings.

Smart, Intelligent, and Autonomous Banking

Smart, intelligent, and autonomous banking is being driven by the adoption of Intelligent Virtual Agents and robo-advisors by the financial enterprise as well as the increasing adoption of digital personal assistants by customers.

Intelligent Virtual Agents: Automated self-service mechanisms like Intelligent Virtual Agents (IVA) are proving to be highly beneficial to banks as well as customers. For the banking enterprises deploying IVAs, the benefits revolve around improved service metrics like better first call resolutions (FCR), faster turnaround time (TAT), higher productivity of customer service representatives, and lower costs due to automation, apart from higher customer satisfaction. IVAs have the ability to record every conversation with the customer for better analytics. The analytics provide a feedback mechanism for the enterprises to understand the voice of the customer and fine-tune their customer support strategies.

For the customers, the benefits revolve around better understanding of their needs, simplicity of usage, and personalized and contextualized service.

As per leading analysts, by the beginning of the next decade, over a quarter of the enterprise interactions with customers will involve IVAs.

IVAs are software programs or bots that leverage artificial intelligence (natural language processing) to provide personalized and contextualized service to the customers across different digital channels. These can be embedded as widgets in the banking websites and can also be triggered through voice-based or text-based queries from mobile devices or kiosks. IVAs can concurrently handle multiple customers.

With the number of mobile apps increasing rapidly and becoming unmanageable for the customer, IVAs have gained quick adoption from millennials as there is no need to download or install additional software. The earlier generation of chatbots, which were largely triggered by text-based queries and could answer only a limited number of simple queries (for which rules were defined), are evolving into powerful IVAs that can perform complex tasks. They are increasingly becoming smart enough to understand the intent and the context behind customer queries and provide a contextualized response, thus ensuring that every customer feels special. In this section, we treat chatbots and IVAs synonymously.

IVAs can be considered as the next generation of digital technology adoption with the coming together of social messaging, artificial intelligence, and conversational user interface (CUI). CUIs are simple user interfaces that can strike "human-like" conversations with the end customer. The customer can either text their queries or talk to the interface to get a response from the interface. CUIs are considered the next generation of user interfaces. Similar to app stores, we can find bot stores for "specific-purpose" chatbots.

IVAs are increasing seeing higher success rates in answering common queries and have a mechanism to bring in human interaction once the customer queries and issues become more complex. They are thus seeing higher adoption by banks.

Figure 7.3 depicts a high-level component view of a typical IVA. It needs to be noted that not all the components depicted in Figure 7.3 need to exist for building an IVA. Less complex IVAs may not need multiple integrations with enterprise systems. Based on the data architecture of an enterprise, more systems or data stores may also have to be integrated.

They can be integrated with enterprise systems and cognitive (and conversational/natural language processing) services. Trained with information from existing customer conversations (that are largely in an unstructured format), over a period of time (with more conversations with the customer) they understand the customer better. Advances in natural language processing also lead to better understanding of the language of the customer requests and higher accuracy of responses. Many IVAs support multiple languages (other than English).

IBM Watson, Botego, and Creative Virtual are popular platforms for IVAs. Custom IVAs (and chatbots) can also be built leveraging bot frameworks from Slack and Facebook Messenger.

Federal Bank, a leading private bank in India, and leading banks in the United Kingdom like RBS, Santander, and NatWest, are examples of banks that are adopting (or have already adopted) IVAs for servicing their customers.[8–12]

While IVAs are helping banks support customers on digital channels, humanoids or Intelligent Robotic Agents (IRAs) are being explored for servicing customers in branches. The Japanese Bank of Tokyo-Mitsubishi UFJ (MUFG), with their humanoid bank teller Tao, and IRA, the intelligent robotic assistant from HDFC Bank (a leading Indian private bank) are prime examples of how intelligent banking is gaining adoption even in bank branches.

Robo-advisors: Wealth management functions, which involve advisory services to high net worth individuals (HNIs) related to portfolio management, tax planning, retirement planning, and estate management planning, have traditionally been serviced by wealth managers employed by financial institutions. These services involve advisory fees and have not been leveraging the power of technology for long.

Of late, the profile of HNIs is changing to digitally savvy younger customers who need personalized service 24/7. These customers have a preference for the self-service mode and prefer to cut advisory fees to as low an amount as possible. Traditional wealth management financial institutions have been slow to respond to the needs of the newer generation

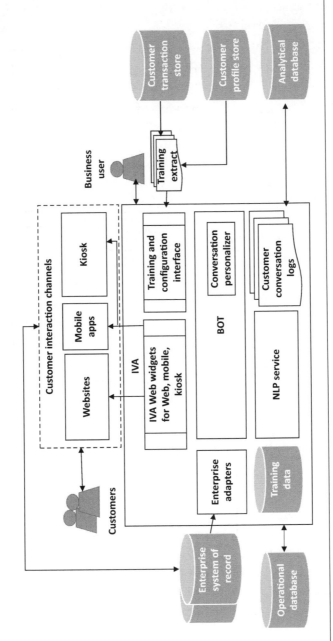

Figure 7.3 Components of an intelligent virtual agent.

of HNIs, thereby providing an opening for digitally savvy fintechs to enter this lucrative area. Apart from payments and lending, fintechs are increasingly seeing success in disrupting wealth management. Fintechs like Wealthfront and Betterment are prime examples of disruptors in this segment. These fintechs have come out with robo-advisory platforms that specialize in portfolio management services. These platforms are fully or partially automated and can be directly accessed by the customers (and/or financial aid advisors) 24/7 through self-service. They provide data-driven advice to their customers and leverage big data analytics.

The high level of technology and automation associated with robo-advisory platforms is enabling fintechs to cut advisory fees and provide self-service and better customer service, as well as be available 24/7, thus attracting a large number of customers. As per analysts, the assets under management of robo-advisors have risen from less than US$5 billion in 2013 to US$50 billion by the end of 2015 and are poised to rise to more than US$2 trillion by the end of this decade.

Robo-advisors collect the profile and preference information of their customers. In addition, they also gather information about the financial goals of the customers, along with their risk-taking appetite. They identify the financial products matching these attributes, recommend the financial instruments that the customers should make investments in (based on specific financial models and algorithms), monitor these investments, and provide value added services like alerting the customers of specific market events that can impact their investments through their platforms. The user interface is intuitive to the customer with informative dashboards displaying granular information about their investments.

Figure 7.4 depicts the high-level components of robo-advisors.

Apart from an intuitive customer interface, robo-advisors rely on data lakes and real-time or streaming analytics/complex event processors. Data lakes serve as the single shared repository for the customer, the market as well as the investment data required by the robo-advisor, and these data lakes reside on big data infrastructure like Hadoop file system. The robo-advisor platforms also have an interface for risk management groups to model risk and data scientists to build, test, and execute algorithms.[13-15]

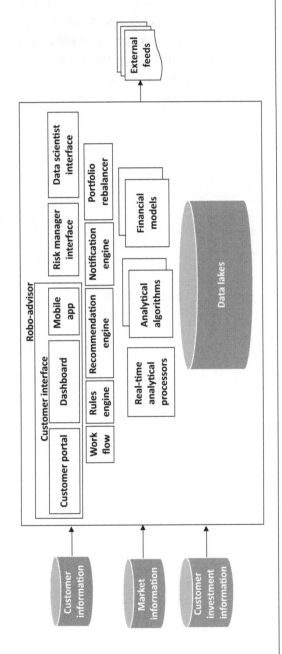

Figure 7.4 Components of a robo-advisor.

Personal digital assistants (PDAs): Personal digital assistants are typically background agents on devices that can listen to what the end consumer tells them to do and provide an appropriate response. For example, the user can activate Apple Siri (on Apple Watch or iPhone) by voice and ask it for today's weather report. Siri would immediately query external services and provide a response of the local maximum and minimum temperature, along with rainfall-, sunset-, and sunrise-related information. PDAs get better in understanding the needs of the customer over a period of time as they converse more and more with the customer. They can automate tasks like setting up calendars, calling contacts, and downloading music on behalf of their user.

Google Now, Microsoft Cortana, Apple Siri, and Amazon Alexa are all examples of how artificial intelligence is being leveraged in the consumer space and making consumers' lives easier. PDAs are typically agents available on devices and can talk to external Web services to fetch information for users. Machine learning enables the agent to learn more about customer behavior by gathering information about the customer from the apps installed on the device as well as the contacts stored.

PDAs can be trained to conduct transactions autonomously on behalf of the user. In other words, we are moving toward a world where customers will increasingly instruct their PDAs to perform banking transactions on their behalf, and banking systems must gear up to execute these transactions securely.

In the emerging bot world, we will have PDAs, which can be considered personal bots, supervise other bots on behalf of the device consumer and get tasks done. Mizuho, a Japanese bank, has already begun research on building a platform for connected cars, wearables, and smart home kits to make secure payments in collaboration with SORACOM, a Tokyo-based startup.[16]

The Short-Term, Part-Time Employee

One of the economic models spawned by digital technologies is the sharing economy, a data-driven model in which employees need not be dedicated to the same enterprise full-time and can also work for a partner, a competitor, or for other independent gigs. Part-time employment and short-term gigs have not been favored by businesses due to higher costs (for the enterprise) as well as security and non-compete reasons.

With enough security and analytical tools available in the cloud for enabling control of those who work for the enterprise, enabling part-time employees (especially for those profiles not requiring creativity) is not a stretch for the enterprise, although this would need tweaks in the HR policies and culture of the enterprise.

Banks and financial enterprises only need to take a look at how Uber and Airbnb manage their staff (and their businesses) success-fully. Tomorrow's financial enterprises need to have a pull mecha-nism to attract and onboard employees. Role-based enterprise digital agents, digital workspace, IDaaS and cloud-based user and resource (desktop/laptop/virtual machine or container/workspace) provision-ing, and part-time employee task and activity instrumentation, com-bined with big data analytics, serve as the technical foundation for enabling part-time employees and short-term stints while ensuring security and confidentiality for the enterprise. Given the extent of digitization and automation that is being implemented today, a dedi-cated office space for the part-time digital worker may also not be needed for many roles.

Figure 7.5 depicts of the capabilities needed by a financial enter-prise for employing short-term part-timers for noncreative tasks.

From an enterprise HR process perspective, the employee life-cycle process would change from *Job Posting→Recruitment→Onboarding→Employment→Offboarding* to *Task Posting→Self-Service Sign-Up→Quick Onboarding→Instant Resource Provisioning→Short-Term Employment or Gig→De-Provisioning→Offboarding*. Instead of posting jobs in the marketplace, tasks can be posted for part-timers to sign up and execute. Role-based enterprise digital agents would aid the part-time employee in accomplishing the tasks needed for the role. The role-based enterprise digital agent would preserve the security and confidentiality of any enterprise information or asset. In other words, a part-time employee cannot access the enterprise secrets without going through the role-based enterprise digital agent. On the completion of the employment contract, the part-timers can be instantly offboarded, thereby ensuring security and protection for enterprise and customer assets.

Figure 7.5 Financial enterprise capabilities needed for employing short-term, part-timers for noncreative tasks.

More Opening of Data and APIs Due to Regulation

Government regulators today are more open to disruptive technology than they ever were. With financial inclusion always being on top of the priorities for most governments across the world, they are increasingly looking at supporting processes, practices, tools, and technology that reduce the cost of financial transactions as well as encourage companies who support them in achieving these goals. They are increasingly seeing the role of financial innovation in achieving their financial inclusion goals, and they are adopting multiple approaches like regulation and tweaking policies to foster financial innovation, setting up infrastructure, and supporting an ecosystem for fintechs to thrive and to rollout financial innovations through their own subsidiaries or agencies.

The Open Banking Standard, as well as PSD2 directives that force established banks to open up their account information for third-party providers (and fintechs) through secure and open APIs, can be seen as examples of the use of regulations to foster financial innovation.

LATTICE80, the world's largest fintech hub in Singapore, Israel's The Floor, London's Level39, and Australia's Stone and Chalk are examples of government- (or semi-government-) backed infrastructure that foster an ecosystem in which fintechs thrive.

The National Payments Corporation of India (NPCI), owned by a consortium of banks and promoted by the Reserve Bank of India, the country's central bank, is an example in which a government-backed organization is involved in rolling out cost-effective payment innovations for financial inclusion.

The Indian government's financial inclusion program revolves around the creation of a unique identifier (called Aadhaar) for each citizen, the opening up of zero-balance-no-fee bank accounts (called Jan Dhan, which have a process that ensures that accounts are opened within 90 seconds) for poorer segments of the country who have been excluded from the banking system, linking of the unique identifier with Jan Dhan bank accounts and digital payment initiatives like unified payment interface (UPI), which enables simplified instant money transfers between accounts, BHIM app, a mobile wallet built over the UPI platform, and Aadhaar Pay (that enables customers without a debit or credit card or mobile wallet to specify their unique ID, authenticate biometrically, and make payments to retail vendors). NPCI has played a key role in the rolling out of UPI and the BHIM app as well as Aadhaar Pay. The success of their initiatives can be gauged from the fact that the BHIM app recorded 10 million downloads within nine days of its release and was the number one app on the Google Play store.

We are thus seeing governments across the world coming out of the thinking that established banks are too big to fail. They are trying to encourage alternatives for established banks and are forcing them to come out with financial innovations and also to support external parties who would want to come out with derivative financial innovations.

From Omnichannel Experience to Optimum Channel Experience

Customers often have a preference for specific channels for specific needs. For any problem-solving needs, they still approach branches or call centers, though they may transact through Web or mobile for their other transactional needs. Positive experiences during every interaction with the bank engage the customer more than the multiplicity of channels available for interaction (with the bank). This is borne by a recent Gallup survey.[17]

As per this survey, the satisfaction the customer has with their interactions with a bank (in their preferred channel) results in a higher engagement than the number of channels the bank has for interacting with the customer. The attitude of employees when interacting with the customers, the consistency of messaging from employees across channels, the consistency of the employee messaging with the brand messaging and positive channel experience during their interactions with the bank all have a bearing on the satisfaction levels experienced by the customer.

There is a stark difference (more than 60%) in satisfaction levels experienced (by customers during their interactions with their banks) when comparing a highly engaged customer with a disengaged customer. Highly engaged customers tend to deposit more in their banks, remain loyal, and tend to buy more products of the same bank when compared to disengaged customers.[18]

Thus it is imperative for banks to focus on providing an optimal experience for their customers in their channel of preference and keeping the messaging consistent rather than trying to engage the customers through multiple channels. This can to be achieved by use of analytics to determine the preferred default channel for specific needs of individual customers, training the employees on brand messaging and the need for consistency of messaging when dealing with the customer, putting the best foot forward, that is, having the best among employees in the front-end for servicing customers, and keeping the employees motivated (only motivated employees motivate customers).

Business Clouds

Horizontal services of most industries like procurement, sales, marketing, commerce, and supply chain are already available on the cloud. Thus the entry barriers for setting up an organization are very small as compared to earlier days. Provisioning the above clouds can be completed within minutes, and the organization (needing the above functions) can get started within a few hours. In the next few years, we will witness the common functionality related to wealth management, merchant banking, wholesale banking, retail banking, and so on move to the cloud or be available on a SaaS model. Setting up a bank (after the necessary government approvals) will not take much time, and those wanting to set up can provision (and customize) the banking services they wish to offer within a short time. Agility, flexibility, faster end-to-end process, better understanding of customers, simplicity, and great experience is what will differentiate the leaders from the laggards in the digital world.

Real–Time Digital

Technological advancements related to blockchain, aggregator services, APIs, complex event processing, and streaming analytics have incubated real-time business cases for banks. Instant payments and real-time fraud analytics are the most popular use cases that are seeing increasing adoption. Bank of America, JPMorgan Chase, and U.S. Bank have signed up with Early Warning's clearXchange network to offer real-time peer-to-peer (P2P) payment services. More than two dozen countries are planning to implement or are in the midst of implementing or have already implemented a real-time or near-real-time payments mechanism. Fintechs like Venmo offer real-time P2P payment without charging any fees, and TransferWise and Xoom are already offering instant cross-border payments for a low fee.[19]

Fintechs are chipping away at banking customers as they are trying to think through how to embed themselves into the digital lives of consumers whenever they may need money and are designing services accordingly. Most of the digital initiatives of banks so far are focused on how to enable consumers to access banking services digitally rather than how to make themselves useful in scenarios whenever customers may need money. Banks will need to start thinking about when customers will need money rather than when customers will need a bank and embedding themselves into the digital life of their customers in order to capitalize on the emerging trends. This will require them to partner more with the ecosystem apart from building innovative solutions of their own.

Conclusion

In the next few years of this decade, banks will witness interesting trends that will disrupt the way they work.

Bank branches will not be disappearing in the near future, but what we know as a branch in the next few years will be different from the bank branches that exist today. Augmented reality, virtual reality, digital walls, intelligent robot assistants, and sensors for detecting gestures would drive the "phygitalization" of branches.

Advances in artificial intelligence would drive "hyper personalization" of branches and result in the dawn of the era of "smart branches."

Robots and bots are set to learn how humans work on repetitive tasks involving multiple legacy systems and automate the execution of boring, repetitive tasks.

While we will see the established banks closing a few branches, we will also see the challenger banks open physical branches for scaling up their operations. However, these branches will be smart branches and more phygital in nature.

The adoption of virtual agents and robotic advisors would make banks smarter and more intelligent.

Blockchain and distributed ledger technology is set to aid the dawn of secure borderless banking and real-time transfer of money.

More banks are going to be pressurized by regulators to open up their internal data through secure APIs and bring in greater financial inclusion.

Cloud-based provisioning mechanisms would encourage exploration of "task-based, short-term, part-time employee," a constituent of the Sharing economy.

Advances in blockchain, real-time payments, and streaming analytics will drive adoption of instant payments.

More fintech and SaaS providers will incubate the growth of banking business clouds.

Faster networks, the increasing power of the browser, and techniques like Progressive Web Apps will enable the shift toward every time, everywhere, every device banking.

By 2020, we will also see enterprise-wide adoption of real-time analytics and real-time risk management for business risks such as credit and market risks.

Partnership-wise, we expect closer collaboration between financial institutions and retailers as well as telcos by 2020. Financial institutions will partner with retailers for selling and distributing the banking products and partner with telcos for managing the IT infrastructure of the bank.

As more and more banks go the digital way, the employees of financial institutions will need more education, awareness, and investments on protecting the information assets and data of customers. By 2020, we expect the use of machine learning, apart from comprehensive security infrastructure, to be used for protection against cyber-attacks.

By 2020, we also expect banks to change their business processes for evaluating customer credits. The customer credit rating and scoring will go beyond the traditional parameters, such as financial data and repayment capacity, to include social profiles and social community rating, similar to what Sesame Credit uses today.

By 2020, we believe that the interest rates and fees for the customers will move toward dynamic pricing rather than fixed pricing for a segment of customers.

We believe that by 2020, the customers will be developing and designing the banking products on their own and the same will be either crowd-approved or sourced before actual launch to larger customers by the bank. Customers will become part of the banking product definition process.[20]

Thus tomorrow's bank will need the capability to support human-to-human, human-to-machine (bot), and machine-to-machine conversations. It's up to the banks to capitalize on these trends through partnership with the ecosystem, faster technology adoption, and culture change needed for tomorrow's digital world.

Points to ponder:

- Future of banking
- Impact of artificial intelligence and augmented reality on bank branches
- Impact of blockchain on banking
- Impact of robotic process automation on the workforce
- Shared economy capability demands
- Real-time banking

References

1. LeadershipNOW. LeadingThoughts—Building a Community of Leaders (Quotes on Vision). http://www.leadershipnow.com/vision-quotes.html

2. Ajay Gupta and Vik Sohoni. 2016. Digital Marketing Really Matters for US Banks Even as Branches Show Significant Staying Power. McKinsey (Insights). Dec 1. http://www.mckinsey.com/business-functions/digital-mckinsey/our-insights/digital-blog/digital-marketing-really-matters-for-us-banks-even-as-branches-show-significant-staying-power?cid=other-alt-mip-mck-oth-1612

3. Jim Marous. 2015. Robots and AI Invade Banking. The Financial Brand. Jul 7. https://thefinancialbrand.com/52735/robots-artificial-intelligence-ai-banking/

4. Oscar Williams-Grut. 2016. Challenger Bank Metro Is Opening New "Stores" While Big Banks Are Closing Hundreds of Branches. *Business Insider India*. Dec 14. http://www.businessinsider.in/Challenger-bank-Metro-is-opening-new-stores-while-big-banks-are-closing-hundreds-of-branches/articleshow/55983450.cms

5. Wipro. The Virtual Workforce. Applying Robotic Process Automation in Banking. http://www.wipro.com/documents/the-virtual-workforce-applying-robotic-process-automation-in-banking.pdf

6. Aboli. 2015. FinTech Is Scaling Up: UK Banks to Enable International Remittances in Mobile App Using TransferWise's API. Let's Talk Payments (LTP). Dec 24. https://letstalkpayments.com/fintech-is-scaling-up-uk-banks-to-enable-international-remittances-in-mobile-app-using-transferwises-api/

7. Finextra. 2017. Ripple Lands First Middle-Eastern Bank. Feb 1. https://www.finextra.com/newsarticle/30069/ripple-lands-first-middle-eastern-bank?utm_medium=newsflash&utm_source=2017-2-1

8. Nick Ismail. 2016. RBS, Natwest and SEB Banks Are Deploying a Virtual Assistant for an Artificial Intelligence-Driven Customer Service. *Information Age*. Oct 6. http://www.information-age.com/virtual-assistant-rbs-natwest-seb-banks-deploying-chatbots-123462511/

9. Reuters. 2013. (This URL has been archived) http://www.reuters.com/article/2013/04/10/idUSnMKW5746a+e0+MKW20130410

10. Beerud Sheth. 2015. Forget Apps, Now the Bots Take Over. TechCrunch. Sep 29. https://techcrunch.com/2015/09/29/forget-apps-now-the-bots-take-over/

11. Doug Overton. 2016. The Rise of Virtual Agents: The Future Banking Experience. *Finance Digest*. Sep 20. https://www.financedigest.com/the-rise-of-virtual-agents-the-future-banking-experience.html

12. Mandy Reed. 2016. Virtual Agents and Human Agents Join Forces for Customer Service in 2016. LinkedIn. Jan 21. https://www.linkedin.com/pulse/virtual-agents-human-join-forces-customer-service-2016-mandy-reed?articleId=8851892874697973961#comments-885189 2874697973961&trk=sushi_topic_posts_guest

13. Vamsi Chemitiganti. 2016. Design and Architecture of a Robo-Advisory Platform. Vamsi Talks Tech. Oct 15. http://www.vamsitalkstech.com/?p=2354&

14. Vamsi Chemitiganti. 2016. How Robo-Advisors Work. Vamsi Talks Tech. Jul 1. http://www.vamsitalkstech.com/?p=2418&

15. Vamsi Chemitiganti. 2016. Big Data Driven Disruption—The Robo-Advisor. Vamsi Talks Tech. Jun 10. .http://www.vamsitalkstech.com/?p=2329&

16. Finextra. http://www.finextra.com

17. Daniela Yu and Bailey Nelson. 2016. Bank Customers: Are Channel Experiences All That Matter? Gallup (Business Journal). Nov 9. http://www.gallup.com/businessjournal/197345/bank-customers-channel-experiences-matter.aspx

18. Daniela Yu and Bailey Nelson. 2016. Bank Channel Experiences Make or Break Customer Engagement. *Gallup (Business Journal)*. Nov. 16. http://www.gallup.com/businessjournal/197363/bank-channel-experiences-break-customer-engagement.aspx?g_source=FINANCIAL_SERVICES&g_medium=topic&g_campaign=tiles

19. Paul Schaus. 2016. BankThink the Real Promise of Real-Time Payments (It's Not the Fees). American Banker. Jun 30. https://www.americanbanker.com/opinion/the-real-promise-of-real-time-payments-its-not-the-fees

20. Bryan Yurcan. 2017. USAA Opens User Experience "Design Studio." American Banker. Feb 10. https://www.americanbanker.com/news/usaa-opens-user-experience-design-studio?utm_content=buffera26c0&utm_medium=social&utm_source=twitter.com&utm_campaign=hs

Appendix

More Social

In this section, more of the terms, tools, frameworks, and processes used in social technology world are described.

Figure A.1 describes the enterprise maturity model for handling social media.

Social Engagement[1-5]

There are different definitions for "engagement" for a marketer. Broadly, most of the definitions tend to define engagement as the effectiveness of communicating with the intended audience and gaining their attention. While one school of thought defines social engagement as all about businesses publishing content on social media channels to elicit maximum response from fans and followers, a broader school of thought defines social engagement as a bi–directional communication between businesses and their customers with the communication content being more focused on helping the customers solve their problems rather than being merely communicative of the brand benefits. The intent of the communication is to influence the customer to stay loyal to the brand. The engagement of a customer is cultivated over a period of time, by providing experiential and useful content to the customer through social media channels.

Social capability maturity

	Basic	Standard	Advanced	Optimal
Objective	• Connect with customers through social channels	• Engage with customers on social channels • Listen to customer feedback through social channels	• Engage with customers on social channels • Listen and act on customer feedback through social channels • Lead generation • Real-time interaction with customers on social channels	• Engage with customers on social channels • Listen and act on customer feedback through social channels real-time • Engage with employees and partners on social channels. Listen and act on their feedback real—time
Social presence	• Accounts on popular social networking platforms like Facebook, Twitter, Instagram, Pinterest	• Accounts on popular social networking platforms like Facebook, Twitter, Instagram, Pinterest	• Accounts on popular social networking platforms like Facebook, Twitter, Instagram, Pinterest • Own social community sites enabling customers to interact with each other. These are linked to existing customer-facing websites	• Accounts on popular social networking platforms like Facebook, Twitter, Instagram, Pinterest • Own social community sites enabling customers to interact with each other. These are linked to existing customer-facing websites • Social collaboration platforms for employees and partners
Technology and tools	• Social content publishing tools	• Social content publishing tools • Social listening tools	• Social content publishing tools • Social listening and response management tools • Social insight tools • Social CRM • Automated integration with big data platforms (for analysis) and customer–facing enterprise systems • Community creation tools/social collaboration platforms • Websites with social login support • Social identity management tools	• Social content publishing tools • Social listening and response management tools • Social insight tools • Social CRM • Automated integration with big data platforms (for analysis) and customer-facing enterprise systems and HR systems and internal systems for employees • Community creation tools/social collaboration platforms • Websites with social login support • Social identity management tools
Capability	• Social marketing and communications	• Social marketing and communications • Customer engagement	• Social marketing and communications • Real-time customer engagement • Co-creation with customers • Social media response management	• Social marketing and communications • Real-time customer engagement • Co-creation with customers • Social media response management • Employee and partner engagement

Figure A.1 Maturity model for handling social media.

For most enterprises, social engagement activities span across a mix of channels. They include sharing informative brand–specific videos on YouTube, tweeting posts on Twitter from multiple handles, periodically publishing blogs on corporate sites or blogging sites, posting knowledge–sharing content on public and social communities specific to the brand, posting expert articles on LinkedIn or setting up groups on LinkedIn, posting updates on Facebook, or sharing "behind the scenes" photos on Instagram.

Different social media channels have different ways of measuring engagement levels. While for Twitter, the engagement score is dependent on the number of replies, retweets and mentions, for Instagram, it is based on the number of followers and hashtag mentions. For Facebook, the engagement score is dependent on shares per post, likes per post and comments per post, while for LinkedIn, it is dependent on the number of interactions per post, the clicks, the followers, and the number of impressions. Broadly, social engagement metrics describe the measure of the popularity and usefulness of the content based on the number of end users reading (and responding to) the content as well as the interest shown by the users by sharing the content to their network. Most of the social media channels themselves provide analytics to measure engagement in their channels as they too have an ulterior motive in publishing the social engagement metrics. The more interesting and useful the content, the greater the number of active users and the greater the time spent by these users, thus reflecting on their revenues. Most social engagement, listening, and analytics tools also provide a view of the return on investment (ROI) on social engagement efforts based on conversation rate (a metric that provides an understanding of the audience and its preferences and is a measure of the number of comments elicited by the post from the audience), amplification rate (the rate at which followers share the user's post), and applause rate (a metric that helps understand the kind of content liked by the engaged audience and is a measure of the number of likes, +1s, or favorite clicks per post).

Social media engagement metrics drive social engagement across different channels as per the planned branding goals. The goals may be to largely understand what type of content is liked by the target audience and what type of content goes viral across different channels and tailor the publishing of content across different channels as per this analysis. The goals may also include driving traffic to the brand websites from social media, for which we will need to leverage Web analytics tools like Omniture, Google Analytics, and so on to identify metrics like click–through and traffic originating from social media channels.

Different departments in an enterprise need different metrics from social media. For example, metrics like number of followers and click–through may be needed more for marketing and brand communications department while a product development department may need derived metrics like "Number of Product Ideas" from social media.

Social Media Channels Leveraged by Enterprises

Social networking platforms facilitate connections between their users. These platforms facilitate the sharing of experiences, opinions, likes, and dislikes through textual, pictorial, audio, or video content. These platforms have the underlying capability to track the content creators and content consumers. Based on the privacy settings configured, the content creator's comments can be consumed by any number of followers or friends of the content creator, who are registered users in the platform. Registered users with large numbers of followers are considered to be influencers.

Social networking platforms like Facebook allow businesses to also have profile pages for their brands to help them connect and engage with their customers or build a community of fans who can potentially turn into customers later. Citi leverages its Facebook presence to engage with their fans by announcing the sporting events they sponsor in different cities and asking them questions about sporting events in their cities, thereby facilitating conversations and interactions with them.

Engagement with users is built by publishing content that may not be typically expected from banking enterprises. When banks engage with a potential customer or a customer on a social network platform, their interest lies beyond the user. Their engagement with the user through contents and questions and answers sessions is also to enable recommendations by the user to their network.

Since Facebook needs actual identities of their registered user, banks and financial institutions are also trying to leverage Facebook to assess the credit worthiness of the immediate friends of the Facebook user and determine their capability to pay back borrowed money and then recommend products or offers.

Micro-blogging platforms also enable registered users of the platform to connect with each other with the restrictions being more related to the number of characters in the text they share. The users can also upload photos and videos and share the Uniform Resource Locators (URLs) through micro-blogging platforms.

Micro-blogging platforms aid more immediate information-sharing when compared to social networking sites like Facebook (where content is considered to be fresh for a longer time). Content published by the creator can be disseminated to all the followers of the content publisher within a few seconds.

Businesses planning to engage their customers through Twitter need to have the capability to respond within a few minutes of any event. Micro-blogging sites are used more by businesses to announce the occurrence of an event or spot "what is the trend currently." Twitter provides users with the facility to prefix their posts with a hashtag (#) and group their posts. Businesses also love the fact that Twitter enables "direct messaging." A number of leading banks like Bank of America, Wells Fargo, Citi, and HSBC have adopted Twitter for providing customer service. Some of these banks have multiple Twitter accounts. Westpac has leveraged Twitter to warn users of fraud. Given the "immediate" and "near real-time" nature of Twitter, a few banks like ICICI Bank and Axis Bank have also leveraged Twitter to enable money transfers between their customers who are Twitter users.

Businesses also assess the influence of the user based on the number of followers.

Weblogs (or blogs) are online personal diaries or journals published by experts or anybody with knowledge on any topic to share their expertise and experience with the general public. Most blogs are searchable through search engines. Blog posts appear in reverse chronological order and allow the readers to comment and also enable the bloggers (or publishers of the blog) to respond back. The fresher the content of the blogs, the higher the popularity of the blog and the greater the number of readers of the blog. Blog consumers use blog readers to read blogs from multiple source. These readers use rich site syndication (RSS) feed readers to keep the blogs up-to-date.

Blogs can be hosted or self-hosted (by renting servers and installing blogging software on this server) and may involve having to buy a domain name. Popular blogging platforms include Wordpress.com and Tumblr. Blogging platforms like Tumblr allow different types of content like text, links, audio, video, and photo to be added to blogs before publishing them. They allow all users to search blogs based on their tags and allow registered users to tag the blogs or follow specific bloggers as well as to share blogs with the network. LinkedIn also provides a good platform for bloggers.

Blogs are useful for a business or an individual to build their brand as an expert or as somebody who can be of help in solving specific problems in which they have expertise. Many financial research firms make use of blogs to publish insights from their research. J. D. Power and Associates Banking Blog, ACTON's Financial Marketing Insights, Banking.com, Bank Innovation, and NetBanker are examples of popular banking blogs.[6]

Video-sharing platforms like YouTube enable marketers to upload video content. This content can be commented upon by users, and the URLs can be shared by users to their connections through social networking sites or even through emails. Video-sharing sites like YouTube go beyond being just a database of videos and provide a social networking site-like infrastructure. They allow every registered user to have a personal channel, similar to a Facebook wall, and allow the user to follow other registered users who have uploaded videos and subscribe to their updates. The personal channel can be customized and will typically contain all the videos uploaded by the user as well as the videos uploaded by the users they have subscribed to.

Businesses leverage video-sharing sites to share information about their products and share knowledge about how to use the product or how the product works. Interesting videos, mostly the success stories of their products or services, are uploaded to YouTube to generate buzz and make them viral, increasing their brand recognition in the process. A number of banks and financial service enterprises have their own channels on YouTube. Wells Fargo leads the pack among these enterprises, with more than 14,000 subscribers to their channel and more than 37 million all-time YouTube views.[7]

Live streaming social platforms like Meerkat, Twitter Periscope, and Facebook Live are the latest social channels to gain widespread popularity. These live-streaming platforms are proof of how social media platforms have evolved from text to multimedia content to the streaming of live video feeds. Users can use their smartphone cameras to live stream events to their followers and fans through the apps belonging to these platforms. Twitter's Periscope has more than 10 million subscribers. The user telecasting the event is called the Scoper, and the subscribers viewing these events after logging in to the platform are called Viewers. These platforms can be leveraged by banks and financial services to provide investment and financial management tips to their customers and engage them live.

Photo-sharing platforms like Instagram (as well as Tumblr and Pinterest) provide a social networking platform for visually appealing content. They enable their registered users to upload photos, tag them for discovery by others, and share them with their network. Registered users can like the photo, comment on them, follow other users, and receive updates from the ones they follow. These platforms also provide a search interface to enable users to search based on tags. A few of them support photo editing activities like cropping of the photo. Business users can leverage analytical tools available as part of these platforms to measure engagement metrics like comments and likes.

Banks and financial institutions are taking to Instagram as a medium to engage with their fans and customers through visual communication and promote themselves among the millennial fans and customers. Creative content, more related to those customers benefiting from their financial astuteness, is being uploaded on these sites to engage the users. American Express (Amex) has more than 20,000 followers on Instagram. Amex leveraged Instagram to engage their followers with unseen behind the scenes photos of various events (concerts, fashion shows, and sporting events) they had sponsored.

Social messaging platforms like WhatsApp, Facebook Messenger, Google Hangout, Skype, Snapchat, and WeChat enable one-to-one or one-to-group instant communication. Text, photos, audio, and video can all be instantly shared through these platforms. Given that messaging platforms are valuable largely for instant chat with friends, the maximum usage come from mobile devices.

The user interface for such platforms are usually apps on mobile devices, and these platforms largely serve as a replacement for short messaging service (SMS). There is thus a very thin line dividing social messaging platforms and mobile messaging platforms.

More and more banks are leveraging messaging platforms to enable money transfer. This is essentially useful if the user needs to transfer money to another user instantly but does not know the account number to which the money should be transferred. Axis Bank has launched a service called Ping Pay, which enables money transfer through WhatsApp. Singapore-based Fastacash has partnered with Xpress Money, a global money transfer company and launched a mobile remittance app called XOPOTO. This app allows users to transfer money internationally via Facebook, Twitter, and WeChat. Facebook Messenger and WeChat allow peer-to-peer payments within the app.[8]

Online-review platforms are websites that provide user-generated ratings and feedback for the products and services they use. Yelp, which is more of a restaurant review site, made online-review sites popular. For financial institutions, MyBankTracker, Credio, and Credit Karma serve as examples of sites that provide user feedback on products and services offered by different banks.

Online review sites are leveraged by banks and financial services for social listening and analytics.

Discussion forums like Quora and Digg are social platforms for knowledge-sharing. These are helpful for users who wish to know about any particular topic. These are platforms where one registered user helps another registered user. These forums are categorized into various sections and allow users to comment, upvote, or downvote the answers or share with others.

Many businesses look at these forums as a platform for users to help other users. Businesses can identify brand advocates from these forums and encourage or reward them for answering more questions from users. BankersOnline is a good example of public discussion forums for banking services.

Many businesses integrate private social community sites, a variation of discussion forums, with their customer websites. These private social community sites enable customers to ask questions on any aspect of the product or service they have used. Most answers are provided by other users who might have faced similar problems or by identified experts or brand advocates. This approach reduces the volume of calls going to call centers for resolution, thereby reducing the cost of customer service.

A user of a discussion group can be an *admin* or a *group owner* with the ability to create different categories, topics for conversation as well as user groups. Users can be *moderators* with the ability to ensure that conversations take place as per the rules set or they can be remain just a *user* with the ability to create a post within a topic or comment on the post. The users with a higher number of posts can be deemed to be highly active users. Active users who have their posts read by a high number of users can be deemed to be influencers.

Social bookmarking sites[9,10] help in building folksonomy or "user-generated taxonomy." These sites contain the list of URLs of websites or images that are bookmarked and tagged and facilitate search of the URLs or images based on the name of the bookmark. These bookmarks can be shared with others in the network. The primary value of these bookmarks lies in understanding the category to which the content should belong to as per the user or a group of users. These bookmarks aid content discovery, especially from an image perspective, and suggest related links or images.

Pinterest is an example of a visual social bookmarking site that enables users to pin photos or images to their account on the platform. This pinned photo can be tagged and shared with others. A series of pinned photos can be grouped together to create a story and form a Pinterest board (Pinboard). This content can be private or public. Pinterest also supports links to websites, thus helping drive social media traffic to their specific websites.

Businesses can leverage bookmarking sites to create their own Pinboards from third-party sources as well as to showcase internal content. Banks like Bank of America and Wells Fargo are discovering the benefits of engaging millennials as well as mothers through their Pinboards of rich content related to better money habits or saving for vacation.[11]

As seen, the lines between different types of social media channels are blurring, but for the banking and financial service enterprise, success in leveraging social media lies in identifying the right channels to engage with and the right way to engage with them.

SOCIAL MEDIA REPUTATION MANAGEMENT

Given that what's said on social media about a brand, a product, or a service cannot be controlled, the next-best option for most companies is to monitor the social media conversations, identify potential situations when reputation of their brand, product, or service can take a beating and act early by responding in appropriate social media channels proactively before there is a crisis. Apart from popular social networking channels, online review sites are the source of data for social reputation management for conversations or feedback related to a brand, product, or a service. Reputation management may need the involvement of public relations department and legal department, and may involve workflows.

Social Media Response Management

Increasingly, enterprises have also realized the value of using Twitter and Facebook for customer services. Customers too realize that defects about a product or service, when discussed on Twitter and Facebook, have a high chance of going viral and hence a higher chance of gaining attention from the product or service vendor. Hence, they prefer Twitter and Facebook as channels for customer service instead of having to reach out to call centers. Enterprises must have a process in place to respond to customer complaints on social media. The process would include guidelines on how to be sensitive to customers on social media.

Social Currency

Currency is something that moves around, that is shared for a benefit to the giver. The concept of social currency can be looked at through the same lens. It is about information-sharing, experience-sharing. This sharing (of information and experience) is the currency of social media, and describes whatever accessible gets created virtually, actually and potentially due to being present in online or offline networks and communities[12–14]

Quite often, marketers use the term "social currency" as the degree to which consumers share information about a brand or a product with others. Vivaldi Partners, a global consulting firm, has come up with a measure of social currency score, to determine how effectively companies are using social media for their brands. The social currency score is based on social buzz generated, the social media audience size, and engagement[15,16]

SOCIAL DATA PROVIDERS

Most social networking platforms impose restrictions on either the number of queries or API (application programming interface) calls that can be performed on their sites daily or impose a limit on the number of days (preceding the current date) for which data or content can be obtained from these sites. They also change their public APIs often, leading to resultant code changes in custom applications.

This has led to various social media data aggregators coming into the market. These data providers have commercial partnerships with social media channels (or owned by the channels themselves) for providing both real-time social data as well as historical social data from multiple social media channels through a developer-friendly single API. Popular social media aggregators include Gnip (which has now been acquired by Twitter) and DataSift. Enterprises can leverage these data providers for building custom social intelligence applications. Even if Facebook or Twitter change their public API for querying, the code for the custom applications need not change if they are programmed against social data APIs. However the use of social data aggregators does come with a licensing cost as well as a cost for provisioning the cloud-based infrastructure for processing the volume and velocity of data (big data infrastructure).

Many of the social listening and analytical tools too leverage social data providers as their input source.

SOCIAL APP REVIEW PROCESS

In order to ensure uniformity and foster adherence to security, user experience, and app behavioral guidelines standards, the developer platforms also provide a sandbox testing environment for the social apps.

They also require the developer to submit the social app for a detailed review process in advance (before they go live) and do not permit the developer to go live until their review recommendations are addressed. For example, one of the key requirements of a social app is the need to request the user's permission for use of their data from social networking platforms. If the app tries to access the social data of the user before his or her explicit permission, the app review process would make recommendations to the developer to ensure that the app's workflow is changed to seek the user's permission before accessing social data of the user.

OPENSOCIAL CONTAINER

During the first decade of this century, one of the key challenges for the developers of social apps was the non-interoperability between different social networking platforms, that is, a social app developed for one social networking platform cannot be used as it is for another social networking platform. With support from Google and a few other social networking sites, OpenSocial was touted as the answer for a "more social" Web. If any website needed to be available as a social app in Orkut as well as, say, Hi5, leveraging OpenSocial helped. In other words, any website implementing OpenSocial would expose the same API for third-party websites to retrieve people (user profile and friend information) and their activity information, as well as standardize the approach to persist this information.

Apache Shindig framework was open sourced to the developer community as a reference implementation of an open social container. Developers (and enterprises) could develop their own social apps hosted in containers and develop their social networking websites leveraging Apache Shindig. Apache Shindig provides server-side components, client-side components, and templates for accelerating development of social apps.[17]

OpenSocial containers also expose activity streams as a collection of actions a user has taken. They support activity templates to allow application developers to define messages with placeholders.[18,19]

Usage Application Capability Framework for Social Technology

The usage, applications, and capabilities (UAC) framework for social provides an overview of how social media is relevant to enterprises (Figure A.2). It provides a depiction of the value of social media to an enterprise, the areas where it is used, the areas where it is applied (product research and development, marketing and public relations, service [customer]), and capabilities needed by the financial enterprise to benefit from social media.

Best Practices for Social Media Management

The power as well as the pitfall of social media lies in the fact that content once posted ceases to be under the content publisher's control anymore. Even though the content publisher has the option to delete the post, there is always a risk that somebody else would have copied the post before it was deleted and would try to use this against the poster for ulterior motives. Hence it is necessary for the risk-averse financial enterprise to come out with guidelines for their social media management team on how to respond and how not to respond on social media channels so that there is no damage to their brand reputation.

Best practices for social media management of course start with having an integrated enterprise-wide social media strategy. Strategic best practices include the building of capabilities outlined in the UAC framework for social, having the right mix of properties in appropriate social media platforms based on analysis of customer presence, leveraging appropriate tools for social media management, having the ability to integrate social tools with enterprise systems,

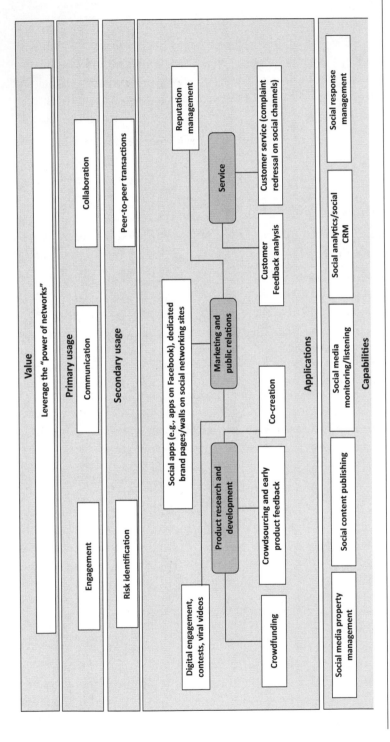

Figure A.2 UAC framework for social technology.

having a dedicated team to monitor social media, having a social media response management strategy (and team) to ensure protection of brand reputation (which may include investing in a social media command center), investing in analytical capabilities to identify the influencers, brand advocates and detractors, having a strategy to reward brand advocates, and having a strategy for managing lifecycle of social content.

Social content lifecycle comprises the entire process starting from the creation of content for social media followed by listening to user-generated content (real time or at scheduled intervals) followed by analysis of user-generated content right through to the application of user-generated content or feedback to campaign content. One strategic best practice for an enterprise is to have a mechanism to provide feedback from its social channels to different departments across the enterprise so that the concerned department can act on the feedback of the users within a short time.

Operational best practices include keeping the content fresh and updated at regular frequency on the social media properties (Facebook walls, blogs, etc.), posting content that is highly engaging for the customers, ensuring two–way communication with the fans and followers who may be existing customers or potential customers, acknowledging any negative feedback about the brand or company products, and not being abusive with detractors. Better research and analysis of customer (or fan or follower) behavior can help identify the type of content that can be highly engaging as well as the right time for posting content to ensure better reach and engagement.

More Mobility

Usage Application Capability (UAC) Framework for Mobile Technology

In this section, more of the terms, tools, frameworks, and processes used in mobile technology world are described.

Figure A.3 depicts how mobile technology is used and applied by the enterprise (for servicing their employees and customers), as well as the capabilities needed by the enterprise.

Mobile technology is valuable to any enterprise for serving the needs of customers as well as employees and partners. The primary

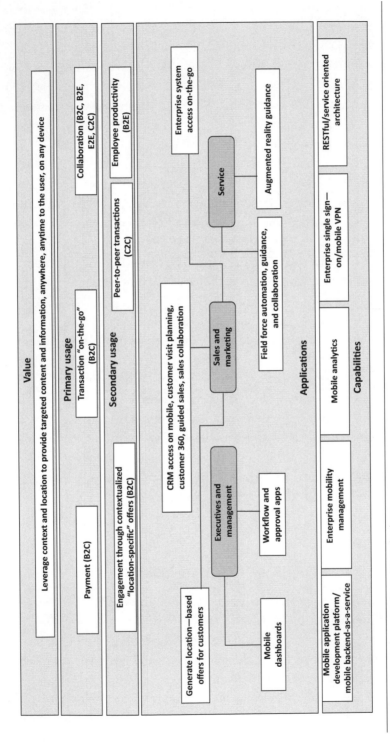

Figure A.3 UAC framework for mobile technology.

value of mobile technology lies in the contextual information it provides, based on which the customers can be serviced with targeted recommendations.

From a business-to-consumer (B2C) perspective, mobile technology enables the enterprise to serve the transactional and engagement needs of the consumer.

From a business-to-business/partners (B2B) and business-to-employee (B2E) perspective, mobile technology helps enterprises in increasing the productivity of employees and partners as well as fostering collaboration between employees and partners.

Sales and marketing and servicing department personnel are the primary beneficiaries of mobile technology. The ability of mobile apps to address the demands of sales force and field force automation (especially for wealth managers and investment advisors) have enabled better targeting of customers, better sales, reduced time to service, and better productivity for the financial enterprises. Senior managers and executives can provide their approvals on the go through mobile apps.

To leverage the benefits of mobile technologies, the financial enterprise must have capabilities related to mobility infrastructure (like mobile application development platforms or mobile backend-as-a-service, enterprise mobility management, mobile analytics, and enterprise security infrastructure like single sign–on), apart from an enterprise integration infrastructure.

References

1. Sunil Saxena. 2013. 7 Key Characteristics of Social Media. Easymedia. Aug 11. http://www.easymedia.in/7-key-characteristics-of-social-media/
2. Fusionfarm. (This URL has been archived.) http://blog.fusionfarm. com/what-is-social-media-engagement-and-why-it-matters-for-your-business
3. Charlie Harper, Kimberley Thelwell, Patti Neumann. 2016. What Exactly Is Social Media Engagement? Why Do I Need It? Social Media Fuze. Jan 7. http://socialmediafuze.com/social-media-engagement/
4. Avinash Kaushik. Best Social Media Metrics : Conversation, Amplification, Applause, Economic Value. Kaushik (blog). http://www.kaushik.net/ avinash/best-social-media-metrics-conversation-amplification-applause-economic-value/

5. Jasmine Jaume. 2013. What IS Social Media Monitoring? Answers to Common Questions and Misconceptions. Brandwatch. Feb 20. https://www.brandwatch.com/2013/02/what-is-social-media-monitoring-answers-to-common-questions-and-misconceptions/

6. Jeffry Pilcher. 2012. Top 10 Best Banking Blogs – Readers Choice 2012 Winners. The Financial Brand. Nov 8. http://thefinancialbrand.com/26152/best-banking-blogs-readers-choice-2012/

7. Jeffry Pilcher. 2014. Top 100 Hottest Bank & Credit Union YouTube Channels. The Financial Brand. Oct 3. http://thefinancialbrand.com/42904/power-100-2014-q3-youtube-banking/

8. See Kit Tang. 2015. How Social Media Is Reshaping Global Money Transfer. CNBC. Nov 12. http://www.cnbc.com/2015/11/12/start-up-fastacashs-xopo-app-lets-users-transfer-money-through-social-media.html

9. Sysomos. Different Types of Social Media Channels. SlideShare. http://www.slideshare.net/sysomos/different-types-of-social-media-channels-sysomos

10. Curtis Foreman. 2017. 10 Types of Social Media and How Each Can Benefit Your Business. Hootsuite Blogs. Jun 20. http://blog.hootsuite.com/types-of-social-media/

11. Mary Wisniewski. 2015. Pinterest Is Paying Off for These Big Banks — Here's Why. American Banker. Aug 5. http://www.american-banker.com/news/bank-technology/pinterest-is-paying-off-for-these-big-banks-heres-why-1075878-1.html

12. Wikipedia. Social Currency. https://en.wikipedia.org/wiki/Social_currency

13. Incite group admin. 2013. What Is Your Social Currency? INCITE GROUP. Jul 16. www.incite-group.com/customer-engagement/what-your-social-currency

14. HRzone. What Is Social Currency? http://www.hrzone.com/hr-glossary/what-is-social-currency

15. Kurt Badenhausen. 2013. Subway, Google and Target Are Top Brands for Social Currency. Forbes. Mar 12. http://www.forbes.com/sites/kurt-badenhausen/2013/03/12/subway-google-and-target-are-top-brands-for-social-currency/

16. Samuel Hum. 2015. Example of Social Currency Used in Marketing. Referral Candy. Feb 6. http://www.referralcandy.com/blog/15-examples-of-social-currency-used-in-marketing/

17. Patrick Chanezon. 2008. How Do We Socialize Object Online without Having to Create Yet Another Social Network? SlideShare. Mar 4. http://www.slideshare.net/chanezon/open-social-presentation-gsp-west-2008/15-Integrating_Community_Feedback

18. Wikipedia. Activity Streams (Format). https://en.wikipedia.org/wiki/Activity_Streams_(format)

19. Wikipedia. Activity Stream. https://en.wikipedia.org/wiki/Activity_stream

Additional Resources

1. BrainyQuote. Tim Berners-Lee Quotes. http://www.brainyquote.com/quotes/quotes/t/timberners444503.html
2. Chris Howard, Daryl C. Plummer, Yvonne Genovese, Jeffrey Mann, David. A. Willis, David Mitchell Smith. 2012. The Nexus of Forces: Social, Mobile, Cloud and Information. Gartner (currently archived). Jun 14. https://www.gartner.com/doc/2049315/nexus-forces-social-mobile-cloud
3. TechTarget (SearchCIO). Nexus of Forces (Definition) http://searchcio.techtarget.com/definition/nexus-of-forces
4. Commander. 2013. What Is the Third Platform? Oct 30. http://blog.commander.com/platform/
5. O'Reilly. What Is Web 2.0? http://www.oreilly.com/pub/a/web2/archive/what-is-web-20.html?page=5
6. Sprinklr. 2011. (The Getsatisfaction blog URL has been archived and redirects to Sprinklr blog site.) http://blog.getsatisfaction.com/2011/05/25/network-effect/?view=socialstudies
7. Pascal-Emmanuel Gobry. 2011. How Strong Are Network Effects Online, REALLY? Business Insider (Tech Insider). May 19. http://www.businessinsider.com/network-effects-2011-5?IR=T
8. Jasmine Jaume. 2013. What IS Social Media Monitoring? Answers to Common Questions and Misconceptions. Brandwatch. Feb 20. https://www.brandwatch.com/2013/02/what-is-social-media-monitoring-answers-to-common-questions-and-misconceptions/
9. Giselle Abramovich. 2013. Inside Mastercard's Social Command Center. DigiDay. May 9. http://digiday.com/brands/inside-mastercards-social-command-center/
10. Crowdsourcing http://www.crowdsourcing.org
11. Microsoft. 2015. Align Enterprise Social Tools with Business Needs. https://www.microsoft.com/itshowcase/Article/Content/506/Align-Enterprise-Social-Tools-with-Business-Needs
12. Wikipedia. Gamification. https://en.wikipedia.org/wiki/Gamification
13. Ryan Dube. Characteristics of Social Networks. LoveToKnow. http://socialnetworking.lovetoknow.com/Characteristics_of_Social_Networks
14. Sprinklr. 2011. (The Getsatisfaction blog URL has been archived and redirects to Sprinklr blog site.) http://blog.getsatisfaction.com/2011/05/25/network-effect/?view=socialstudies
15. Sunil Saxena. 2013. 7 Key Characteristics of Social Media. Easymedia. Aug 11. http://www.easymedia.in/7-key-characteristics-of-social-media/
16. Chris Howard, Daryl C. Plummer, Yvonne Genovese, Jeffrey Mann, David. A. Willis, David Mitchell Smith. 2012. The Nexus of Forces: Social, Mobile, Cloud and Information. Gartner (currently archived). Jun 14. https://www.gartner.com/doc/2049315/nexus-forces-social-mobile-cloud

17. Ryan Dube. Characteristics of Social Networks. LoveToKnow. http://socialnetworking.lovetoknow.com/Characteristics_of_Social_Networks

18. Sprinklr. 2011. (The Getsatisfaction blog URL has been archived and redirects to Sprinklr blog site.) http://blog.getsatisfaction.com/2011/05/25/network-effect/?view=socialstudies

19. Patrick Chanezon. 2008. How Do We Socialize Object Online without Having to Create Yet Another Social Network? SlideShare. Mar 4. http://www.slideshare.net/chanezon/open-social-presentation-gsp-west-2008/15-Integrating_Community_Feedback

20. David Nattriss. 2010. Facebook Platform. SlideShare. May 11. http://www.slideshare.net/davenatts/facebook-platform

21. Karl Flinders. 2014. CaixaBank Facebook App Unites Social Media with Banking. Computer Weekly. May 7. http://www.computerweekly.com/news/2240220234/CaixaBank-Facebook-app-a-further-blurring-between-social-media-and-banking

Index

Printed and bound by CPI Group (UK) Ltd, Croydon, CR0 4YY

24/10/2024

01778284-0006